# IN THE SAME VOICE

# IN THE SAME VOICE

## Women and Men in Law Enforcement

Deborah Parsons

Paul Jesilow

SEVEN LOCKS PRESS
*Santa Ana, California*
*Minneapolis, Minnesota*
*Washington, D.C.*

Seven Locks Press
P.O. Box 25689
Santa Ana, CA 92799
(800) 354-5348

Printed in the United States of America

Library of Congress Cataloging-in-Publication Data
is available from the publisher

ISBN: 0-929765-92-3

Cover and Interior Design: Richard Cheverton/Waypoint
Editorial Services: PeopleSpeak

*For our families*

# Contents

# PREFACE

Women have made enormous progress in their representation in the labor force, increasing nearly 200 percent since 1900.[1] While this statistic is impressive, women, in general, remain in less-powerful occupational positions that are often boring, subservient, and low paying, with few real prospects for promotion. Female employees remain concentrated in traditional occupations such as clerical, retail sales, and waitressing.[2]

A desire for higher pay, independence, and personal rewards has led many women to cross the occupational segregation line into jobs not traditionally held by women. They are seeking employment in both professional and blue-collar fields. Although their motivations may differ, women are pursuing new and challenging opportunities, often entering what were once male-dominated occupations in greater numbers than in earlier years.[3] Additionally, more women are earning degrees in higher education, which translate into greater impact on public policy from a feminine perspective. Female physicians, for example, although relatively few in number only 30 years ago, now comprise more than 20 percent of all doctors[4] and about 40 percent of students entering medical schools.[5] Public policy implications include more research into the effects of ailments and drug therapy on women. Large numbers of women are also attending law schools and seeking careers in the legal profession.

Women, however, have not made significant inroads in all occupations. Police patrol work is notable in this regard, with police departments continuing to be male-dominated. Nine decades after the first woman was given the title of "policewoman," a large portion of society still perceives female officers as oddities, perhaps because of their few numbers or the notion that police work should be a male occupation. Because of their sparse representation, women who enter policing continue to be seen as pioneers.

Some argue that women are more likely to possess the traits that are needed by today's officers. They believe that women are more likely to use their intellectual rather than physical prowess to control others and from that viewpoint are a natural match for modern police work.[6] They argue that a larger female presence in policing would have a positive effect—that women bring a nurturing, cooperative spirit into their police roles, which mediates the aggressiveness underlying much volatile police behavior. Carol Gilligan is probably the most often cited for her assertion that men and women have different moral orientations; women conceptualize moral questions as problems of care involving empathy and compassion, while men see such problems as matters of rights.[7] Other studies have found women to be supportive and men to be argumentative and competitive.[8]

The argument that the presence of women in policing will change the occupation is compelling on its face, but we will show that self-selection, police department screening, and officer socialization currently produce female officers who differ little from their male colleagues and, except in rare instances, who do not utilize a different style. Based on interviews with male and female officers, we explore the reasons for behavioral and attitudinal similarities between male and female officers. Central to the argument is the notion that policing is perceived as predominantly involving law enforcement activities and that fulfillment of this role requires characteristics usually attributed to men, for example, aggression, physical prowess, logic, and stability of emotions. Characteristics commonly considered feminine, such as compassion, empathy, nurturing, and strong emotions, are frequently perceived to be weaker, less appealing, less successful, and especially in terms of policing, possibly dangerous and life-threatening. The perpetuation of the law enforcement model prevented women initially from entering policing and continues to keep their numbers low. The limited number of women who do enter policing either possess or assimilate the values already established in the system.

Organizational efforts to change the police, such as professionalization and bureaucratization and more recent attempts to emphasize and implement community policing, have had very limited success. In chapter 1, we address these attempts in some detail by focusing on the history of U.S. policing. We follow the establishment and growth of the law enforcement ideology and associate its existence with limiting the success of organizational reforms.

Women have a long history in police departments. Their introduction into the occupation was one of the earliest substantial alterations to policing. They filled a special role in many agencies early in the 20th century: they were hired for their distinctive skills in mediating problems associated with women and children. Chapter 2 reviews the past of women in police work and illustrates how favoritism toward the law enforcement component of the occupation hindered their integration and effect.

In chapter 3, we discuss the officers we interviewed and the cities for which they worked. While doing this, we also provide a more general description of the types of police departments that exist and give the reader some information on how we did the research.

Many public-minded individuals have been concerned that those who are attracted to police work may be drawn by dark interests. They fear that officers are little more than fascists who have discovered a convenient occupation for their dictatorial interests. We found no such inclination among the 80 officers we interviewed. Rather, a majority of the 40 men and 40 women had joined the police to escape a boring lifestyle. The opportunity to do exciting, outdoor work that they felt was worthwhile was a major lure. Chapter 4 reviews the history of officers' decisions to join law enforcement and the reasons our interviewees had for joining the police.

Training is another of the traditional areas where efforts to improve the police have occurred. We wanted to learn what officers liked best and least about their academy education and how they thought it might be improved. We also wanted to discover whether there were differences between the way women and men perceived the instruction they received. In chapter 5, we review the history of police training and discuss the association between the cultural favoritism toward crime control and our interviewees' attitudes about their academy educations.

Chapter 6 presents the features of police work liked best and least by those we interviewed. Their answers indicate that they are not all of a like mind. But their responses also indicate a strong cultural favoritism toward law enforcement activities. Both the men and women enjoy the autonomy they experience while on patrol. People and rules that hinder their freedom are disdained.

In chapter 7, we discuss the social life of officers and how it is affected by their jobs, because this, too, is a major concern for them. The police occupation is an isolating one. New officers soon find that it is difficult to keep old friends and to make new ones. They feel rejected by the general society and turn to the companionship of other officers. For the most part, the attitudes they hear and internalize are those of the police culture. We present this material in some detail in this chapter.

We were specifically interested in whether there were differences between the way men and women did their jobs. Historically, male and female officers have had different roles within policing, their activities determined in part by gender stereotypes. We asked the officers how they liked to handle situations that involved women or juveniles; specifically, we queried them about domestic disputes and an incident in which they catch youngsters spray-painting gang slogans. Surely, we assumed, if there were differences between male and female officers' behaviors, they would appear in their responses to these scenarios. We learned, however, that the genders felt similarly about the situations and that their attitudes were guided by their loyalty to the crime control component of policing. In chapters 8 and 9, we describe how officers handled these situations in the past as well as what our sample of officers reported.

In our concluding chapter, we argue that to change policing and increase the percentage of women in the occupation, it is necessary to focus on transforming the value system from one that overemphasizes law enforcement to one that more closely reflects the need for problem solving, empathy, and communication. To alter the rigid value system of the police and facilitate long-term resolution of law enforcement dilemmas, changes have to occur in two areas: the projection to society of the actual police role and the attraction to police work and selection of individuals who understand and accept that image. This would ultimately bring about a new police force, one that would promote different skills and ideas. Such modifications, however, will not be easy. The police organization and the officers who belong to it are highly resistant to change. Reforms will be grudgingly accepted only if they offer advantages to the officers. They must, therefore, be the result of negotiations between street officers and their superiors and not unilateral decisions from above. In the final chapter, we offer some suggestions as a starting point in the discussion, including a substantial change away from the command-and-control model of the job.

# ACKNOWLEDGMENTS

The endeavor of writing a book involves more people than the authors. Support and inspiration come from various sources and individuals. We are deeply grateful to our families and friends for their love, guidance, and support. We would like to thank friends (now colleagues) Susan Will and Jon'a Meyer. Other significant people who provided necessary support included Dan Lincoln, Steve and Linda Saldana, Julianne Ohlander, and John Sykes—so that our time could be spent writing. A special thanks is owed to Judy Omiya, who always is able to make the impossible happen. Our greatest source of love and thanks goes to our wonderful parents and family members: Eunice and Stuart Parsons; Rosalie and Ted Jesilow; and Judith, Kathleen, Nancy, David, Kym, Jason, Liam, and Zackary Parsons.

We would like to acknowledge and thank our colleagues who have imparted words of wisdom when we most needed them. A special thanks to Kitty Calavita for her guidance in the research and writing of the original dissertation. Henry Pontell and John Dombrink also played an important role in the creation of this work. Thanks to Eve Buzawa for numerous discussions on the police and domestic violence and to Gil Geis, who always gives freely of his time and is a truly remarkable source of knowledge and academic know-how.

Finally, this book could not have been accomplished without the participation, knowledge, and experiences of the dedicated women and men in law enforcement, who must remain anonymous. The police administrators, the patrol officers, and the administrative staff are all to be commended for their role in making these pages talk. Along the way, we have met many inspiring heroes and hope to honor their duty and service to humanity through this book.

# CHAPTER ONE

## Police Administrative Models

Throughout the 1990s, policing suffered reoccurring losses of public respect and trust in the wake of publicized acts of brutality against citizens, of which the videotaped beating of Rodney King was but one. Other incidents, early in the decade, included controversial cases in Miami and Detroit, involving fatal shootings and beatings by police officers, which increased racial tensions and dissatisfaction with law enforcement. More than two-thirds of respondents to a survey at the time said that when they hear of an allegation of police brutality, they feel that the charge is likely to be justified.[1]

Corruption and brutality proved common elements in several large, urban departments during the decade. In 1990, indictments of seven Los Angeles sheriff's deputies for skimming money from large drug arrests shocked citizens. The deputies owned expensive houses, luxury cars, and extravagant yachts.[2] Near the middle of the decade, members of New York's, Philadelphia's, and New Orleans's "finest" were all found wanting. In New Orleans, the citizens feared the police as much as they feared violent criminals. More than 50 officers were involved in various unlawful activities, including rape, beatings, drug sales, and murder. One shocking tale involved an officer charged with ordering the murder of a mother of three. He had her killed because she had filed a "confidential" complaint against the officer, alleging he had pistol-whipped her friend.[3] In another New Orleans incident, an officer, while robbing a family-run Vietnamese restaurant, murdered the son and daughter of the owners and, by chance, her former partner, who was moonlighting as a security guard. A third sibling was able to escape death by hiding in a freezer and was able to point out the killer to other officers when she returned to the restaurant in her role as an officer answering an emergency call. The officer's indictment for murder was the fourth brought against New Orleans officers in the previous 12 months.[4]

In Philadelphia, at about the same time, a half-dozen officers admitted that they had framed people, stolen money, and lied to judges to obtain search warrants. Their actions had resulted in scores of individuals being wrongfully imprisoned. In New York City, some 50 officers, many as members of crews, were involved in drug trafficking, extortion, and thefts.[5]

As the new millennium began, attention to police corruption once again focused on Los Angeles. Informants told of unjustified shootings, the planting of evidence, false arrests, beatings, intimidation, and perjury. In one case, two officers shot and paralyzed an unarmed gang member. They planted a gun on him and testified in court that he had attacked them. The 19-year-old was sentenced to 23 years in prison.[6] More than 70 officers have come under suspicion and more than 20 had to leave their jobs because of the scandal. As this book went to press, more than 40 criminal convictions had already been overturned because of the officers' actions, and hundreds of other cases are yet to be reviewed. Many of those who have been released had originally pled guilty, despite the fact that they were innocent of the charges. They had prior criminal records, which, if convicted, would have resulted in longer sentences under California's severe three-strikes law. For example, one individual pled guilty to selling drugs because he would serve only eight years in prison. If he had been convicted at trial—a likely circumstance given that the police planned to lie—he would have been given a life sentence. Similarly, another former felon found it easier to plead guilty to possessing a weapon, although he never had it, and to be sentenced to 16 months in prison as opposed to going to trial and facing the possibility of at least four years of incarceration.[7]

Such reports of brutality and corruption subvert the foundation of trust from which police agencies derive their legitimacy to control behavior and, ultimately, have caused many Americans to lose faith in their own local law enforcement services. The acquittal of O. J. Simpson for the murders of his ex-wife and her friend, for example, was in part due to the fact that the jury believed that Los Angeles police officers were not above planting evidence.

The urban uprising in Los Angeles following the acquittals of police officers who had beaten Rodney King underscored the fact that the police maintain order only with the consent of the public. When citizens no longer view the law and its agents as legitimate, control can be achieved only by an armed military response, and by then it is too late to prevent extensive personal, property, and social damage. These facts are not wasted on leaders, both those within the immediately affected communities and those who will eventually feel the sting of the political and economic aftermath. Efforts by the criminal justice system to maintain its publicly granted legitimacy are therefore imperative.

Public concern with police misbehavior is not new. Throughout the last 100 years, law enforcement has repeatedly been under community and governmental pressure to modify its conduct, and numerous attempts have been undertaken to alter it. Some of these efforts include administrative changes, standardization of equipment and policies, advanced training, and higher levels of qualification in the areas of recruitment, selection, and promotion. We argue, however, that these efforts to modify officer behavior have fallen short, in large part, because they have not altered the police value system, which supports certain attitudes and personality traits—some which police recruiters look for and some which are learned in the training process and on the job.

Police officers view their occupation as primarily law enforcement oriented, emphasizing crime fighting over other services. Studies, however, reveal that their focus may be misplaced; only 10 percent of policing involves the law enforcement component,[8] and dangerous activities represent less than 1 percent of citizen-initiated complaints.[9] The police value system, with its emphasis on crime fighting, does not mesh well with what police work actually consists of—service activities and problem solving. This dilemma, we argue, has undermined most attempts to reform policing, including the integration of women into the occupation. In this chapter, we chronicle the history of policing and the entrenchment of the police favoritism toward crime control.

## HISTORICAL BACKGROUND

Historically, police departments have attempted to upgrade the quality of their personnel and the manner in which officers reach decisions as a means to control the darker side of officer behavior and to improve the delivery of services. Political and administrative pressures have been responsible for some of the changes. The public also wants to exert some control over the inception, development, and philosophies of police departments.

The first large, metropolitan U.S. police department was created in New York City in 1840. A police historian wrote of the causes of its inception:

> A wave of riot and disorders swept American cities. The cause of the disorders was the revolutionary transformation of American society, including urbanization, industrialization, and immigration. The largest cities had grown into huge complexes, creating a crisis in all public services. Industrialization had altered the daily pattern of work and created extremes of wealth and poverty. Finally, immigration brought to the United States people of different ethnic and religious backgrounds. Many of the riots were clashes between different ethnic groups: the newly arrived Germans, or Irish Catholics versus the established anglo saxon protestants. Economic problems generated disorder as banks were attacked by rioters. Americans used violence to settle questions of morality; rioters objecting to new medical practices attacked hospitals. Finally, race was a source of disorder: white rioters attacked abolitionists and free black citizens in northern cities.[10]

New Yorkers initially balked at the idea of a standing police force as the solution to the growing disorder because they feared a military presence in the city. The only recollection of such a body the young nation had was the memory of English soldiers patrolling colonial streets. New Yorkers did not want a return to such monitoring. In holding with their hard-won independence and democratic values, Americans wanted their police to be less intrusive than the English had been.[11]

To establish the New York Police Department (NYPD), the city fathers selectively copied from the London Metropolitan Police. The London police, created in 1829, was a centralized, bureaucratic office of the national government in which personnel operated under exacting guidelines instituted by the department's hierarchy.[12]

The London police emphasized impartiality and legality in order to create a dispassionate organization. The autonomous officer was detached from the local citizenry and behaved according to the policies of the bureaucratic central office, which was, for the most part, free from partisan persuasion.[13]

Americans, however, wanted the police to be under local supervision and not a centralized government arm with authority over them. New York and other American police departments, in contrast to the London model, were radically decentralized. "Not only were they agencies of city government, but effective control was exercised at the neighborhood and ward level. . . . [M]ayors and chiefs of police had little real power; power lay with city councilmen and police captains at the neighborhood level."[14]

London, in fact to a large extent all of England, had a homogeneous population, whereas America was heterogeneous with a constant flow of new immigrants. Each U.S. officer had to establish his own authority among the citizens he patrolled. Officers gained respect only by upholding local standards and expectations in contrast to enforcing impersonal bureaucratic ideals.[15] They patrolled on foot and enjoyed a great amount of autonomy in performing their duties. Headquarters and other officers were rarely close by, and the men needed the support of the community in order to perform their job. Accordingly, officers' decisions fit within the prevailing ideology of the area's citizens, an ideology that they probably shared. To do otherwise would be to risk losing community support. Such democratic policing was not entirely positive. Police might, for example, brutalize minorities or other groups deemed unacceptable by the local residents or immediately punish wrongdoers that they caught on the streets. (Officers and the citizens they served agreed that judges were too lenient.) Officers gained respect by upholding local standards and expectations[16] even as their actions trampled the rights of the relatively powerless.[17]

Officers in New York, Chicago, and other large U.S. cities embodied a personal, informal authority, which allowed them to operate among a population that mistrusted institutional, formal control. Departments in urban areas decentralized command and granted their poorly trained officers a wide range of discretionary power. By the end of the 19th century, however, a change-minded country was having second thoughts about these practices.

## A Need for Reform

As the country entered the 20th century, public criticism of officers arose in response to police handling of neighborhood problems. Reform legislation to restrict gambling, Sunday drinking, and other perceived vices were enacted as a result of pressure group action, but police and other parts of the criminal justice system paid little attention to the new prohibitions.[18] The reforms' backers were often Christian, middle-class individuals, whose values differed from those of the immigrant, working-class members, whose behavior the legislation was meant to control. A writer of the period explained well the quandary with respect to alcohol: "On the one side are the extreme temperance advocates, to whom the business is anathema; on the other side, in most large cities, are a majority of the people, who habitually use intoxicating liquors socially, in their homes, clubs, churches, unions, and outings."[19]

Officers could do little to change the behavior of local citizens in immigrant and working-class neighborhoods. Officers on the beat were isolated from other police and had to satisfy the desires of local community members. Automobiles, the telephone, and two-way radios were decades away. Out of necessity, officers developed friendships and other close ties with the citizens they policed. When problems arose, the officers used these personal arrangements to better handle some of the communities' problems, but this also meant that they were "unable to act against [local citizens] with the vigor prescribed by law."[20] Policemen who attempted to enforce the new middle-class reforms jeopardized their ability to use their friendships to mediate local disputes. Moreover, the rare department or officer who did try to implement the laws found it no easier than do today's police. The new crimes lacked identifiable victims. Lacking complainants, law enforcement could only function with the aid of informants or illegal searches, and such illicit police actions were met with bitter criticism and legal suits.[21]

Middle- and upper-class citizens were irked by the lack of police activity. They envisioned that if laws were enforced, the evils of the day would disappear.[22] The police, in the reformists' view, were hindering the moral transformation of society. The reformists were unaware of the impossibility of the police task and frowned on what they saw as corrupt law enforcement.

The view that the police were corrupt did have a legitimate basis. Many officers, as well as other public officials, used their positions to obtain illegal income.[23] The newly created vice offenses coupled with public zeal for their enforcement made it easy for officers to pressure shady businesses into illicit payments.[24] A turn-of-the-century commissioner of the NYPD, for example, surmised that "[h]undreds of gambling houses and pool rooms exist . . . [that pay] immense sums of money in order to secure immunity."[25] These establishments were thought by the reformists to be breeding grounds for crime. Of particular importance to the former commissioner and other reformers was the plight of women and children.

> Respectable families are compelled to suffer without redress. . . . [T]he children of the tenement houses were condemned by the government of New York City to grow up under the most demoralizing conditions without assistance from the police authorities, who were in the pay of criminals. The decoying and abducting and ruining of girls was, and in many places continues to be, a regular trade in houses and by persons obviously under the protection of the police.[26]

The public's image of officers was that they were sloppy, ill disciplined, and poorly managed.[27] A commentator of the day called them "ignorant men of violent passions, placed in positions of seemingly great authority."[28] The standing of the officers in the eyes of the communities' elites may have also suffered because it was probably easy for the population to tie such officers to the criminals they policed. An expert on the subject noted that "a stigma attaches to police work because of its connection with evil, crime, perversity, and disorder. Though it may not be reasonable, it is common that those who fight the dreadful end up being the dreaded themselves."[29]

The public's view of the police had a factual basis. Initial urban departments were besieged with difficulties. Writing in 1920, a historian commented about the earlier period, noting that "Department reports of the time indicate a condition of utter lawlessness on the part of the police themselves. Assaulting superior officers, refusing to go on patrol, releasing prisoners from the custody of other policemen, drunkenness, extorting money from prisoners—these were the offenses of daily occurrence committed with impunity under the protection of a political overlord."[30]

A lack of officer preparation was considered part of the problem. Early police departments offered low pay and little training for their officers. Men were hired haphazardly and sent out to do the job, many using their own equipment.[31] At best, in the late 1800s police work was a high-status blue-collar occupation.[32] Departments had their historical roots planted in a period of antiprofessionalism, spawned by Andrew Jackson, who had noted that professional office holders would "acquire a habit of looking with indifference upon the public interest and of tolerating conduct from which an unpracticed man would revolt."[33] The politically cognizant Jackson exalted the common man, probably because he knew there were more of them.

Antiprofessionalism resulted in administrators and patrol officers receiving little, if any, training before going on the job. Individuals who sought employment in the newly formed departments also lacked formal education. They were mechanics, skilled industrial workers, shopkeepers, clerks, transportation workers, and a few unskilled laborers.[34]

## THE PROFESSIONAL MODEL

During the first years of the 20th century, innovative police administrators pushed the idea of professionalism in policing to eliminate the influence of local standards and politicians and to improve the image and actions of officers.[35] They were most likely impressed by the increasing prestige and salaries enjoyed by members of the medical profession.[36] Physicians in the 1800s had few skills and little success in treating illness. They, too, suffered from antiprofessionalism. States did not license doctors and almost anyone might enter medical school. Pay was low and few members of the educated class chose it as an occupation. The medical elite were able to change all that in the first 20 years of the 20th century. Licensing laws and medical school requirements for a college background before admission, in part, changed the social class and image of doctors. They were soon granted the final trappings of a profession: autonomy—the right to decide for themselves whether a member had acted correctly or wrongly.[37] Police hoped that professionalization would bring them similar success.[38]

Professionalization was initially viewed as a means by which officers could escape the dilemma of middle-class calls for full enforcement versus the need to satisfy local neighborhood standards. A key element in the strategy was to convince politicians and the public that officer discretion was necessary and that full enforcement was unwise, if not impossible. Acceptance of officer discretion would allow officers to legitimately tailor law enforcement to the community.[39] Discretion went hand in hand with the police reformers' goal of professionalization.[40] A professional officer, because of his training, the argument went, could effectively utilize wisdom.

Included in the argument for professionalization was an expansion of the officer's role to include a service component.[41] Citizens had long approved of such an enlargement of police duties, and at least one early police administrator in England, Edwin Chadwick, recognized that the expansive role might improve the police's image. By 1868, "Chadwick argued that the service role had become the main stay of police legitimacy."[42]

August Vollmer, the chief of police in Berkeley, California, from 1905 to 1932, is commonly recognized as the leader of the movement to professionalize the police as a means to overcome its negative image as a corrupt and brutal force and to seize power from local political bosses and gain autonomy.[43] He argued that, as with doctors and lawyers, "inefficiency and all the ills that follow in its wake may be expected until this professional status is recognized by the public."[44] Vollmer's objectives included standardizing the selection and training of police officers and improving minimum requirements to include college education and special technological skills.[45] He wanted policemen to be of "superior intellectual endowment, physically sound, free from mental and nervous disorders; they must have character traits which will insure integrity, honesty, and efficiency; their personality must command the respect and liking of their associates and the general public."[46] Each officer, from Vollmer's viewpoint, should be independent and detached from political affiliation or allegiance to special interest groups. Education, Vollmer believed, imparted autonomy, dignity, and respect to professional policemen. An educated officer would be an efficient crime-fighter, and his occupation would go beyond the reach of partisan political interference.[47]

During the time Vollmer was implementing changes and creating a "new" Berkeley police department, many academic fields were addressing the causes of crime. Vollmer, hungry for new knowledge, accepted various theoretical perspectives and very much wanted police officers to learn the causes of crime so that they could be viewed as experts. As experts they would be called upon to identify "criminals" before they committed crimes. Crime prevention would be a primary police function. In order to accomplish this end, Vollmer believed it necessary to "raise the educational and intellectual standard of our police departments, elevate the position of policemen to that of a profession, eliminate politics entirely from the force, and secure the people's confidence and sympathy, respect and cooperation." Vollmer concluded that "when we have reached a point where the best people in society are selected for police service, there will be little confusion regarding the duties of the members."[48]

Many observers outside law enforcement agreed with Vollmer that there was a need to improve police standards, in part because officers made judgments on their own, having the unique and awesome responsibility of life-and-death decisions. A public administration specialist of the period wrote:

> The police department, as the direct crime prevention agency, is concerned with a social problem that is interrelated with all the social and

economic conditions in the community. . . . [T]he task of combating
crime calls for superior abilities together with training and education.
Since effective law enforcement may require the exercise of more power
than is actually conferred by law, the authority of police to use personal
discretion should be increased and the character of personnel improved
so that this discretion will be wisely exercised.[49]

Vollmer's philosophy and innovative ideas, however, were criticized.
Many remarked that what might work for a college town like Berkeley
would not necessarily work in big urban areas.[50] In addition, there was
little money to support Vollmer's proposals. Physicians had been able to
raise their social and economic positions with assistance from the
Carnegie and Rockefeller foundations.[51] No such philanthropic energy
was aimed at the police.

Many powerful police reformers, unlike Vollmer, had no law enforcement experience of their own and were raised in upper socioeconomic
households. They viewed the police as public servants. Advanced education, they believed, was important for police administrators but not for
patrol officers.[52] By 1931, only 20 percent of cities conducted training
for their officers.[53] Thirty years later, advanced education for officers was
still rare; less than 1 percent of departments dictated some college education for their recruits and many did not require a high school degree.[54]

But more structural components of police work probably doomed
efforts to raise the individual officer to the level of a professional. Most
notable, officers then and now begin their careers as patrol officers and
remain in that position from one to five years before promotion. A
police task force described the inherent difficulty:

> Since a police officer serving in this capacity must respond to all demands
> upon police, whether they involve removing a cat from a roof or arresting
> a robbery suspect, his status is adversely affected both within and outside
> the police agency. Police work, therefore, tends to attract persons who
> are willing to perform in mechanical aspects and to accept in its status a
> compensation.[55]

Individuals who had the education and skills needed to be professional
police officers probably had numerous other career opportunities and the
quasi-military police organization was unable to attract highly capable

college graduates, who remained unwilling to begin their posteducation careers at the lowest level of a department, squandering years executing "mechanical, undemanding duties."[56]

The dilemma just described has not changed much. Recruitment and retention of the college educated remains problematic. Proficient workers require "continual job opportunities to keep them interested and satisfied. If the opportunities do not exist, some of them will be frustrated and become knockers and cynics in their work."[57] A police expert noted:

> Ideally, an occupation improves the quality of its personnel by making the pay, the nature of the work, or the prestige of the work so attractive that the number of persons seeking the occupation is greater than those who can be accepted. The existence of high standards makes the occupation doubly attractive because the potential candidates are selected after a series of sharp and competitive eliminations. Those who make it are the elect.[58]

The police job has not reached such high status; it ranks low in occupational prestige—47th on a list of 90 occupations according to one study.[59]

Also preventing the move to police professionalization is the historical fact that the professional model of autonomy is at odds "with the American philosophy of government."[60] The idea that officers should make independent decisions about citizens, and that disagreements between the public and police should be reviewed by an organization of officers, is incompatible with history. Residents and legislators have long reviewed police activities. The rise of the professional model was itself a reaction to public criticism of officer behavior in the preceding years.

Officer autonomy has also been limited by numerous judicial decisions. Court determinations have, for example, stipulated when an officer can use force to affect an arrest and take evidence,[61] limited the scope of police searches,[62] and required police to inform suspects of their right to legal counsel prior to questioning.[63] In addition, lawsuits brought against officers, their departments, and the municipalities that paid their salaries have resulted in officers being much more cautious about their decisions and actions. Officials fear lawsuits and they often change policies to avoid them, even when no clear decision requires them to do so.

Concern by police departments about the consequences of lawsuits has spawned a journal called the *National Bulletin on Police Misconduct*, devoted entirely to these issues, and officers, in general, are knowledgeable of the cases that direct their decision making.[64]

Vollmer's dream of a professional police force never reached fruition. Rather, police departments became bureaucracies, and only the leadership of the forces obtained the skills and education Vollmer had envisioned for all officers. A police expert concluded "that most attempts to make a profession of police work have led to a professionalization of the police department, to a lesser extent a professionalization of those in staff positions, and only to a relatively minor extent to professionalization of the rank and file officer in the line."[65]

## THE BUREAUCRATIC MODEL

By 1930, bureaucracy was well on its way to being the accepted archetype for police administration. The implementation of its ideals into the police organization was another attempt to address problems associated with poorly trained and uneducated personnel. Samuel Walker, discussing the period, wrote:

> Public concern about police brutality had been rising since the turn of the century. Magazines devoted an increasing number of articles to it, while victims of police misconduct brought suits in increasing numbers. The Wickersham Commission report created a sensation and aroused public opinion even more. The leaders of American policing were deeply embarrassed: the stories of widespread brutality damaged their claim that policing was a profession. This public pressure forced police departments to take steps to eliminate the worst kinds of misconduct.[66]

In many ways, the new police standard resembled the London model and closely paralleled the relatively newly emerged writings of Frederick Taylor and Max Weber,[67] whose ideas were affecting sizable portions of the private and public world. By the time bureaucratization was clawing at policing, writers were proclaiming that the model had created a "managerial revolution" and that it would one day be universally accepted.[68]

Bureaucracy was not born in the 20th century but rather had its modern-day roots in the managerial structure of the Catholic Church and European armies. Frederick Taylor urged the application of its concepts to the corporate world, positing increased efficiency as the outcome. He argued that in any trade there was little uniformity in the methods used by workers. There was no accepted standard but rather "fifty or a hundred different ways of doing each elements of the work." Methods were "handed down from man to man by word of mouth" or were "learned through personal observation."[69] Taylor argued for a new way of doing things, one in which managers would be more important. He wrote:

> Under scientific management . . . the managers assume new burdens, new duties, and responsibilities never dreamed of in the past. The managers assume, for instance, the burden of gathering together all of the traditional knowledge which in the past has been possessed by the workmen and then of classifying, tabulating, and reducing this knowledge to rules, laws, and formulae which are immensely helpful to the workmen in doing their daily work. . . . [T]hey develop a science for each element of a man's work, which replaces the old rule-of-thumb method.[70]

Max Weber had been dead a decade when the depression of the 1930s was in full stride. His writings, however, must have sounded fresh to police administrators of the day. He provided a blueprint for bureaucracy to those who were interested, a blueprint that must have seemed as if it had been designed for police work. Of utmost importance, bureaucracy, according to Weber, was based on a "belief in the 'legality' of . . . rules and the right of those elevated to authority under such rules to issue commands." Obedience was "owed to the legally established impersonal order. It extends to the persons exercising the authority of office under it only by virtue of the formal legality of their commands and only within the scope of authority of the office."[71]

Weber posited that an efficient bureaucratic organization has a clear division of labor with a hierarchy or chain of command; "that is, each lower office is under the control and supervision of a higher one."[72] Officials were to be selected for technical competence, which was based on their training. The rules, which governed the acts of the office holders, were to be "formulated and recorded in writing, even in cases where oral discussion is the rule or is even mandatory."[73] And, of great importance to police administrators, the bureaucrat was to be "subject to strict and systematic discipline and control in the conduct of the office."[74]

Police leaders saw the benefit of a bureaucratic, paramilitary organization in which officers followed orders.[75] They wanted to limit patrolmen's discretion and gain more control over their behaviors, thus reducing individual error in decision making and deterring corruption. By limiting options through strict policy guidelines, administrators purported to dispense justice more fairly and uniformly to the citizens. The type of choices officers made had to fall within prescribed limits, otherwise they would be disciplined and penalties might be considerable. An expert on the subject explained:

> Since the courts evaluated an officer's actions according to his conformity to or variation from departmental policy, the rules and procedures became tantamount to law. If an officer deviated from standard procedures, he opened himself up to civil suits, departmental discipline, or criminal prosecution. As long as the officer operated within the department's rules and procedures, neither he nor the department could be charged with corruption or incompetence.[76]

Although patrolmen could not be under constant scrutiny by supervisors, all officers' actions were to be evaluated and all reports reviewed. The officers' daily patrol logs were to include descriptions of work hours and breaks, climate, radio calls, pedestrian and vehicular stops, and miles driven while at work. In addition, officers were to submit detailed reports on all police activities in which they were involved, such as crime or traffic accident reports. These data were to be used by supervisors to control officer discretion.[77]

Foremost among police leaders pushing for bureaucratization of the occupation was O. W. Wilson, a former student of August Vollmer. Early on, Wilson decided that police were to be evaluated on a "daily, weekly and monthly summary of arrests by each officer for the various offenses, as well as average daily mileage." He contended that these items provided "a fair picture of their [officers'] relative production."[78] His use of these criteria to make decisions on issues such as job promotions clearly fixed arrests as a primary determinant of an officer's success.

In the field, Wilson emphasized officers' "appearance, conduct, courtesy and a square deal." Patrolmen were, he wrote, "never permitted to forget that there is no law against hurting a police officer's feelings." As a result, "an officer must not arrest a man because his actions or his manner or his appearance displeases, or because of what he says, but must permit only the offense to determine his action."[79] The bureaucrat, according to the model, does not let feelings or emotions interfere with decision making. Rather, rules are to govern behavior. The bureaucratic officer is aloof. Television made the image of the detached officer an icon in the persona of Joe Friday, the fictional star of the television series *Dragnet*.

> [Friday] has no connection with the manhole-disappearing, Model-T reversing Keystone cop of our youth, . . . Friday is not the private and perhaps even amateur sleuth; he is the public, and certainly professional gum-shoe. As such, he plays a more impersonal, bureaucratized role . . . he is oriented toward the police profession and not toward its clients.[80]

The bureaucratic model also purported to deal with the difficulty that police work requires extensive skills. Office holders gain expertise through specialization, which allows for skills to be sharpened by repetition. O. W. Wilson, as chief of the Kansas City Police Department, created separate departmental units in which assigned officers could specialize in one activity, such as vice control, homicide investigation, or traffic.[81] These distinct crime-fighting units garnered additional civil support for bureaucratic departments by furthering the public perception of police expertise in crime control.

The bureaucratic model required centralized command and control. Policy had to be uniform to insure officer compliance, and the only way to insure uniformity was to place decision making in the control of key administrators within departments and to make them autonomous from neighborhood control. The removal of local influences from police practices, reformers felt, would limit the public perception of corruption.

All in all, implementation of the bureaucratic model emphasized the crime control component of policing. Officers were evaluated on arrests, tickets, and other law enforcement activities. Social service work, such as talking with youngsters or helping a family, were ignored in the evaluation process. An aloof officer could not be bothered with personal problems of citizens.

## THE BUREAUCRATIC MODEL AND TECHNOLOGY

Prior to the 1930s, implementation of the bureaucratic organizational model would have been difficult, at best. During that early era of police work, controlling patrolmen's decisions was problematic. Communications between officers and supervisors were difficult. Officers patrolled on foot and signaled each other for help by rapping their clubs on the sidewalk or by blowing a whistle.[82] Contact with a supervisor was nearly impossible. The introduction of the telephone improved the matter somewhat. Police call boxes were erected in neighborhoods and officers were required to communicate with their headquarters on a regular basis. During the 1930s, however, officers were increasingly put into automobiles outfitted with radios that could receive messages from supervisors and allow the overseers to direct the officers.[83]

The technological advancements were also used to "sell" the new police to the public. Most notably, automobiles and radios were pinpointed as invaluable aids to the apprehension of criminals. Illustrative is a piece that appeared in a 1927 issue of *Literary Digest*, which described the "quick-eyed neighbor who had telephoned" the police. "While the trail was still hot, the police were already off for the chase before the wise neighbor had hung up, and within twenty minutes of the theft, we are told, a swift police car with two officers had picked up the thieves."[84]

Also of importance in convincing the public of the benefits of bureaucratic policing were the potential cost savings. Max Weber had noted that "bureaucratic work is not only more precise but, in the last analysis, it is often cheaper,"[85] a detail that did not go unnoticed by police administrators who faced declining revenues due to the depression. An article examining Cambridge, Massachusetts, at the time, for example, pointed out that the introduction of the automobile would modernize police patrolling and "make it possible to reduce the police force from 235 to 194 men."[86]

The new technology that made the model salable to the public also required unique skills and training, many of which had not existed in earlier decades.[87] It was during the 1930s that departments, for one of the few times in their history, were able to recruit extensive numbers of college-educated individuals, who possessed the prerequisites for the distinctive new activities. It is understandable that police departments did their best at attracting college graduates during the Great Depression, when a secure government job was preferable to unemployment.[88] The depression severely limited the number of employment positions in the private economic sphere, which enhanced the desirability of a police job. Police officers earned $3,000 a year and could own houses and automobiles. They were "middle class" and they were never laid off. Young men chose police work because of the salary and security; "it was lucrative and less expensive to attain than the position of lawyer or teacher."[89] Municipalities were delighted to get better-educated middle-class candidates and slanted entrance examinations in their favor.[90]

Middle-class citizens approved of administrators' moves to implement bureaucratic policing. The public felt that officers should treat them with a formality that included civility and respect, that officers should be military in their appearance and have little contact with politicians—all characteristics of the new model.[91]

By 1950, large, urban centers were dominated by bureaucratic police departments that utilized centralized command and control. Where previously police buildings and operations had been scattered over miles, departments were increasingly building large stations to house their personnel under one roof. Administrators argued that better police protection and service could be attained in this fashion. Radio-directed patrol cars, they told the public, had made neighborhood stations obsolete, and "a major source of avoidable waste in our largest cities" could be eliminated.[92] Regional police operations, advocates posited, are "economically and administratively sound and can be realized at a great savings to the taxpayers."[93]

## Problems

Initial concerns with the bureaucratic model centered on departments' failures to train officers and to develop policies that might provide "police personnel specific guidance for the common situations requiring exercise of police discretion."[94] Officers could hardly be faulted for not following guidelines when none existed. These issues did not seem insurmountable to those favoring the bureaucratic model. Police academies coupled with procedural manuals were seen as solutions. It was expected that law enforcement experts would establish a group of diagnostically related groups of behaviors from which officers would, with computer quickness, select an appropriate response. An American Bar Association study, for example, commented that an officer should be "equipped with numerous alternative forms of action from which he can, based upon carefully established guidelines and training, select the response most appropriate to the situation at hand."[95]

Police officials focused on selection and training as the best means to obtain qualified officers. They argued that they needed officers who would "reduce exposure from litigation concerning negligent hiring, negligent retention, and negligent entrustment" and "who are able to understand the problems of the community and who relate well to its members."[96] The aim of the training was to transform the individual into a "standardized product."[97] Recruits received coaching in physical conditioning, but their formal instruction was "heavily weighted toward the technical aspects of police work including criminal and procedural laws, departmental rules and regulations, the care and use of firearms, and techniques of arrest and apprehension."[98] In one 1960s study, 70 percent of the recruits felt that their academy manual on rules and procedures was the most useful item they received in their training, presumably because adherence to its instructions would protect them from departmental discipline and citizen suits.[99]

Successful implementation of a bureaucratic model of policing that directs officers' decisions and actions is unlikely. One reason is that the nature of policing does not lend itself to complete standardization. The bureaucratic model sets out to restrict and curtail the use of discretionary power at the patrol level. Yet without discretion, officers would be forced to handle every situation by the letter of the law, allowing for no exceptions. The implications of such a course are great. An already overburdened criminal justice system simply could not survive a policy of "full enforcement" of the laws. Nor would the public tolerate such a policy, as evidenced by the pressures not to enforce certain statutes and the public outcries that arise with increased traffic law enforcement.[100]

Discretion is also important for accomplishing many aspects of the job. Most police activities do not involve law enforcement but rather are order-maintenance functions "for which legislative or judicial direction is either vague or nonexistent."[101] Because police departments are open 24 hours, 7 days a week, they are the only government agency that many people turn to for help. And people call with all sorts of problems. Illustrative of their duties, a survey conducted by the Public Administration Service for the President's Commission on Law Enforcement and Administration of Justice concluded in the mid-1960s that Kansas City Police Department patrol officers "devoted only 32 percent of their time to criminal matters."[102] Other studies have reported much lower figures.[103] A comprehensive study of patrolmen in one city during a 54-week period, for example, revealed that of 599,211 assignments, crimes against persons accounted for less than 3 percent of officers' time, and crimes against property involved about 14 percent of their day. The rest of their hours were spent on other matters.[104]

The extent of conditions that confront officers prevents complete cataloguing of possible responses, and if a circumstance is in a manual, the patrolman may not know "what the instructions mean when he faces a situation that appears to call for action."[105] As one researcher noted:

> Policing will never become a science in the sense of having closely and logically set rules governing each situation, in which the predictability of each outcome is very high. . . . human interactions and human beings being what they are, the degree of uncertainty about any police-citizen encounter will remain fairly high.[106]

Another difficulty associated with bureaucratization of the police was it hindered the recruitment of highly qualified personnel. Once the depression had passed, those seeking professional careers found unrewarding the prospect of a highly supervised position. Under the quasi-military, authoritarian style of command, police officers were "treated like robots whose duty is simply to follow orders. This approach, it is argued, fails to provide sufficient job satisfaction for police officers."[107] And when departments were able to attract the college educated, police administrators found them more likely than less-educated officers to doubt orders, to seek reassignments, to exhibit lower morale, and to become easily frustrated with bureaucratic procedures.[108] Departments were little impressed with educated recruits and preferred to choose personnel based on "rigid physical standards" that reflected "the popular image of what the police do rather than a careful analysis of job requirements."[109]

The idea that officers operating under the bureaucratic model could be controlled is also suspect. Officers do not perform their duties under constant supervisorial scrutiny. Rather, patrol personnel make decisions throughout their day and take actions, which may never be seen or evaluated by superiors. The only record of a specific action may be an officer's report, turned into the supervisor at the end of the shift, which will be reviewed in retrospect of officer actions already taken. "For many patrolmen, the task of decision-making in police work becomes seen as a problem in selecting an alternative that can be later described to a supervisor in terms consistent with the rules and regulations of the department."[110]

Many of the problems of the bureaucratic police plan are similar to difficulties found in any large bureaucracy.[111] Personnel develop loyalty to the organization, which separates them from the rest of us and becomes an obstacle preventing meaningful suggestions for change.[112] Among law enforcement personnel, rookies learn from veterans "that the way to get along in a police organization was to never rock the boat."[113] Officers were "expected to internalize norms and the value system of the department, and to accept the operating principles of maintaining the status quo."[114]

The centralized bureaucratic police organization was isolated from the community. Its leaders perceived themselves as crime control experts and resisted input from the lay public. Technological changes, such as helicopters, motorcycles, and radio-dispatched patrol cars, had "removed the officer from the street and ended informal contacts between officers and law-abiding citizens. The police became increasingly isolated and police-community relations suffered. To many people, especially racial minorities, the police seemed like an alien occupying army."[115]

Following urban riots in the mid-1960s, police relations with minority communities came under intense criticism, primarily because the conflagrations had all been sparked by law enforcement actions. In 1967, the Task Force on the Police of the president's commission commented that an obstacle of "major proportion" confronted the police in such neighborhoods; they faced "widespread hostility and resentment" because "the police and citizens living in impoverished conditions" failed "to understand each other's problems."[116]

The task force recommended that departments develop minority recruitment as one method to increase understanding. In addition, they advocated that all recruits receive training in community relations.[117] Neither of these two efforts, however, substantially changed matters. Qualified minority members often found jobs in less controversial occupations than police officer, and those individuals who were attracted to law enforcement were selected by and soon socialized into a police subculture that rejected change and prized loyalty to the system. Community relations instruction in the academy was no more successful in changing officer behavior. Once on the streets, recruits conformed to the subculture.

The failure of law enforcement agencies to learn and respond to the public doomed attempts during the 1970s to change the constabulary. An underlying ideology of policing is that it will reflect societal values, demands, and needs. The legitimacy of law enforcement, to some extent, rests on the acquiescence of the public to be controlled. In some respects, policing exists because the public wants it. Ultimately, public acceptance of police actions is the result of negotiations between departments and citizens.

All too often, law enforcement agencies failed to respond to public and private attempts to change policy and practice. Efforts by members of poor neighborhoods to modify patrol officers' behaviors did occasionally result in departments instituting policy changes, but officers on the street were known to often disregard official edicts because they believed that such changes were a halfhearted effort by the administration to appease whatever community group had complained.[118] Under the bureaucratic model, police perceived themselves as the crime experts. Public efforts to change their activities were unwanted infringements. Indeed, officials have been more likely to attempt to change community perceptions to be in line with a strict crime control agenda. Rather than establishing a dialogue with the citizenry to learn their concerns, administration efforts have more closely resembled public relations techniques, in which police leaders, conforming to their bureaucratic roles, have done their best to convince the population that their policing procedures were appropriate and necessary.[119]

## COMMUNITY POLICING

The failure of the bureaucratic model of policing with respect to community relations rekindled the 19th century U.S. philosophy that police should be under neighborhood control. Today, numerous departments have instituted community policing programs that decentralize decision making and actively seek citizen input. Beat officers are expected to respond to neighborhood concerns in a way that solves problems.

Community policing is not a single program. Numerous activities have been defined within its rubric, and varying measures have been suggested to evaluate its effectiveness.[120] A community policing program should at least

> include some type of community involvement in decision making which focuses on specific priorities and needs of the community; a relatively permanent assignment of police officers to a neighborhood in order to instill mutual feelings of trust and responsibility between the officers and the community; and a commitment of resources and personnel to meet the needs of the community.[121]

Team policing and foot patrol are two tactics that have been commonly associated with the evolving community policing model. Team policing is generally described as an early failure, although some of its components are still thought to be important elements in an effective community policing strategy.[122] Its major components were

> decentralization: decisions are made by middle level supervisors in charge of particular teams; geographic focus: teams are assigned to

neighborhoods. Officers remain assigned to particular neighborhoods for extended periods of time; unity of police services: the team handles all services in an area. Follow-up investigations are handled by team members, not by centralized experts; team or task force decision making: policy is largely affected by team members; community input: residents have major impact upon policy.[123]

Decentralization was to encourage "responsiveness to the community by identifying, both within the department and for the community, one person who was to be held responsible for policing a particular area."[124] It was to improve problem resolution because those making the decisions were more familiar with the neighborhoods where the issues occurred.

The implementation of the team policing model was not an easy task.[125] Initial trials did not prove to be great successes.[126] Bureaucratic organizations are highly resistant to change, and paramilitary organizations, such as the police, are probably more so. Early efforts at team policing tried to invoke ways of working and thinking that were contrary to existing police culture and failed as a result. In most cities, team policing was implemented within specific geographical areas, which created additional conflicts between the few officers assigned to the programs and the vast majority of officers who continued to exist in a bureaucratic environment in which administrators attempted to tightly control their behavior.

Foot patrol and "storefront" police stations have enjoyed a greater longevity than team policing and have been deemed successful. These programs began to appear in the 1970s with the announced goal of lowering the extent of crime. Lessening the distance between citizen and officer, the argument went, would result in residents being more willing to provide the police with information about malefactors, which would lead to arrests and decreased crime. Whether foot patrol actually lessens crime is unclear. An expert on such matters, in a review of the experience in Newark, New Jersey, concluded that the results

> indicate that the addition of intensive foot patrol coverage . . . can have considerable effects on the perception of residents concerning disorder problems, crime problems, the likelihood of crime, safety, and police service. Such additional patrol, however, appears to have no significant effect

on victimization, recorded crime, or the likelihood of reporting a crime.[127]

The results from a program in Flint, Michigan, were also less than clear with respect to reducing crime, but the foot patrol did improve residents' feelings of safety.[128]

Another program that falls within the rubric of community policing, problem-oriented policing (POP), was enunciated by Herman Goldstein.[129] The model has been widely implemented, but "researchers have conducted only a few controlled evaluations to assess their effects on the police or the community."[130]

Goldstein urged police administrators to work with the communities they serve to define the problems that need addressing. He argued, "at least initially in the development of a problem-solving approach to improved policing, to press for as detailed a breakdown of problems as possible."[131] The police should then work with the neighborhood and other civic agencies to solve these problems. This is of utmost importance to Goldstein. As he noted, the public "usually want[s] to know if the community policing initiative has had an impact on the problems of concern to them."[132]

Implementation of community policing programs, such as problem-oriented policing, is not easy. At least, communities that mistrust the police may be hesitant to offer advice to departments.[133] But without "development within the minority community of the capacity and willingness to communicate views and dissatisfactions to the police," efforts will fail.[134]

In other communities, groups established to convey attitudes to the police about their neighborhoods may not be representative of all individuals within the locale.[135] It has long been noted that the police do not fully enforce all laws.[136] Rather, the "laws which are selected for enforcement are those which the power structure of the community wants enforced."[137] Similar to the situation of a century past, police relying on such sentiment may trample the rights of the powerless in the name of community policing. For example, complaints from residents in one very influential neighborhood about prostitution, drug sales, and vagrancy that were occurring along its perimeter resulted in the closing of a motel that had provided low-cost housing. The voices of the very poor were ignored in this instance, and the burden of their social exclusion was compounded.[138]

The difficulty with programs such as problem-oriented policing stems from their reliance on "local standards of conduct and acceptable levels of enforcement."[139] Behavior may be tolerated in one neighborhood, while the police may be called upon in another. A retirement community, for example, may complain bitterly about the noise caused by teenagers gathered in a local park, hoping that law enforcement will drive the youth away. Other communities may seek to eradicate from their streets older vehicles that are perceived as bringing down property values and pressure their police to step up ticket writing or towing policies. It is arguable whether significant police resources should be invested to enforce local standards of conduct in this way. Just because a community wants change does not necessarily mean the change is desirable.

Another hurdle for implementation of the community policing model stems from the public's belief that police should do something about crime. Departments have been very successful at convincing the public that they are crime control experts and should be evaluated on their law enforcement efforts. As the new millennium begins, many politicians and police chiefs have credited their community policing programs with reducing crime rates. The evaluations, however, seem self-serving. Crime rates have declined throughout the United States in cities that have (or claim to have) community policing and in those that do not. The general decline in reported crime is due to other factors, but police agencies have been quick to take advantage of the downturn by claiming responsibility. Community policing, however, requires the police to perform tasks other than law enforcement, and the public may not accept officers' newly adopted service role.

A consequence of implementing the community policing ideal rests on the very backbone of the paradigm: officers are assigned regular beats in hopes that they will merge into their neighborhoods as trusted civil servants. Controversy might well arise, however, as officers become responsible for policing smaller territories and become more sensitive to neighborhood standards. One hundred years ago, local control of the police resulted in cries of corruption and a reform movement. Similarities between the community policing model and early U.S. police organizations suggest that associated problems may resurface. Decentralized departments grant greater autonomy to individual officers, and this may improve esprit de corps among many law enforcement personnel. Supervisors, however, fear "their officers might become less productive or even corrupt."[140] The bureaucratic model, with its emphasis on centralized command and control, was adopted by police leaders as a means to eliminate corruption and control officer discretion. Placing power back in the hands of citizens raises the potential for a decrease in official accountability by officers.[141] Evaluating community policing based on public surveys of their performance is apt to exacerbate the dilemma.[142] Officers are likely to differentially enforce laws to conform to community wishes. Cities within the United States remain heterogeneous, and each neighborhood may need and demand differing activities from their police force. Not all community members will approve of the new police agenda, and they may view it as breeding corruption.

It seems unlikely that officers will abruptly embrace community policing. Too many of them joined the force for the excitement of the job; they want to catch the bad guy and put him in jail.[143] Community policing, however, requires different abilities. Officers are expected to be "creative and innovative" and to possess "certain skills, including problem conceptualization, synthesis and analysis of information, action plans, program evaluation, and communication of evaluation results and policy implications."[144] Patrol officers, who are socialized into a culture that mistrusts outsiders,[145] will not suddenly seek the advice of community members in order to do their job. In many places, community policing may be little more than a new title, while department administrators and street officers continue to do the job in the same fashion as before.[146]

That being said, there is some evidence of success for the community policing model. Santa Ana, California, home of the oldest community policing program, has benefited from interactions between citizens and officers at neighborhood meetings.[147] Recent results from Indianapolis are similar. "As police-citizen cooperation increased, residents considered the neighborhood to be safer."[148]

Community policing seems to work best when its policies are established after negotiations. In a give-and-take atmosphere, officers and citizens can come to understand each other's perspectives. Because front-line officers are involved in decision making, they may be more likely to accept and support new department trends. Citizens may empathize more with their officers and give them high marks for effort. Research suggests that law enforcement agencies that take the time to learn and deal with their constituents' irritants and troubles will be perceived in increasingly positive terms.[149] Certainly, the public should be more likely to have confidence in a department that values its input and addresses the concerns it feels are pressing.

## Discussion and Summary

Differing organizational styles have failed to rid the police of problems. The police continue to attract criticism, in part because few people have a clear concept of the police's role, duties, and constraints. A source of public criticism of police actions, for example, stems from differences between citizens' and officers' perceptions of the correct method for handling a situation for which the police have been called. The public often summons the police to deal with situations that turn out to be civil matters.[150] The responding officer faces the difficult task of explaining why no action can be taken.[151] The result is that citizens frequently have something negative to say about their experiences with the police.[152]

The dilemma of popular perception versus police's reality stems from the public's comprehension of the police's role. Law enforcement elite, such as August Vollmer and J. Edgar Hoover, stressed the crime control component of the occupation—some argue out of a macho image but more likely because our society was and continues to be frightened of crime. As with all professions, the police needed a specific area of expertise that they could dominate.[153] Police promised to do something about illegalities so we granted them a certain amount of expertise and autonomy with respect to crime.

In reality, police officers have much less of an effect on crime than the general public believes. Studies of increased patrols have reported they are ineffective at lowering crime rates,[154] and much of what we label as crime is beyond police capabilities. We have criminalized too many behaviors that have as their cause basic societal dilemmas. Social quandaries cannot be eliminated by police, just as medical doctors cannot eliminate the causes of cancer. They are much too rooted in our system. Until society and police understand this impasse, law enforcement will remain a lightning rod for public disapproval.

In reality, the police have many roles. More than 65 years ago, the complexity of the position was noted by the Wickersham Commission:

> On the one hand we expect our law enforcement officer to possess the nurturing, caretaking, sympathetic, empathizing, gentle characteristics of physician, nurse, teacher, and social worker as he deals with school traffic, acute illness and injury, juvenile delinquency, suicidal threats and gestures, and missing persons. On the other hand we expect him to command respect, demonstrate courage, control hostile impulses, and meet great physical hazards. . . . he is to control crowds, prevent riots, apprehend criminals, and chase after speeding vehicles. I can think of no other profession which constantly demands such seemingly opposite characteristics.[155]

It is unlikely that any single officer can fulfill all of these roles. The patrolman who can calmly handle a family fight or a juvenile spray-painting walls may not be the same individual who enjoys the adrenaline rush of high-speed chases and shootouts. Differing models of policing simply cannot handle this dilemma. In particular, police emphasis on the law enforcement or crime-fighting role produces individuals suited to some activities and not to others, and a change in policing strategies will not alter this fact.

In the remainder of this book, we illustrate how the crime-fighting image of policing has affected almost all aspects of officers' careers. We begin in chapter 2 by chronicling women's activities in departments. Their introduction into policing early in the 20th century was one of the first changes to the occupation, and it is women who have been most affected by the emphasis on the law enforcement role. The difficulties they have faced in policing are similar to the hurdles that other minority members have had to overcome to become police officers.

# CHAPTER TWO

## Women in Policing: A Tale of Cultural Conformity

Nine decades after women entered policing, a large number of people still perceive a female officer as an oddity. Perhaps this is due to the few numbers of female officers or the notion that police work should be a male occupation. Because of women's sparse representation, a career as a police officer remains an uncharted frontier, and the women who enter policing are seen as pioneers.

The perpetuation of the crime control ideal continues to limit the number of female officers. Policing is perceived as predominantly involving law enforcement activities, which require characteristics usually attributed to men, for example, aggression, physical prowess, logic, and stability of emotions. Characteristics commonly considered feminine, such as compassion, empathy, nurturing, and strong emotions, are frequently perceived to be weaker, less appealing, less successful, and especially in terms of policing, possibly dangerous and life-threatening.

Early in the 20th century, middle-class reformers entertained the notion that hiring large numbers of women into the occupation would bring about needed changes in policing. They argued that women would bring empathy and compassion to policing, thus mitigating violence believed endemic in the job.

The argument that the presence of female officers would change the occupation is compelling on its face. However, we argue in this chapter (and throughout the book) that self-selection, departmental screening, and socialization produce female officers who differ little from their male colleagues and, except in rare instances, who do not utilize a different style. Women who do enter policing and are successful either possess or assimilate the values already established in the system.

## Policewomen

Early policewomen held unique positions, different from those held by their male counterparts. The advent of women in policing was a cooperative effort, one in which men and women worked in separate spheres, although they had similar goals. Policewomen developed a distinctive place and gained some acceptance within, as well as outside, the law enforcement community. In early times, the special qualities of womanhood were celebrated as a valuable difference between men and women in police roles. One of the female pioneers in the occupation argued that "no woman can really be a good policewoman, unless she works as a woman and carries with her into a police department a woman's ideals."[1]

Women's entry into police work was part of a larger social reform movement that took place during the Progressive Era of the late 19th and early 20th centuries. As in more recent social movements of the 1960s and 1970s, women in the early 1900s were actively attempting to alter their place in society, as well as working toward the reformation of major social institutions.[2] Concerns during the earlier reform movement included women's right to vote, regulation and abolition of alcohol, child worker laws, and regulation of food and drugs.

Post-Civil War industrialization in the United States created the economic conditions that galvanized the problems that policewomen[3] wanted to address. The same economic conditions also gave rise to women seeking the position of policewoman.

Industrialization created opportunities for individuals to leave farming communities and seek employment in cities. Such jobs also lured immigrants from Europe to the United States. The prosperity associated with the period created an expanded middle class, largely consisting of white Anglo-Saxon Protestants. The women of this socioeconomic group viewed with displeasure the lives of the growing working class.

Laborers often were young and alone in the cities. Although most of their moments were spent working, by the end of the 19th century they did have some leisure time, and commercial efforts to satisfy their desires for recreational activities expanded. Professional baseball, for example, became a well-liked spectator pastime for the workers. In addition, centers of amusement became popular, offering attendees a variety of entertainments. Arcades, featuring moving pictures and other newly created attractions of the period, were particularly popular, as were dance halls.

The recreational centers attracted both male and female workers, who might attend events alone or in groups with other laborers. The sight of women out on their own was a new situation and conflicted with the values of the American middle class. "Respectable" women of the period simply did not go to public places without a man.[4]

Alterations to conditions in jails and prisons were the women's first motivation to seek a career in law enforcement. The Christian reformers were concerned with protecting women in the jails, many who had not broken laws. Illustrative were newly arrived females to the city, who often found life there less than what they had expected. A chronicler of the history of policewomen noted that "police stations often also functioned as homeless shelters, and many of those who sought refuge were women and their children." The upper-middle-class female reformers urged that females "should be available to assure that women seeking shelter, almost always poor and frequently intoxicated, were not vulnerable to advances by the men responsible for them."[5]

Another matter were suffragettes, who, as a result of their participation in demonstrations to win the right to vote, were sometimes arrested and jailed. They too sought reform of the penal institutions. Their middle-class sensibilities were stunned by the treatment they received when arrested and jailed for even a few hours. Middle- and upper-class "women were horrified to be touched by men, even when no violence, excessive force, or sexual assault threat was present."[6] Cultural norms dictated that only a spouse or immediate family member might be that intimate.

The reform-minded, middle- and upper-class Christian women, active in civic concerns, launched efforts to improve prisons and end the mistreatment of women and children. In their view, female officers were needed to handle the growing moral problems, and they urged the hiring of women into the occupation.[7]

Law enforcement employment became an avenue for women to work as part of the "Child Saving Movement," designed to rescue wayward youth and women from the depravities of industrialism, alcoholism, and sexuality.[8] Members of the movement argued that degenerate women and children should fall under the jurisdiction of a social worker with police officer powers. They assumed that women were a natural choice for handling miscreant youth, since at home this was their domain.

Another issue for the reformers was the image of "white slavery"—the belief that virtuous women were being captured and sold into sexual slavery. Prostitutes of the day were seen as fallen women, but "the female reformers agitating for policewomen weren't really interested in these women. It was, in part, a class difference,"[9] but the religious leanings of the middle-class women probably played a substantial role in how they viewed women "with a past." Protestants believed that God was not a forgiving sort; one did not sin, seek absolution, and then sin again. Rather, one trod a consistent religious path. People were predetermined to go to heaven or hell. The elect could be recognized by their stern religious performance, while the damned, including delinquent women, were to be avoided.[10] The reformers were more interested in preventing good women from being led astray and sold into sexual bondage than they were in changing the ways of existing prostitutes.

The first American policewoman was Lola Baldwin, who was hired by the city of Portland, Oregon, in 1905 to protect women who were attending an exposition,[11] but the most important early individual was Alice Stebbins Wells, appointed to the Los Angeles Police Department (LAPD) in 1910. Prior to Wells's commission, she was a religious student and worker who "became interested in the scientific study of crime."[12] For her, the handling of crime was "one of the greatest fields of applied Christianity." She posited that the "police department represents the strategic point at which virtue can meet vice, strength can meet weakness, and guide them into preventive and redemptive channels."[13] A few years after her appointment, she preached:

> The battles of the future will be intellectual and moral battles, and a vast
> army of women have been studying and working to prepare themselves as

no body of soldiers has ever done before to help wage victorious warfare
against the forces that would destroy the race.[14]

In order to carry out her religious mission, Wells acquired "signatures to
a petition asking for the necessary change in police regulations to admit
a woman to the force," and she enlisted "the influence of various organizations of men and women to secure her appointment."[15]

On the job, Wells did her best to maintain a separation from traditional, male policing. She wore no uniform and carried no weapon and
kept her badge in a handbag.[16] But she must have been a strong-willed
individual. Besides forcing the city fathers of Los Angeles to create her
position, she established the parameters of the policewoman's job for
decades to come.

Wells inspected the new palaces of leisure: "penny arcades, moving
picture shows, skating rinks, dance halls, and other places of public
amusement, including the parks on Sunday," and in these locales she
saw sin and the potential for wayward youth to turn to crime. For her,
the prevention of crime and the prevention of immorality were the same
activity. For example, she believed most of the short films in the penny
arcades were "suggestive of evil." To protect the young, she used her
police powers to coerce the amusement center owners to abide by her
Victorian standards. Despite a lack of law to back her up, she was able to
persist. A writer of the day noted, "Where there is no ordinance, she
suggests the elimination of undesirable features and the introduction of
protective measures, and since these places are dependent on the police
commission for a license to continue in business, they hardly dare
ignore her requests."[17]

During the ensuing decade, Wells gave talks around the country urging other cities to hire policewomen. In 1915, she helped form the
International Association of Policewomen (IAP), which had as a primary objective the promoting of the concept of policewomen to police
departments and communities.[18]

Following the appointment of Wells to the LAPD in 1910, news
accounts describing policewomen grew steadily. Despite the press they
received, the actual number of paid policewomen expanded very slowly.
Seattle appointed five in 1912, and during the same year, women were
commissioned in Omaha and Denver. The next year Topeka, Kansas,

and Rochester, New York, appointed policewomen. By 1915, 70 women were earning police salaries in 26 different cities—a sizable percentage of growth but hardly a meaningful dent in the male-dominated occupation.[19] Their number increased during World War I, when men were in shorter supply. The rise in England totaled thousands, but growth in the United States "was on a limited scale."[20]

Policewomen were very compatible with the professional model of policing that August Vollmer was urging to be adopted at the time. Most of the women had higher educations, many with advanced degrees in nursing, teaching, and social work, which they incorporated into law enforcement—all matters that improved the professional image of policing. The women recognized and promoted their unique differences in philosophy and ability from their male counterparts. They viewed themselves as social workers and not as "cops."[21] Illustrative are comments made at a national meeting of social workers in 1919:

> The police woman does not go out to arrest disorderly men, or to apprehend women who are soliciting on the streets for prostitution; from the very beginning, the chief duty of the police woman has been to protect and safeguard youth, and today her latest opportunity lies in the direction of protective work.[22]

New York City, in particular, took advantage of the women's missionary fervor. The city hired 18 policewomen but, according to written accounts from the period, also had a volunteer force numbering 5,000, which consisted of "prominent social welfare workers."[23] The women were organized into precincts and trained by paid officers. They were

> to safeguard the morals of young women in the vicinity of cantonments and camps; to investigate crimes affecting women, such as compulsory prostitution, abortion cases and fortune-tellers. They also look after the wayward and missing girls, juvenile delinquents, and cases of improper guardianship. They secure employment for worthy girls and women, act the part of peacemakers in family difficulties, and, in fact, do general welfare work.[24]

Most of the women felt a strong calling to help humanity, to bring dignity back to women's lives, and to prevent crime by keeping a watchful eye on children. It was said that the "position of a woman in a police department is not unlike that of a mother in a home."[25]

During the early reform years, the average male officer believed that the concept and use of policewomen was a passing fad.[26] The success the women achieved was minimal. The social worker role that the early female leaders wanted to fill was not appreciated by male officers, who resented the new image being imposed on policing. The women recognized that to be accepted into the male-dominated world, they had to have a function that differed from that of the men.[27] Their evaluation of the situation reflected an astute knowledge. One of their number wrote:

> The rules and regulations, customs and traditions of police departments, having developed completely under the regime of men, do not always function according to a woman's way of doing things. To attempt to accomplish everything one would like to do by disregarding the system in operation, would be very unwise policy for policewomen to adopt. Effective service depends largely upon the extent to which the women cooperate with the men, for after all, policewomen have taken up police-womanship, not with the idea of replacing men in this work, but for the purpose of aiding and assisting them by seeking in a quiet, unassuming way to prevent crime.[28]

The women believed that male officers would accept females into the occupation as long as the women did not threaten male dominance and the role they sought fit within the traditional view of female activities. For these social activists, the "duties of the policeman and the policewoman must always be different."[29] Crime fighting and law enforcement were male domains. Crime prevention, the women hoped, would become the female function. The measure of a policewoman's "success should not be the number of arrests made," they urged, "but rather the number of arrested prevented.[30]"

Crime prevention activities focused on youngsters because police believed "that the causes of crime were to be found in the effect of certain existing institutions upon the young people of the country, and that the attack on crime must be made among the young."[31] In general, it was felt that unsupervised juveniles would commit crimes; however, if they were watched more closely, crime would be prevented.[32] Policewomen were expected to deter or diminish the determinants of vice, gambling, and lawlessness,[33] as well as give attention to

> The protection of young girls and the prevention or minimization of
> social evils . . . the return of runaway girls to their homes, the warning of
> young girls, the suppression of dance hall evils, . . . petty gambling in
> stores frequented by children . . . the sale of liquor to minors, service at
> railroad depots, the conducting of investigations and the securing of evi-
> dence.[34]

Women were grudgingly accepted into police work but almost exclusively
because they handled situations disliked by the men, in particular, incidents involving women and children. Almost everywhere they existed,
for example, policewomen were called upon to patrol theaters in search
of truants and disruptive children. An inspection report for a 1925
department reported that its policewomen had visited "moving-picture
houses" 2,446 times, removing 259 truants, 14 disorderly juveniles, and
37 children who were found asleep late at night. In addition, during
their tours of the theaters, the female officers arrested 13 men and 1
woman for indecent acts.[35] Male officers probably disliked monitoring
the activities of theatergoers and willingly surrendered such assignments
to the female constabulary.

Efforts by the women to define their mission as crime prevention were
often disregarded by police chiefs, who would occasionally send their
female officers to assist in "discovering thieves and even murderers and
to get evidence against criminals."[36] Not every department saw fit to use
their female officers as quasi-social workers. In Chicago, for example,
the superintendent of the police wrote in a letter that "the scope of the
duties of police women in this city consists principally in ascertaining
violations of the law" and that their "duties do not differ materially from
those of police men."[37]

Across the United States, policewomen were required to perform
many tasks that resembled standard police work, such as interview sexual assault victims, interrogate women felons, keep records, disseminate
information to the public, take complaints, serve as decoys, and patrol
areas of prostitution. For the female officers, working undercover was
particularly "difficult because mingling with people after dark was just
not a normal activity for respectable women."[38] One policewoman, who
resigned because of the assignments, complained that she "had joined

the force to help fallen women and wayward children." But instead she "was forced to accompany men of the lowest type, professional stool pigeons, around town, to enter dives of the worst type and do work which could be done much better by men."[39]

The women who received praise within departments were those who fulfilled the law enforcement goal of policing. Illustrative was Josephine Roche, who was appointed to the Denver police in 1912. A year later, the Denver chief referred to her as "the best man" on his force.[40] Roche concentrated on enforcement and not social work activities, although she believed women had methods that differed from men. She wrote about her endeavors:

> [W]e no longer believe in the old theory that law must be enforced by the club or by the revolver. You cannot force people to do right. You cannot beat goodness into them. You have to show them why they should obey the law. Just because a woman is a woman and disassociated from the idea of force, she can frequently enforce the law with more ease than a man.[41]

The efforts of the female activists to create a crime prevention role for policewomen were only minimally successful, and by the 1930s, growth in their number came to a grinding halt. For one reason, the depression reinforced traditional gender roles; women returned to the home, and the diminished number of jobs went to men.[42] But a change in the archetype of the police force had a more long-term effect.

## BUREAUCRACY AND POLICEWOMEN

During the 1930s, a new wave of police administrators infused departments with bureaucratization. The social worker–oriented policewoman had matched well the educated police professional urged by Vollmer 20 years earlier. But she had only a minimal role in the police order envisioned by O. W. Wilson and J. Edgar Hoover, who were actively pursuing law enforcement as the police goal.[43] Crime prevention activities were relegated by the male leaders to minimal importance. Wilson "did not advocate expanded roles for policewomen. To the contrary, he believed that women were ill-equipped emotionally for leadership positions."[44] Hoover was much harsher. While he was director of the FBI (Federal Bureau of Investigation), no women were hired as agents. He argued, "The Bureau's responsibilities were too taxing, too physically demanding, too complicated and serious for women, except insofar as they could help out in menial or subservient roles."[45] He wanted his agents to be "tough, fearless crime fighters," trained to use "the latest scientific crime fighting techniques."[46] He used the media to portray this image and to glorify himself and his agency.

As a result of the police leaders' endeavors, the bureaucratic police department of the 1930s emphasized crime fighting over the "order maintenance and service aspects of the police role," and officers on the street ridiculed such duties "as not being 'real' policework."[47] Women who had the same law enforcement goals as their male colleagues could survive within police departments.

By World War II, the major distinction between the work of male and female officers was not between law enforcement and crime prevention. Both groups of police officers probably emphasized crime-fighting activities. Rather, the differences between male and female activities stemmed from the belief that the police function required the use of authority and force and that women lacked the physical presence to fill that role.[48] Moreover, the specter of assault and possible death hung over the patrolmen's job, and women, in general, were to be protected from such situations and not shoved, badge first, into them. These matters limited the opportunities for women's employment by law enforcement agencies. By 1938, there were slightly more than 500 policewomen nationwide; most probably worked a normal police officer's 48-hour, 6-day workweek for which they received compensation comparable to that of male officers.[49]

Following World War II, few policewomen were given the fanfare that had accompanied their introduction 40 years earlier. A study conducted by the Woman's Bureau of the United States Department of Justice in 1949 concluded that policewomen were less than 1 percent of force personnel.[50] An estimated 1,000 were employed by about 140 cities with populations of more than 25,000; New York led the way with 174 followed by Chicago's crew of 79. In most cities, policewomen continued to work with women and children. But indicative of the crime-fighting role that many policewomen filled was the report that in 40 cities the women were required to carry a firearm while 36 cities made it optional.[51]

During the economic boom of the 1950s, the number of women hired into police work increased dramatically. By 1960, 5,617 female police officers and detectives were serving U.S. municipalities. Their number in New York City had grown to 253. There, and in other large departments, policewomen had the same powers as policemen, received the same salary, and had the opportunity to become detectives.[52] Most of the women were involved in law enforcement activities. Working in teams, the policewomen, in civilian clothes, patrolled locales where complaints indicated "the presence of degenerates, shoplifters and jostlers." The women, it was argued, were better suited for investigations involving "degenerates" because "the direct evidence necessary for a court conviction can best be obtained by a policewoman."[53] The women were also involved in surveillance, at times "tailing" suspects or finding employment in a suspect's social world so as to spy on him. And, of course, in rape cases, the women were used because they were "successful in obtaining information from women who may be reluctant to discuss delicate or sordid matters with male officers."[54]

Not all the new policewomen, however, were involved in the crime control arena. Some had found employment because of expanding police responsibilities. The rapid postwar increase in automobiles, for example, quickly overburdened downtown parking capacities and police departments needed to increase the number of individuals assigned to traffic and parking duties. Female officers made handy "meter maids." A sergeant praised them, noting that they "are 'three times as rugged as men'—they don't complain so much about their feet and they hand out more tickets."[55] Some of the traffic officers were paid the same as their male counterparts, carried revolvers, and worked the same 48-hour week. Those who were limited to checking for parking violations, however, received lower salaries.[56]

Women also entered police work during the 1950s because administrators found them useful support staff within the bureaucratic police world. One superintendent of communications, for example, noted that his staff of female dispatchers handled a call, on average, in nine seconds. "The girls seem to stand the pace much better than men," the reporter noted.[57]

By the middle of the 1960s, the president's commission, in the half page it devoted to them, urged an expanded role for women in policing:

> Police women can be an invaluable asset to modern law enforcement and their present role should be broadened. Qualified women should be utilized in such important staff service units as planning and research, training, intelligence, inspection, public information, community relations, and as legal advisors.
>
> Women could also serve in such units as computer programming and laboratory analyses and communications. Their value should not be considered as limited to staff functions or police work with juveniles; women should also serve regularly in patrol, vice, and investigative divisions. Finally, as more and more well-qualified women enter the service, they could assume administrative responsibilities.[58]

Nationally, however, potential positions for women remained limited, primarily because women were perceived as being unable to handle the physical and emotional rigors of patrol, where most police jobs exist (and from where future administrators are chosen).

## WOMEN ON PATROL

Revolutionary changes occurred in women's roles during the 1960s and 1970s, both in the larger society and in policing. Women sought equal access to employment opportunities, including jobs generally held by men, such as police patrol work. Rather than stressing their differences, these women pushed against what they correctly perceived to be artificial barriers and sought occupational equality to men in patrol work. Of primary political importance, in 1972 Congress passed a number of pieces of legislation that have directly impacted women's opportunities for achievement. Title IX, because it opened school athletics to women, is the most celebrated. But the same year, Congress enacted the Equal Employment Opportunity (EEO) Act, which unlocked the door that had kept women out of patrol. Municipalities were legally liable if they failed to hire and place on patrol worthy female applicants.[59]

In Indianapolis in 1968, and then with great fanfare in 1969 in Washington, D.C., policewomen were reassigned to patrol work. Some women, who had entered policing to do social work, were not happy with their new positions and objected.[60] But increasingly from that moment, women entered policing as equals to men, to perform identical duties and receive identical rewards. The terms "policewoman" and "policeman" were dropped, and the more generic term of "police officer" was adopted. The unique professional position of quasi–social worker, which the pioneer policewomen had worked so hard to create, vanished, leaving the crime control function of police unchallenged from the ranks of officers.

## Problems

Since women's integration into patrol, efforts to attract and hire women into law enforcement have been minimal and often required litigation to bring about change. Women wishing patrol assignment were not readily accepted into the bureaucratic police organization. For one, a general belief existed among the men that women were incapable, or at least less capable, of police work. Basic to their belief was the notion that men and women are different and that police work requires some ability only men possess. In general, those in society who hold this and similar views argue that behavior is, in part, biologically determined and further assert that gender-based roles in society are rooted in biological makeup. Simply put, men, because they were hunters in earlier societies, are more aggressive and better suited for the conflict of modern life. Women, because they gave birth and had to nurse their offspring, are nurturing and better suited for domestic careers. Women who identified with their "traditional roles" were "commended for competency and ingenuity in problem solving."[61] But women performing or desiring "male" occupations were considered abnormal. In order to do men's work, it was posited, they must deny their feminine nature. They must be tough, unemotional, and decisive—traits not stereotypically assigned to women.

In general, individuals who choose occupations not traditionally associated with their gender, such as female police officers, will feel great pressure from many in society to reconsider their decisions. Those who conform to societal expectations gain a feeling of solidarity by urging deviants to conform. Punishing deviants further reinforces this sense of solidarity or "group" and demonstrates the "evils" of nonconformity.[62] Male officers accomplished this function by ridiculing female officers or excluding them from activities in the hope that they would quit.[63]

Women's entrance into patrol coincided with an expanded interest across the nation in law enforcement. Beginning with the presidential election of 1964, crime control became a high priority on the national agenda. The potential for violence had always been a core element of police work; the period that surrounded women's entrance into the male world of patrol was particularly so and probably further hindered their acceptance. Media presentations focused on law enforcement as the goal of police work and stressed the occupation's perils. Officers were portrayed as "ill-paid" and facing "danger and hardship"[64] in a world in which they had to deal with "criminals who would not stop at murder to carry out their purpose."[65] There was, according to some, "a war against the police," which involved "vicious attacks on officers, the murder and maiming of lawmen."[66] Citizens were instructed that the police "detect crime and apprehend criminals" and that "[it's] not their job to be involved in private disputes such as landlord-tenant problems, or quarrels between neighbors, or in family disputes."[67]

Foremost among males' verbal complaints about the entrance of women into patrol was that they would not perform well in potentially dangerous situations.[68] Some men maintained that women might cause violence.[69] Their diminutive size and strength, the argument went, were not conducive to physical confrontation,[70] and suspects might challenge a female officer. For male officers, being tall and intimidating was an important police tool.[71] (The same philosophy had excluded shorter males from police acceptance.) Priority was given to men, who were perceived as having "the brawn to deal with police problems."[72] A woman on patrol threatened the status quo of the police culture and in particular the officers' self-image as fierce individuals doing a job only tough men could accomplish. Male officers insisted that they would hesitate to call the "weaker sex" to back them up in violent situations.[73] Moreover, the men feared that their fellow officers might abandon a chase of fleeing felons if any female officers got in trouble. The male instinct, they posited, would be to protect the women from harm.[74]

Antagonism also developed between male officers and vocal feminists of the day, who were demanding equal rights and equal pay. Feminist demonstrators, along with criminals and civil rights activists, were perceived of as "enemies" by the officers.[75]

All in all, women who entered policing as patrol officers had a tough time of it, in large part because they were not accepted by their male colleagues. Their continued small numbers suggests that the situation has not changed much.

## ARE FEMALE OFFICERS DIFFERENT?

Beginning in the 1970s, numerous studies were conducted on hypothesized differences between male and female officers utilizing measures of job performance, such as arrest rates, self-initiated activities, dependability, observation skills, and stress control and composure.[76] Many of the investigators concluded that there was little difference between the way male officers did the job and the manner in which women accomplished it.[77] Some analysts, however, have suggested that men and women do differ. Men made more arrests than did their female counterparts[78] and were overrepresented among officers who had been disciplined for brutality.[79] The lower rates of arrests and violence among female officers hint that they seek alternative ways to handle citizens' problems.[80]

Illustrative of the better studies was a pilot project conducted in New York City during 1975 and 1976. Patrol performances of 41 women officers were compared to a matched sample of 41 male officers.[81] Police and civilian personnel observed the officers while they did their jobs. The authors of the research reported:

In general, male and female officers performed similarly: they used the same techniques to gain and keep control and were equally unlikely to use force or to display a weapon. However, small differences in performance were observed. Female officers were judged by civilians to be more competent, pleasant and respectful than their male counterparts, but were observed to be slightly less likely to engage in control-seeking behavior, and less apt to assert themselves in patrol-decision making. Compared to male officers, females were less often named as arresting officers, less likely to participate in strenuous physical activity, and took more sick time.[82]

The report noted that some of the differences may have been the result of the women "holding back," as they were new to the areas and riding with males who often wanted to take control of the situations. Although not mentioned in the report, many, if not most, of the male officers were former military men who viewed women as unable to lead and did not want to take orders from them. Historically, the exercise of authority and use of force were assigned to men. Women were rarely allowed to command and control others. Other matters likely also affected the situations. Male officers, for example, more often drove the patrol cars, chiefly because women drivers pulled the bench seat closer to the foot pedals, which cramped the long-legged males.[83]

The report explained that when female officers rode together, the women "were more active than when they rode with men."[84] These items and others led the researchers to note that the matter of yielding may be "a reflection of traditional male-female role behavior."[85] They determined that

> The results of this study offer little support either to those who hold that women are unsuited to patrol or to those who argue that women do the job better than men. By and large, patrol performance of the women was more like that of the men than it was different.[86]

## ACCEPTING THE CULTURE

The results of the studies of police performance by gender were analogous to investigations done at about the same time of women's execution of other leadership roles. Where women were accepted, they performed their jobs as well as men.[87] For women entering police work (and other male-dominated occupations), the problem was not so much having the physical ability to do the job but rather the lack of approval from male colleagues. To be appreciated, the female recruits had to

> accept the standards and the style of the male world. The male world, that is, will admit them if they can pass male tests and perform just as well as or better than men. They must become competitive, achievement-oriented, and reject the patterns characteristic of the woman's world.[88]

To be successful, the female officer, or for that matter any officer, must share the values and norms of the police culture. The female recruit who wants to win the approval of her colleagues must either bring with her to the job the values and norms of the police culture or she must adopt them early in her career. Rookies who do not conform to the group's norms are shunned or ridiculed by orthodox members of the culture[89] and can expect their police careers to be difficult and probably short-lived. Certainly, they would have little chance for promotion since they would be excluded from the departments' informal social networks, which "are the keys to opportunity for mobility within the organization."[90]

## DISCUSSION AND CONCLUSION

Pervasive negative beliefs concerning the abilities of women to perform the police role continue to exist, despite research findings that women perform equally as well as their male counterparts in the role of police officer. These attitudes appear resistant to change for a number of reasons. Some biological differences are unchangeable. Reproductive abilities—getting pregnant, carrying a baby, and giving birth—are biological realities with which women must deal. Those in police departments and the general society who disapprove of female officers likely have their prejudices reinforced by these biological facts.

It is doubtful that all recruits will be capable in both the crime control and service functions of police work. Unfortunately, as we will show, those individuals who become police officers prefer the law enforcement component of their jobs. Subverted is the hope that female officers might differ from their male counterparts and elect the service role. Individuals who are attracted to the police occupation are selected by and soon socialized into a police subculture that rejects change and prizes loyalty to the system. In the following chapters, we explain the research upon which our conclusions are based and explore their consequences with respect to police behavior.

# CHAPTER THREE

## *How This Study Was Conducted*

We could have studied male and female officers in a number of ways. One of the best might have been to travel with them through their workdays and record how each individual handled various situations, as was accomplished in New York City at the time of women's entrance into patrol.[1] If men and women did the job differently, we ought to have noticed. Such work, however, is unusually arduous. Most days, officers do little more than patrol an area, and it would be unlikely that we would often view situations that might differentiate the genders. Moreover, an extensive number of personnel (and the associated expense) would be needed for such an undertaking. And in the end, we might have only concluded that men and women did the job similarly or differently, but we probably would have been unable to say much about why such conditions existed.

A far easier method for studying officers is to present them with a survey that asks them to agree or disagree with various statements. Numerous such studies have been conducted.[2] They are relatively easy to do, and the officers' answers can be statistically analyzed to determine if differences exist between the groups. Surveys, however, also suffer from their inability to uncover the underlying causes of measured distinctions and similarities. The researcher knows that they exist but is often left to speculate about the basis of their existence.

We decided to interview officers to determine their attitudes and impressions with respect to their jobs. Similar previous research has utilized interviews with officers from single departments or of the same gender or ethnicity.[3] Our sample, we hoped, would represent a wider group of officers and, as a result, be more reflective of general police attitudes and practices.

## ACCESS

Access to the police departments was problematic. Officials have good reason to feel threatened by studies, particularly ones that in part use gender as a basis for understanding. Civil suits brought by female officers against their departments, claiming harassment by other officers and superiors, have proved expensive and embarrassing. During the time of our study, for example, several Southern California departments were immersed in such episodes. In one city, male officers were said to have coerced female officers into having sex with them while on the job.[4] In another action, the city of Newport Beach ended up paying off police employees not to file suit.[5] Departments could hardly be blamed for fearing that our inquiry might stir up trouble and lead to similar legal entanglements.

But the problem we expected in obtaining permission to meet with officers was exacerbated by "poor timing." We had completed interviews in one city and were about to begin efforts in a second when the videotaped police beating of Rodney King became public. During the next weeks, the footage was shown daily on newscasts, talk shows, and television magazine programs. Police administrators, because of the negative publicity, were likely more cautious than usual about admitting outside researchers, and we were fearful that we might have no one to interview.

Department chiefs, however, were very cooperative. Nine police agencies, located in three Southern California counties, were contacted regarding participation in this study and seven consented. Since we were requesting to interview male and female officers, one chief turned us down because he currently had no women on his force. Another official with a large department declined participation for his organization. He did not cite the reason for the decision, but his force had suffered a number of recent scandals and was under a substantial measure of political pressure. It seems likely that he was avoiding the possibility of adding to his problems.

## The Departments and Cities

The seven participating departments are located in three Southern California counties. It was our belief that officers' answers would be reflective of differing police styles. Organizational structures and objectives of police departments are presumed to create similarities among officers within a unit as the philosophical goals of each agency and its administrators determine the types of people they select to be recruits. Officers within a unit should reflect its established profile and therefore tend to resemble each other in terms of attitudes and behaviors. Studies comparing police forces reveal that phenomena such as supervisorial and organizational structures influence police decision making[6] and that certain neighborhood characteristics together with organizational structures produce systematic patterns of police behavior.[7]

We utilized classifications developed by James Q. Wilson.[8] He proposed three styles of police department behavior: legalistic, watchman, and service. Wilson's policing modes are only ideal types. Departments may, in fact, utilize overlapping styles. He warns the lay reader that "departments categorized together are not identical in all respects" and that his classification "can only suggest, it cannot prove, that a particular operating style is associated with certain organizational characteristics."[9]

We wanted to include departments from each of Wilson's categories because we believed that legalistic, watchman, and service departments differ with respect to whom they select to be officers, what they stress in training, and what officers learn while in service. Because of these variations, we expected that officers' answers might differ by the type of department to which they belonged. Inclusion of diverse departments and municipalities should increase the likelihood that our study is reflective of a broader band of policing.

Five of the departments in our study patrol large, urban areas with culturally and economically diverse populations. The departments receive a high volume of calls, including homicides, rapes, robberies, and other violent offenses. Four of these five cities have substantial populations of immigrants, many of whom speak little English. This creates an added problem for officers, who need to be sensitive to cultural practices that may be alien to them. Additionally, multicultural gangs are a significant presence in these cities; the fifth urban department also polices gang turf. The five cities also have discernible vice problems. One municipality, for example, prospers because of an extensive tourist trade that has given rise to visible prostitution. Officers must use their discretion in order to provide a friendly environment for visitors while maintaining order.

The five urban departments employ a watchman method of policing. Watchman-style departments stress order-maintenance duties and are concerned with peacekeeping. They are located in cities that generally have high crime rates, and police officers handle a considerable number of calls on a daily basis. In order to deal with the wide-ranging situations that their officers meet, administrators in watchman departments allow their officers a great deal of discretion. As a result, officers often treat family disputes informally, and juvenile misbehavior is generally ignored. Officers do, however, formally address serious crimes. Communities with watchman-style departments are rarely homogeneous and may have pockets of wealth and poverty.[10]

The two remaining units in our study are located in suburban municipalities with homogeneous, predominantly white populations. One department, located in a very affluent area, has a long tradition of legalistic policing. Its reputation is such that officers in other departments, as well as citizens, told us that misbehaving within the city's boundaries is likely to get one arrested. Legalistic departments emphasize law enforcement duties, such as investigating crimes and arresting offenders.[11] Administrators usually restrict the use of discretion by their officers. Legalistic departments, for example, detain or arrest a larger proportion of juvenile offenders. Of course, criminal justice personnel could not do their jobs without some leeway, and so, it is not surprising that patrol officers within legalistic departments do distinguish between major and minor crimes, feel that private disputes are usually less important than public disorders, and are willing to overlook some offenses.[12]

The other department, located in a city with a middle-class to upper-middle-class population, has a "self-defined" service-oriented police force. Officers are hired for this unit because they possess characteristics believed by their superiors to be necessary for carrying out service duties. College degrees, for example, are common among the department's personnel. (For example, the 13 interviewed officers from this department had all taken some college courses, and 6 held bachelor's degrees.) Officers are instructed to respond to and take seriously even the most minor citizen complaints. Service departments, such as this one, are concerned with helping citizens and their communities. Middle-class communities often require police departments to utilize the service style. These suburban cities are usually homogeneous and not deeply divided by class or racial lines. Crime is less obvious. The police do take seriously all requests for help, but officers in the field try to mediate situations and avoid the use of arrest.[13]

## SUBJECTS

The 40 male and 40 female officers we interviewed participated in this study after being given the opportunity to do so by a superior in their departments.[14] Generally, the officers we talked with were educated, comparatively young, with less than 10 years of police experience. The majority of the officers (56 percent) had attended college courses, and more than 40 percent had at least a bachelor's degree (37.5 percent had obtained only bachelor's degrees, and an additional 5 percent had advanced college degrees). It is difficult to determine if they are representative of officers nationally. No state or national information exists on officers' ages by gender. Nor are national or state averages available on officers' educational achievements, although this study's officers did surpass national requirements by a substantial amount, suggesting that our sample of officers was more educated. Eighty-five percent of all police departments require only a high-school diploma of its officers, while 5 percent dictate a two-year degree and 1 percent require a four-year degree. The remaining departments require less than a high-school diploma.[15] The unusually high educational level of our group is most likely reflective, in part, of the voluntary nature of this project. Police officers with college degrees are probably more likely to participate in research studies.

## The Questions

The literature on policing suggests numerous areas for research, ranging from officer recruitment and training to the reasons for retirement. We developed questions to embody the various stages of a police officer's career. The queries were neither controversial nor deeply personal but were developed to learn about officers' motivations for entering police work; perceptions of their training and their current jobs; friendships and relationships; future job aspirations; and responses to two common police situations, one involving juveniles and the other domestic disputes. Early policewomen were assigned the task of taking care of juveniles and handling the domestic sphere; therefore, the final two questions were designed to assess differences or similarities between male and female officers with respect to these matters.

In an effort to generate as much information as possible, the questions were open ended and administered face to face. We wanted to be able to "dig" for answers when officers' responses were incomplete, unhelpful, or vague. Open-ended questions allowed the officers to clarify their answers in their own words and to tell us what was important to them.

## The Interview Process

We expected that the interviewing of police officers would be difficult because they are believed to be suspicious of outsiders and reluctant to talk openly.[16] One author suggested, "Interviewers with tape recorders remind them of prisoner interrogations and internal affairs investigations where anything the subject says may be used against him."[17]

The closeness in time of the interviews to the Rodney King beating, we feared, might make matters worse. Surprisingly, many officers seemed disappointed when they determined that the study was about another matter. Most volunteered their opinions and feelings about the clubbing prior to the interview, and many of them mentioned it in their responses. The general view was that they were upset with the public's reaction, but they were also upset by the incident itself. It remains uncertain whether the officers' answers were influenced by the Rodney King beating, but it did not seem to have an impact.

Officers initially appeared to be suspicious of the research. They asked questions about the nature and purpose of the study before being interviewed. They seemed to relax some after being told that their responses were anonymous.

Occasionally, officers may not have been totally honest with us. They may have provided answers that they believed their superiors or we wanted. The subjects, however, often told us information that would have gotten them in trouble if it left the room. Overall, the officers appeared to do their best to be honest. When they did supply answers that seemed to be fabrications, we pulled from them more forthright explanations. Generally, we were impressed with their candid and sincere responses.

## DISCUSSION

Police agencies are particularly reluctant to open their doors to research concerning gender issues for fear the outside investigation will uncover inflammatory problems. With current public scrutiny, police administrators are also disinclined to permit any research concerning personnel issues—such as hiring and promotional practices and officer misconduct. It is less threatening to invite outside research help in areas such as gang violence or response time to calls. The present study was successful, in part, because of the manner in which it was presented to top administrators for consideration. They believed that the study was somewhat innocuous because it did not ask officers whether they suffer unfair treatment, whether they violate citizens' rights, or whether they follow departmental policies and abide by the laws of the state.

Overall, this study provides unique information. The systematic, in-depth interviews allowed officers to offer personal insights. In addition, the opportunity existed during the interviews for officers to expand and clarify their answers. The sample size was large for interview studies, and we were able to gain insights on a broad range of police topics.

The following chapters use the officers' answers to shed some illumination on, as we see it, the inherent problem with police; that is, individuals who are attracted to police work, hired, and successfully socialized prefer the law enforcement component of police work and shun other activities. This is true for both male and female officers and is the primary reason why we received similar answers from both sexes.

# CHAPTER FOUR

## Why Would Anyone Want to Be a Police Officer?

Most of us have little concern as to why individuals choose their occupations. Overall, it doesn't matter much whether someone decides to be a plumber because the occupation pays well or because the person enjoys working with his or her hands. Two occupations stand out from the rest in this regard: physician and police officer.

Physicians and police officers have an unusual factor in common that makes individuals' motivations for entering these occupations important—specifically, the ability to cause great physical harm by doing their jobs incorrectly. It should not be surprising then to learn that motivations for entering these occupations are probably the most studied.

The original concern with doctors in the early part of the 20th century was attracting high-caliber individuals to the profession. The occupation was glutted with working-class individuals seeking a slight improvement in their standard of living. Medical and corporate leaders professionalized the occupation as a means to improve the financial awards it had to offer and attract better-qualified individuals. The corporate leaders were interested in a healthier (and thus more productive) work force.[1]

Early interest in men's motivations for joining the police were an outgrowth of turn-of-the-century publicity about corruption. Men drawn to police work before the 20th century saw the occupation as a means to integrate the accepted social classes. The police represented the interests of upper-class individuals, who were intent on protecting their property. Men hired into the job came from working-class backgrounds and saw their new positions as high-status blue-collar jobs.[2] Men from established immigrant groups sought the job and did their best to prevent the hiring of more recent arrivals, presumably in order to maintain, at least in their own eyes, their socioeconomic level.[3] It seems reasonable to conjecture that the occupation was apt to be passed from father to son and that those outside the ethnic/cultural circle were unlikely to view the profession as a viable option.

As the 20th century dawned, police officers were increasingly viewed by the middle and upper classes as corrupt and brutal individuals. This issue is discussed more thoroughly in chapter 1. Professionalization was imagined as the cure for police ills. Attempts by police leaders to attract professional men to their departments, however, were largely a failure. The vocation was a blue-collar position for immigrant groups and a social step down for college-educated individuals. Women, however, saw the opportunity the occupation offered to enter the male-dominated work force while maintaining their nurturing self-image. As with immigrant groups, the women most likely perceived police employment as a means to increased acceptance into the working world.

Newspaper and magazine accounts also played a part in determining the type of individual attracted to police work. Nineteenth-century popularized images of the police were not favorable, and writers of the time did little to help the situation. Mystery authors, for example, Sir Arthur Conan Doyle in his Sherlock Holmes stories, portrayed police detectives as less than adequate. Early movie depictions were also not kind. Mack Sennett's Keystone Kops caused more laughs among audience members than awe at their sleuthing ability. J. Edgar Hoover did his best to change the poor image and portrayed to the public a more efficient and sophisticated crime-fighting picture of law enforcement. His success lingers long past his death; college faculty members can attest to the large numbers of students who still see FBI employment as a "crime-busting" activity. More recent media images of the police have represented other facets of police work, but generally they continue to overrepresent and glamorize the law enforcement component.[4]

## The Culture

Researchers interested in learning why one would want to be a police officer face a methodological difficulty: the people they interview are already officers. Individuals who may have wanted to become police officers but were rejected by selection boards are not included for study. Departments' selection criteria are clearly important in determining the composition of a police force. Through most of the 20th century, their choices have produced a fairly homogeneous police force, primarily because selection boards place great emphasis on choosing individuals who conform to the "norms of the department."[5] This is not unusual. All occupations develop their own cultural norms.[6] The important point here is that individuals who already possess the police value system, which includes motivations for entering the occupation, are more likely to be hired than those who hold other values.

The current characteristics of the police subculture have their roots deep within the fertile reform era of the early 1900s. Efforts to professionalize the individual police officer alienated the men from the wider society.[7] Male officers of the period lacked the education to fulfill the role as envisioned by Vollmer and his supporters. They withdrew into their own world, which prized working-class ideals of the time. Their estrangement, combined with their disdain for the social work side of policing, resulted in a strong subculture that overemphasized certain characteristics of the law enforcement role to the detriment of actual police activities. Women's entrance into police work and their handling of police social work activities did not help matters. Males could ignore such activities and concentrate on the law enforcement role. By labeling such actions as "women's work," the men effectively stigmatized the role within the male police subculture.

Preeminent among the male officers' value system was a belief in the necessity of using violence to accomplish the job.[8] Officers never knew when violence on the streets would occur.[9] Since, in their view, the only people they could count on in such situations were their fellow officers, maintaining their allegiance was of utmost importance.[10] They maintained a "code of silence" about police activities, and, if necessary, were willing to lie to protect other officers.[11] A police officer who obtained his doctorate from the Sociology Department at the University of California during the 1960s wrote in his dissertation:

> Solidarity in a police department means more than standing side by side
> in the face of physical danger, it also means lying for your fellow officer

in court, or covering up for him when he is under investigation by the
department itself. This solidarity, often blind, is given to the other officers as men, as individuals, not because they are good, honest, or moral
men, though they may be, but because one never knows where trouble or
danger will strike and one must be able to count on the unhesitating support of any officer near by.[12]

These values presumably have been endemic in departments and are
passed from officers to family members and other residents of the neighborhood. Individuals seeking a patrolman's job who lack these ideals are
likely turned away by those doing the hiring, while individuals who portray the "right stuff" are more apt to be hired.[13]

## STANDARDS

Police departments, as bureaucracies, use tests to initially cull out
unwanted applicants. In a bureaucracy, individuals are hired based on
technical competence or standards. Standards can be used to include certain types of people, while excluding others. During the depression, for
example, departments tilted exams and other entrance criteria to favor
those who had gone to college.[14]

O. W. Wilson's move during the 1930s to bureaucratize police departments helped establish the characteristics used to screen applicants. He
believed that good officers had three important traits: "mental, the physical, and character."[15] Wilson relied on physical requirements and standardized tests developed by academics as initial discriminators.
Applicants had to be at least 5 feet 10 inches in height, weigh a minimum of 160 pounds, and be between 21 and 30 years of age.[16] Three
decades later, the President's Commission on Law Enforcement and
Administration of Justice concluded that

> the dominant concern in the screening of applicants for the job of a
> police officer has been to assure that they met the rigid physical standards
> that were established. Such standards are still applied in many jurisdic-
> tions, despite the fact that they do not bear directly on the most difficult
> problems faced by the police officer today. Emphasis upon physical
> strength and aggressiveness reflects the popular image of what the police
> do rather than a careful analysis of job requirements.[17]

Height and weight requirements began to be relaxed during the 1960s. The change was brought about by several factors. For one, a series of urban riots during the period were all sparked by police activities.[18] Political leaders, as a result, urged departments to seek non-white applicants. They were of the opinion that minority communities would be more responsive to police who looked more like themselves. During the same period, affirmative action decisions required government agencies to hire more minority members. Lowering the physical requirements increased the number of potential applicants, particularly among some ethnic groups whose members were, on average, shorter. By the 1970s, numerous cities had discounted the physical guidelines.[19]

The use of psychological testing was another modification in hiring practices. The psychological profile of aspirants became prominent after World War II because people were afraid that our police officers might too closely resemble the Nazi soldiers who had enforced Hitler's police state. Most research and concern focused on the possibility of an authoritarian personality.[20] Municipalities also endorsed psychological testing of police candidates as a means to protect themselves against civil suits. Departments are liable for individual officer's actions if they fail to test for suitability for the job.[21]

Today, in addition to physical and psychological tests, police applicants must clear a number of hurdles before being chosen by departments. Candidates' schooling, job record, financial and criminal histories, and references are checked.[22]

## Job Motivations

Historically, men and women differed in their motivations for pursuing careers in law enforcement. Some writers have pointed to psychologically oriented reasons for men to join the police. For example, the opportunity to satisfy a need for "manliness" has been suggested as a driving force.[23] But generally, men sought the occupation because it allowed them to work in an exciting environment, with good pay and job security.[24] The men were primarily from working-class backgrounds and saw police employment as a step up the socioeconomic ladder.[25]

Beginning in the late 1960s, police salaries and benefits rose rapidly as a means to attract individuals to understaffed departments.[26] Many recruits looked forward to early retirement at half their final salaries. Police paychecks have continued to rise. New hires, on average, can expect to be paid $30,600 per year, and sergeants make about $47,500.[27]

In early times, women were motivated to join the police by philanthropic crusades. The demise of the unique role of policewomen in social services and their integration into patrol work changed the type of woman attracted to the job.[28] A member of Washington, D.C.'s Juvenile Division at the time of the change commented on the experience:

> Not surprisingly, the majority of the policewomen on the department were not pushing to get into patrol. Many of them, like me, had been attracted to the special assignments where they could use their college degrees doing social service oriented work. Most of the women who were, in fact, fighting for patrol were those who had never been attracted to policework in the past but now wanted to be able to do the same duties as men because that kind of exciting job appealed to them.[29]

The change in policing increased the number of positions open to women and the type of person drawn to the job. Department chiefs increasingly sought female applicants to satisfy public pressures and court orders. These new female officers were recruited in the same fashion and in the same places as their male colleagues[30] and had the same reasons for joining the police. Some differences may have existed,[31] but overall they were "working-class high school graduates who enter policing for its salary, benefits, and career opportunities."[32] And, as did the men, they found appealing the exciting, crime control aspect of the work.[33]

## WHAT WE LEARNED

The characteristics of individuals who become police officers are largely determined by departmental attitudes and hiring practices. This fact is most evident in the answers we received from the women with whom we spoke. Social barriers to women desiring employment in fields that are perceived as male still exist, and despite numerous studies and more than three decades of women's service, some male officers believe that women just can't do the job. Several of the female officers we interviewed, for example, reported that some departments would not hire women, while other departments had reputations for giving women a hard time. One woman told us that she "had an oral interview with another department and they said 'we don't think you can do the job because you are so small; we don't think you can go into a bar fight and actually take action.'" For the members of this selection committee and others, the ability to use violence on the job was of primary importance and, in their view, an ability that only large men possess. As a result, female officers are less likely to be employed by some departments. One officer commented that her preference for her current job stemmed from the department's reputation for fairly treating female recruits. "Its more progressive with women," she told us. "I won't mention other department names," she added, "but some have one or two women for a couple of hundred male officers. They don't really give women a chance to do work in that city."

## EFFECTS OF INCREASED COMPETITION FOR JOBS

Additional minorities and women entering policing swelled the number of individuals seeking officer positions. In the late 1960s, positions often went unfilled. More recently, hundreds have applied for each vacancy in the departments in which we interviewed. The increased competition for the limited jobs has allowed departments to be more selective.

The most evident result of the increased competition is the number of male officers in our sample with a college education; more than half the men had four-year college degrees but only about one-third of the women. Seventy-five years ago, it was rare for male officers to have attended college. A woman had to have a college education to become a police officer, while a high-school diploma was more than sufficient for men. Today, the situation is somewhat reversed; a man without some college experience is at a disadvantage if he wants to become an officer. Departments, as part of their hiring decisions, usually give extra points to applicants who have gone to college. All other factors being equal, the man with the advanced education will get the job.

The situation is somewhat different for women, particularly in departments that are under legal or social pressure to add female officers. Competition for the positions is probably less heated among women. It is probably safe to say that fewer women than men see policing as a viable occupation. At least many more men apply for policing positions. Departments simply do not get many college-educated female applicants, and this is reflected in the lower educational achievement level of the women's side of our sample.

## TEARING DOWN THE WALLS

The increased opportunities for women in nontraditional areas were reflected in the tales we were told. Prior to societal changes of the 1960s, teenagers in high school were placed in gender-stereotypical classes. Men took courses such as wood and auto shop, while women were confined to more domestic activities, such as lessons in cooking and sewing. Legal and social changes during the final quarter of the 20th century have somewhat altered the situation. Today, males and females have a few more alternatives, and the women's answers to our questions reflected this. While still in high school, the young women were able to initiate steps up the occupational ladder. Joining the Explorers was a common first stride.

The Explorers are chartered by the Boy Scouts of America but often housed and supervised by government agencies, such as military installations, schools, and police departments. In the United States, more than 2,500 Explorer units are associated with law enforcement agencies. A typical one in Southern California provides its members with "an 18 week training course on Saturdays at the sheriffs facility."[34] Police department personnel favor such experience, and acceptance of teenage women into the Explorer program has aided gender integration in many agencies. Representative of the experiences of more than a handful of our female subjects in this regard was the background of one. She had taken a law and society class in high school that sparked her interest. She joined a police Explorer unit and soon became a civilian employee within the department. In short order, she joined the police reserves and transitioned into a full-time officer. Fifteen years later, she was well entrenched in the occupation that had attracted her as a teenager.

Entrance of women into the Explorers and increased numbers of women participating in other formerly male-dominated activities, such as team sports or the military, will eventually multiply the number of women interested in policing and balance the current educational discrepancy between men and women. More women will seek police employment, allowing departments to be more selective.

## GROWING UP AT THE OCCUPATION'S KNEE

For both men and women, knowing someone who had some association with police played a role in their choosing the job. On a few occasions, the impact resembled the situation of a bygone era, when all the male members of a family might be police officers. A Hispanic woman, for example, credited her seven uncles, all of whom worked in policing, with galvanizing her interest. "I never thought of any other career," she recollected. In such situations, the older relatives recounted "war stories" to the youngsters—tales of catching the bad guys and aiding the innocent. "It sounded exciting," several officers remembered. At least one of our interviewees provided us with evidence that the practice continues. Her son, nephew, and uncle have all become police officers.

Relatives were not the only people who influenced our subjects toward law enforcement. Neighbors and friends in the police department also played a role. According to a couple of our officers, men in the neighborhood when they were growing up provided their early image of the police. Another told us that her "dad's friends were either cops or firemen," and they were the initial attraction. These people provided positive early images of the police that stuck in the memories of our officers. A 14-year veteran, for example, recalled that she would accompany her "grandparents, when they were alive, to a Croatian fraternity for peace-loving people. And one of the ladies that was there worked at LAPD in their records division. So I talked to her a little bit."

A couple of our officers' fathers were police officers, but the children denied that their parents' profession had led them to the same occupation.

One woman's father and cousin had both been officers in the Chicago area, but when we asked if they had inspired her to enter policing, she exclaimed, "No, absolutely not!" The other officer recollected that his father took him on ride-alongs, but he "never thought of it as a career until after college. When I was growing up, I was a cop's son and I hated that," he lamented. Despite these officers' protestations, their parents' occupation probably played some role in their career choice. Moreover, individuals who learn about policing from friends, relatives, and acquaintances also learn the police value system and, as a result, are more likely than others to be accepted into the occupation.

For more than a handful of the officers we interviewed,[35] the impact of knowing a policeman was not as direct as growing up at the occupation's knee. They knew someone in policing, but the person did not immediately affect their career decisions. Rather, their elders were seldom-seen models who may have planted positive images of policing. Illustrative was a woman who credited the low-key television drama *Adam 12* as the origin of her childhood interest in the police. (A handful of individuals mentioned such shows.) But the fact that she had two uncles who were police chiefs in Germany and two who were officers in Italy must have played some role. It seems likely that having a familiar police image, whether that be a relative, family friend, or neighbor, establishes the occupation as a viable choice in some youngsters' minds.

## DRIFTING INTO POLICING

Some individuals drift into the job. They have had other jobs, but at least for now, they are police officers. A story provided by a veteran who didn't come to the vocation until he was past 35 is indicative:

> I got introduced to it 20 years ago when there was a TV series called *Police Story.* It had a different story every week and it was based out of Los Angeles. I was in my 20s at the time. I already had a career in L.A. far different from policing. I was a talent agent in Hollywood, but I had reached the point in that career where I didn't want to do that anymore. So I reached out for this just for fun. I reached out for this before I quit my other job to make sure I was hired.

The route by which women and men drift into police work is similar and yet different. A plurality of both sexes had civil service jobs before their current positions. Department hiring committees give extra points to applicants who have civil service backgrounds, so those without it are at a disadvantage. For the men, such service was primarily in the military. Those doing the hiring for police departments probably have military experience and look for it among applicants. Former military experience may also help recruits survive the rigors of police academy training and result in such individuals being more likely to be officers and included in research such as ours. (Academy training is described in more detail in the next chapter.)

## THE MEN

The men we interviewed had not stepped into the military with the idea that it was a stride toward policing. Rather, joining the armed forces for them was a means to obtain some other goal. One interviewee told us that he "wanted to do something within the public service sector." He entered the military so that he "could go to school on the GI Bill. But, as it turned out, [he] got a Navy scholarship and got the education while in the service." He majored in criminal justice, and his coursework led him to assignment with the military police.

Another longtime veteran of police work also reported military police assignment, but for several officers, the road from soldier to police officer was not so explicit. After the service, one became a buyer in the aerospace industry and then in pharmaceuticals. He became a reserve police officer and decided he liked it, so he changed careers. Another male was a member of the armed forces for 23 years before leaving to become a high-school teacher. A police department, he remembered,

> put out a call for a civilian beach liaison officer for the summer. They took teachers out of the system and hired them to do beach patrol. Most of the kids in this area go to the beach. We know these kids; we are used to dealing with them. Some of them have cocky attitudes, and so the department liked the idea of having teachers in uniform. The uniform demands a little bit more respect. So they hired us thinking that we

could prevent any problems. The sergeant who was in charge of the detail liked how I worked and encouraged me to apply.

Another officer was an air operations specialist in the military. When he was discharged, he "did odd jobs, worked as a meat cutter." A labor dispute sent him looking for a different job.

> I happened to notice a dispatcher opening. . . . I started riding with the
> officers to see what they went through. The big complaint at the time
> was the fact that as the dispatcher you sit down and you really don't know
> what the officers are exposed to. So I started riding, and then one night,
> I busted out of the unit with an officer, and a subject was breaking into
> the back of a residence. I was ahead of the officer. I thought, "If I like it
> this much, I might as well get paid for it."

Several of the former military men mentioned earnings as a reason to join policing. In this regard, they saw the job as similar to soldiering; it promised a steady salary. Other likenesses also proved attractive. In particular, the uniform gave them "a sense of pride and status." "I like the uniform and I like the responsibility that goes along with it," we were told.

## THE WOMEN

Women also were hired into the job from previous civil service positions. Job security, as with the men, was important for these government workers. "There will always be a city government and a police," we were told.

Many of the civil service jobs the women held were civilian positions associated with police work. For these women, working alongside officers proved the final step in their attraction to the job. Two of the women had been schoolteachers but had been laid off. They then got jobs with police departments, one as a meter maid. She remembered looking at the officers and thinking "Yeah, I can do that." Another woman, the niece of a Scotland Yard detective, recounted her drift into the job:

> When I was younger, I was just going job to job and I didn't really know
> what I wanted to do. This girlfriend of mine worked in police records, and
> that's when a lot of police shows were just coming out. . . . She said it was
> pretty interesting. So I started there typing police reports and talking to

officers and I thought "I could do that." So I started here as a reserve officer first. . . . And then I liked it so I went full time.

Another woman had a similar tale:

I started out as a records clerk here, and what I really wanted to do was be a dispatcher. I tolerated being a records clerk for eight months until I got a position as dispatcher. I was there for two and a half years, and the longer I was there the more boring it got and the more I learned about police work. . . . [Police work] was interesting, and I felt that I could do it and it would be more active than dispatcher, so I did that.

## EXCITEMENT AND ACTION

The lure of an exciting, action-oriented job was the primary draw to policing for both sexes. Twenty-three women and 20 men said "excitement" was most important, although officers defined excitement in different ways. For some it meant a variety of assignments or action-oriented activities. They were tired of the mundane and repetitive tasks they experienced in their previous occupations as secretaries, sale clerks, and dispatchers. This was especially true of female officers who had previously worked at office desks. Remarked one, "I get bored real easy. I couldn't be a secretary." Another recounted a similar desire: "I wanted something challenging, not routine, something new every day."

Female officers did not have a monopoly on wanting to avoid office work. The male respondents also admitted they eschewed employment that confined them to a room. Common sentiments were expressed by one man who did not like the parameters of office work, which he considered a boring lifestyle. "I like working outside," he told us. "I can't see myself sitting in the office all the time."

Most officers made their desire for action explicit, but for some it was a conclusion we inferred from their words. Two officers, for example, had wanted to be aviators but eventually settled for police work; another had become attracted to the job after discussing it with someone he met racing motorcycles.

Many of those we interviewed became police officers because they coveted a dynamic, praiseworthy role in society. They may have seen themselves as Western heroes, suffering from, as one remarked about himself, the "John Wayne Syndrome." "You want to save the world," he told us. One woman expressed well the sentiment while presenting her philosophical underpinning for police work. "I believe in Mom, apple pie, and the flag and the pursuit of happiness and freedom, until that pursuit gets in the way of someone else's," she told us. "I believe there should be a third, neutral party to insure that this freedom is protected." For her, policing meant maintaining that value system. The officers had defined in their own minds the type of person they were, and that portrait agreed perfectly with their picture of policing. As one officer told us, everything he had done "when I was in high school and everything I did up until I was old enough to get into police work" had motivated him to become a police officer. He saw himself as the "neutral party" described by the previous officer. Looking back, he remembered:

> If somebody had a problem, I'd see what I could do. If somebody offered aggression, it was usually easier for me to talk my way out of it than it was to box with them, but if I had to box with them I didn't lose. I was able to look at most viewpoints and say, "Okay, this is fair and reasonable and let's handle it from here."

For officers such as this, part of the lure of policing, for both men and women, was the opportunity to pursue a distinct, useful role in society.

The opportunity for utilizing unique skills, such as problem solving, was also a motivational factor among the officers who were lured by the excitement of the job. "It was the challenge and the problem solving that attracted me," one recounted. "Police work represented something that was exciting and challenging, something where I could try to take control and fix things."

## SECURITY

Job security was the second most mentioned motivation for joining the police force for both men (about 40 percent) and women (about 25 percent). Because they fill bureaucratic positions, police officers, after completing mandatory academy training and a probationary period, can expect that they will be retained in their jobs—a critical concern to some. A single parent, for example, told us she needed an income she could depend on. Starting salaries in urban departments exceed $40,000 annually; with promotions, potential yearly income can blossom to $100,000. These figures plus excellent benefits proved attractive to people accustomed to earning less.

## SERVICE

Only 12 percent of the officers mentioned service to others as an influence in their decisions to enter policing (four women and six men), and they almost always combined this motivation with some other descriptor of police work, usually excitement. Of note, a sizable proportion of the 10 officers who mentioned the opportunity to help others as an attractive part of the job were members of ethnic or racial minorities. They told us they wanted to give something back to their communities. An African-American respondent elaborated on why service to the community meant so much in his decision to become an officer:

> I thought that perhaps I could bring more of a sense of justice to police work. I wouldn't consider my background as disadvantaged, but I did grow up in an area where there were socioeconomic limitations that affected a lot of people around me. But I had a good household. And I saw what was happening in the streets and I saw the contacts that my friends had with the police, which were often negative. . . . I thought I could make a difference.

The expectation that women bring with them to policing a stronger desire than men to help others—to protect women and children, as was their orientation in historical times—was not apparent among our sample. Women did not identify with a particular community. Rather, in general, they looked at police work as an avenue to do exciting work. For example, the only woman who mentioned helping her gender as a reason for entering policing commented, "I wanted to see suspects apprehended, stop seeing women victimized, stop seeing criminals get away."

## CAVEATS

Many officers mentioned more than one motivation as being important in their decisions. Officers were reflecting on choices made years previously. It is difficult for people to remember reasons for specific judgments on most matters. Decision making is a complex process. Given these factors, it is not surprising that many officers recalled multiple reasons for joining the force. Illustrative was one woman, who was most drawn by the variety of the job but whose answer ran the full reach of possibilities. "Variety, nothing is the same; every day is different," she began. But she quickly added not being "penned up inside, being outdoors, and helping the community" to her list. And then she concluded that it was "the variety and excitement of the job. I had always been interested in it. I got a degree in criminal justice and worked as a dispatcher for three years." Her initial desires and those of others were most likely clouded by their current knowledge of the job.

It is also important to reiterate that our sample of officers is reflective of people who have been hired by departments, survived academy training, and are in at least the initial years of their careers. Careful screening of candidates is crucial to the selection process. Legal liability issues compel departments to be extra mindful about the reasons individuals have for seeking this occupation. Central to this concern is the fact that officers have the right to use force. Personnel boards utilize a broad range of information to assess applicants' integrity and character. They select those who fulfill the board members' philosophy of policing. It seems likely that their ideology includes applicants who seek exhilaration. The job does, in fact, afford a level of excitement and risk that only certain individuals seek and police patrol work can provide.

## Conclusions and Discussion

Differences exist between the answers our sample gave to us and what earlier studies have reported. In some regards, the differences are outcomes of affirmative action decisions made 25 years ago. The officers we interviewed reflect the fact that policing is no longer exclusively a white, male occupation filled with individuals who came to the occupation early in life. Today, men and women are drawn and selected from the full spectrum of ethnicities, and many begin the job when they are near or long past 30 years of age. Increased salaries and benefits have further broadened the potential pool of police applicants, and the current televised ride-along programs, which provide audiences with "real life" images of the police, will also most likely increase the number of individuals seeking employment in the occupation. The shows that influenced our officers played on television 20 years ago and rarely featured female police. More recent media fare has depicted women, and the impact on youngsters watching television today will begin to surface in the current millennium.

Increasingly, men and women have similar goals in life and compete for the same jobs. Evidence from our sample suggests that this trend will continue and further impact policing. We have already discussed this matter with respect to women's entrance into Explorer programs, but additional areas promise expanding numbers of women entering nontraditional occupations. For example, men in our sample reported that team sports had played a role in their becoming police officers. As media coverage of women's sports grows, we can expect that the number of females interested in more physical activities, such as policing, will increase.

Still, the answers we received from the female officers indicate that a focus on the law enforcement component of the job limits women's entrance into the occupation. Many department leaders continue to believe that women are unable to function effectively in this role.

# CHAPTER FIVE

## *Training*

When our sample of officers entered the police academy, they shared a view of policing. The occupation, as far as they were concerned, was filled with publicly spirited, outdoor action. In this regard, they probably did not differ from the general population in their view of the job. The recruits' view was substantiated by what they learned at the academy. Some of them, particularly those who had close relatives in policing, may have already known much about the values and norms of the job before their training began. For many, however, it was during their academy experience that they began their socialization into the police world.

## HISTORY OF POLICE TRAINING

Prior to 1900 police received little or no training. During the first years of police reform at the beginning of the 20th century, officers started to get some instruction. Most large cities had schools where officers, according to a writer of the period, were taught "something of grammar and writing and a great deal of marksmanship."[1]

August Vollmer, as discussed in chapter 1, pressed for academic schooling for officers shortly after the turn of the century. Vollmer believed that the job required individuals to be skilled in a number of areas, as policemen had to be "social counselor, parish priest, friend of the down-and-outer, protector of us all."[2] In an attempt to train his officers in these areas, Vollmer began a police school in Berkeley in 1908.

Officers could take courses in a variety of subjects including "police methods and procedures, fingerprinting, first aid, criminal law, anthropometry, photography, public health, and sanitation, as well as occasional lectures on related subjects in criminology, psychiatry, and anthropology."[3] Ten years later, a recruit attending Vollmer's school could follow a three-year program that included courses in physics, chemistry, biology, physiology, anatomy, criminology, anthropology, heredity, toxicology, criminological psychology, psychiatry, police organization and administration, police methods and procedure, microbiology and parasitology, police microanalysis, public health, first aid for the injured, and elementary and criminal law.[4]

Police outside of the university town of Berkeley had little opportunity for extensive training, even in big cities. Chicago had a one-month training program for its officers beginning in 1910. The recruits spent about a week on each of four different areas: close-order drill, weapons training, rules and laws, and tours of courts and specialized divisions of the department. A 1929 study on the school reported "as has generally been the case with police training, no recruit had ever failed a course."[5]

New York's program was less guided by law enforcement ideals and, at least from one report, focused more on the proper use of discretion in immigrant neighborhoods. The police commissioner, who once was a schoolmaster, had his new recruits taken "to visit the Greek, the Italian, the Jewish, the Rumanian, the Chinese quarters." The focus of the officers' education was "on the delicate science of not making arrests."[6]

The New York City's commissioner's ideas about training had other supporters, who believed that officers should be aware of the communities they policed. An article in a popular magazine of the period urged that young men be enlisted into the trade at an early age, then learn about the public while patrolling amusement areas or during traffic watch. The author argued that we should "train into these future policemen, in their impressionable years, a sympathy with people, born of association with them and of helpfulness extended to men and women and children." For him, "Officers so selected and so trained would have a less military, a less professional and arbitrary attitude."[7]

By the 1930s, O. W. Wilson was doing his best to create a bureaucratic police force. His training program had little to do with understanding human misery. His officers were largely trained in the ways of catching and jailing crooks. He told readers in a magazine article that, during lectures and discussions, his recruits were instructed in

> daily gymnasium work and instructions in jiu-jitsu; a thorough course in first aid and resuscitation; extensive studies in local, state and federal judicial procedure, legislation and criminal procedure; presentation of case in court and how it must be prepared; laws of evidence; how to testify; law of arrest; rights of the citizens; rights of the police; the duties, conduct and appearance of an officer; how to approach an offender; besides technical training in investigation and reports.[8]

When it came to dealings with the public, Wilson's emphasis was on appearance, conduct, and courtesy. His officers were not to let their personal feelings interfere with their actions on the job. "Briefly," Wilson explained, "an officer must not arrest a man because his actions or his manner or his appearance displeases, or because of what he says, but must permit only the offense to determine his action."[9] Unlike earlier schools that had made some attempt to allow recruits to learn the use of discretion, Wilson's training forbade it.

Another change in training occurred during the depression and was connected to the influx of college men into policing. Beginning with San Jose State College in 1930 and continuing throughout the decade, colleges began to offer curricula fashioned to ready men for police careers. The programs varied from school to school. The University of Wichita ran a 2-year program in cooperation with the city police. Cadets, who were full-time students, received $50 a month from the police department, good pay during the depression. Michigan State University's program involved 5 years of work, of which 18 months were devoted to internships in various police agencies.[10]

During the decade following World War II, little change occurred in police training. This stagnation may have been due to a belief among officers that experience was the best teacher. Classroom instruction, in the view of those on the beat, was limited and applicable to "matters of policy or matters of general knowledge."[11] Training was seen as a method to improve the public's image of the occupation and, as a result, its status and pay. The public was urged to support training on the grounds that better-prepared officers would wage effective battle with criminals.[12]

The situation had not changed much by the mid-1960s. Some departments still provided no training for their recruits, and small-town police might have received less than a week of instruction before being sent out to do the job among their longtime neighbors. A substantial but minority portion of the remaining cities provided 3 weeks or less of training, while a majority of cities with populations above 250,000 had programs that lasted between 8 and 20 weeks.[13] The primary form of education in all programs was lectures and discussions; less than half of the programs involved recruits in instruction that duplicated actual practices.[14]

The newly established Northern Virginia Police Academy was typical of the training programs of the mid-1960s. Recruits undertook an 11-week course consisting of four segments: academics, firearms instruction, physical education, and driver training. Current officers, who volunteered to teach after they completed their eight-hour shifts, taught the recruits the prevailing ideology on these matters.[15]

A number of factors coalesced during the 1960s and focused public scrutiny on the police and their training. Handling of minorities by officers was one of the items. First, in southern states poor treatment was afforded to civil rights' demonstrators, who found themselves facing police water cannons and night sticks—events that were televised throughout the nation. Then came a series of summer riots in major cities, all sparked by police activities. Rising crime rates, fueled by baby boomers reaching their crime-prone teenage years, also played a role. Other factors, such as increased reporting of offenses, also focused attention on policing matters. Additionally, in 1964, Senator Barry Goldwater made rising rates of wrongdoing the centerpiece of his run for the presidency and placed the "War on Crime" near the top of the national agenda. President Lyndon Johnson appointed a national commission to look at crime and the criminal justice system in the United States. Its report further fueled interest in the police.[16] One result of all this curiosity was an unprecedented number of studies focusing on the police, many of which took in-depth looks at academy training.

## Studies of Academies

The earliest academic studies of police training were conducted by doctoral students working on their dissertations in sociology departments at University of California institutions.[17] Steeped in organizational theory, the researchers aimed their typewriters at the bureaucratic model, beginning with the academy training that recruits received.

Sociological studies of practitioner training were relatively popular during the 1960s. Robert Merton's examination of medical students appeared as the 1950s came to a close, and Howard Becker's inside look at medical training was published a few years later.[18] Those sociologists had focused on the transmission of the medical value system, a system that prized the autonomy associated with the professional role of physicians. The researchers who were studying police education were confronted with something quite different.

The police recruits were taught bureaucratic rules during their training, rules and requirements designed to produce a "standardized product"[19]—a cog to fit in the bureaucratic wheel. Academies taught their students to legally handle situations that might result in liability for their municipalities, in particular the proper handling of defendants and the use of weapons. Failure to teach cadets such activities can result in substantial financial losses for municipalities. For example, a major concern for the Los Angeles Police Department during the trials of the officers who had beaten Rodney King was whether the officers had received proper instruction on the use of the baton. A lack of such instruction would have hurt the city's defense that the officers had acted counter to their training.

The vision that policing requires superior physical skills also played a role in determining the academy curricula. Recruits, for example, did not value information from books, preferring on-the-job training. High scores on written examinations garnered little support, while expert ability at the pistol range was quickly noticed and applauded.

The cultural favoritism by officers and recruits toward the law enforcement component of their job also affected curricula. Lectures given by active or former officers that dealt with law enforcement were appreciated.[20] Training, as a result, focused directly on matters related to catching crooks and putting them behind bars, matters such as evidence and courtroom testimony.

Training had to fit within the bureaucratic command-and-control model. Upper echelon personnel established criteria that instructors taught to trainees. There was, however, a dilemma: within the vast area of police work are many matters for which little or no criteria can be established, circumstances that more aptly require officers to use good judgment. Training recruits to use their discretion in such areas, however, would mean granting street officers more power than the bureaucratic command-and-control model allows. As a result, matters that might best be handled by the use of "good sense" were often ignored in the academy in favor of instruction on "departmental rules, rigorous physical training, dull lectures devoted to various technical aspects of the occupation, and a ritualistic concern for detail."[21]

Academies' focus on meeting bureaucratic criteria meant that recruits were expected to adhere to strictly established boundaries. Unlike professional training, where innovation is rewarded, within the police academy new ideas were discouraged.[22] Outside of class, recruits were expected to closely follow rules. Departments set curfews for their trainees and designated liquor stores as off-limits.[23] A substantial majority of recruits regarded their manual for rules and procedures as "the most useful item they had in their Academy training,"[24] primarily because conforming to its guidelines allowed the enlistees to avoid the wrath of superiors.[25]

During the 1960s, recruits were normally subjected to extreme stress training. The neophytes were chastised for minor indiscretions; trainers often delivered criticisms from within a few inches of the recruits' faces, punctuating their derogation with epitaphs. Military members and team athletes, particularly those participating in football programs, are well aware of this form of disincentive. In the police academy,

the initiate learns that the formal rules and regulations are applied inconsistently. What is sanctioned in one case . . . is ignored in other cases. To the recruits, academy rules become behavioral prescriptions which are to be coped with formally, but informally dismissed. The newcomer learns that when The Department notices his behavior it is usually to administer a punishment, not a reward. The solution to this collective predicament is to stay low and avoid trouble.[26]

More will be said about stress training later in this chapter, but one of its results was to separate the students from their teachers and increase the recruits' solidarity.[27]

Solidarity, or a feeling of belonging, is a necessary factor for the formation of groups,[28] and it is a common feature of schooling, whether among kindergartners, graduate students, or police recruits. Little attention is paid to it in most circumstances, but in police circles, solidarity with other officers is considered a necessity. The occupation can be dangerous, and recruits learn from the tales they are told in and out of class that there are few safe situations.[29] When trouble arises, officers need to know that their colleagues will back them up. Strong solidarity, the ideology holds, will guarantee that support, and numerous academy activities, such as stress training, are designed to increase the group's cohesiveness.

Police training has much in common with military boot camp. Both use ceremony to separate recruits from the wider society. Uniforms and weapons help the neophytes visually perceive themselves as different.[30] Language also plays a part. An official argot helps increase the officers' solidarity. Much as slang identifies members of a group, use of esoteric penal and radio codes identifies police officers to one another.[31]

The content of the stories told by instructors in the 1960s also functioned to increase recruit solidarity. Current or former officers provided the academy lectures, and the instructors soon learned, as university professors do, that examples make material clearer to students and hold their attention. Understandably, some officers found it convenient to spend more time on examples than on substance. During these stories, departmental ideology was passed to the next generation of officers. In addition, the stories provided recruits with an image of a world hostile to police.

The period of the 1960s, when U.S. society was so fractured, was not kind to police. For many, the police represented what was wrong with this country. Despite polls and surveys showing that generally they were approved of, officers felt like a beleaguered minority.[32]

Increasingly militant college students were portrayed in academy lectures as anti-law and order. Minorities, in particular African-Americans, were labeled as potential criminals and antipolice; reporters "distorted the news"; and women, seeking equal rights and half of the patrol car, were irksome to members of the male-dominated occupation. Friends outside the department, some instructors admonished their students, were not to be trusted. "Once a person becomes a policeman," trainers were quoted as saying, "you never know who is your friend."[33] In this fashion, recruits came to view almost all individuals employed outside of law enforcement as the enemy.[34] In kind, members of poor neighborhoods felt the police were secretive and, at best, not caring.

Early in the 20th century, police recruits had been taken to immigrant neighborhoods to learn the use of discretion. As the 1960s came to a close, it was apparent that recruits' training taught them neither to understand differing communities nor to use discretion when policing them.[35]

## REFORM EFFORTS

Increased training and integration of the force were viewed as means to handle the chasm between officers and the communities they policed. During the 1970s, departments extended the length of academy training, and model programs added sociology components, which included instruction on community relations, crisis intervention, and sensitivity training.[36]

Passage of the Law Enforcement Assistance Act (LEAA) in 1965 and strong words from the president's commission on crime galvanized the spread of community relations training programs in police academies.[37] The programs were attractive to administrators for more than one reason. The summer riots of the mid-1960s had clearly pointed out that the police were in a vulnerable position. Sniper fire within urban "war zones" had proved fatal to unprotected officers trying to police the areas. Liability issues also played a role in administrators' favor for community relations programs.[38] They rightly recognized that mistreatment of minorities by police could result in substantial awards by juries.

Today, cross-cultural training for police recruits is mandatory in many states. Across the country, police newcomers average about 13.5 hours of multicultural education during their basic training.[39] Such training need not focus solely on ethnic minorities but can include other groups, such as the elderly.[40] Approaches commonly include group discussions, case studies, or role-playing or some combination of these forms of instruction.[41] Role-playing has been particularly popular, although the activities often emphasize the law enforcement component of the police job. Recruits' suggestions for role-playing in one study included "struggling in order to test the recruit's ability for self-defense." The trainees wanted role-playing to "be applied to every subject such as robbery and assault." "In no case," the author noted, "did I hear a recruit express a desire to learn more about himself or others through role playing."[42]

The success of multicultural approaches is still to be decided. There is concern that officers are turning the programs to their own law enforcement ends or using the programs to learn how to discriminate against minorities without offending them.[43] An in-depth study of a Southern California academy's cultural awareness course was inconclusive.[44] Cadets were surrounded by opinions, offered by instructors, denigrating the policy before they had even left the academy.[45] Only the teacher of the class saw its value. Other instructors did not; they believed law enforcement activities were more important.[46] The dean of the academy, who taught the class, uttered the best that can probably be said about it, while talking with his students: "I know I could never change your value system in the short time I have with you guys, but I may give you something to think about."[47] After a year in the field, there was evidence that any gains from the class were being lost to the police culture.[48]

Academy education may not be able to alter long-held attitudes, and pressuring recruits to change their views might result in rejection of the training as "they are bound to feel defensive and resist, either openly or quietly."[49] Training individuals who already understand the value system of cultural minorities, however, contains no such risks, and their recruitment became a priority for police administrators in their plans to improve relationships with ethnically diverse populations.[50] By 1975, women, college graduates, and members of racial minorities made up substantial portions of recruit classes.[51] It was generally posited that women officers would do better with women victims, minority officers would better relate to the problems of minorities,[52] and a liberal arts college education would better prepare officers for handling diverse cultural situations.

Changing the face of academy recruits may be a good way to improve minority-police relations, and there is some evidence that supports the efforts. As discussed in the previous chapter, the minority officers we interviewed often mentioned service to their ethnic neighborhoods as a reason for their joining the police, a finding duplicated in a study of cadets.[53]

Departments' move to community policing has also affected academy education. Community policing and problem-oriented policing are efforts to integrate police and neighborhood. Bureaucratic policing had isolated officers from the communities they patrolled. Communication between neighborhood leaders and department officials often consisted of the police attempting to convince the lay individuals that the department's wishes were best. Academy students were prepared to perform their jobs "in isolation both from the needs of the recipient and the practical issues of the community."[54] In contrast, the new policing model requires officers to become familiar with the problems of a community and to work with its residents to solve the difficulties the citizens identify. In addition, officers trained for bureaucratic policing had been taught to follow orders and tradition. Community policing requires officers to be innovative decision makers, and academy programs may change to reflect this.[55] One community policing course, for example,

> included collaboration, inclusion and partnership in each lesson. Efforts were made to identify faculty and topics for the upcoming academy classes. In-service classes on problem solving and decision making, and studies on diversities, AIDS and the Americans with Disability Act helped to explore police interaction with normal and mentally disabled citizens.[56]

Changes are needed at police academies so that their curricula more accurately reflect the skills needed by officers working in departments that are attempting to achieve community policing.[57] A structural barrier, however, stands in the way of implementation. Officers are trained at regional sites; a dozen different cities may obtain their officers from a single academy, yet the many departments probably have differing police styles.

As of now, the police culture at the academies has not been affected by the community policing model, and overall educational efforts still focus on bureaucratic policing and law enforcement. Orders flow from top to bottom, technical innovations are applauded, arrests are rewarded, and the vast majority of the material taught to recruits reflects these matters.

## Continuing Problems

We didn't find any reason to expect that police academy training is about to change. The method by which academy curricula are established continues to reflect the bureaucratic policing model. Task analyses, for example, play a major part in the determination of today's academy curricula.[58] First, the different functions of police personnel are identified. These are then used to establish performance objectives, which form the basis for state-mandated requirements. Virginia's task analysis produced more than 400 performance objectives that, when completed, allow a recruit to be certified in the three required areas: basic law enforcement, basic civil process-court security, and basic jailers.[59] The mandated areas do not include community policing, and the officials' lack of trust in their own cadets is clearly evident. During exams, "proctors physically remain at each test site . . . to ensure test integrity."[60]

Despite a stated need for officers who can make good decisions, today's training reflects a lack of faith in cadets' intelligence and ability. For example, concern with weapons continues to remain a high-priority item on the crime control agenda and in academy curricula.[61] A change in instruction is needed, an article in *Police Chief* tells us: "Cadets should be taught to reload their guns before holstering so that they are prepared to defend themselves if they are attacked again."[62] Citizens and officers would be surprised to learn that recruits need to be trained on such matters.

## TODAY'S TRAINING

Recruits' formal education involves a structured academy program lasting approximately four months and field instruction with a departmental training officer for an additional six months. Academies in California follow guidelines entitled "Peace Officers Standard Training" (POST). Other states have similar requirements for police training, which include designated minimum hours and types of instruction. Some variation in standards across the country exists as the result of accessibility to facilities and availability of economic resources. Officers may receive only rudimentary firearms instruction before being assigned a patrol job, or they may receive a full scope of academic, physical, and tactical instruction. Departmental field training programs have similar inconsistencies and economic restrictions.

Academy training is divided into blocks of instruction. Throughout their schooling, recruits receive an overview of criminal law, which includes penal and vehicle codes, health and welfare codes, and business and professional codes. The basics of report writing are also taught. As one would expect, given the emphasis on the law enforcement component, a large part of instruction deals with physical fitness and tactical training, such as officer safety strategies, citizen and suspect contacts, arrest techniques, and the use of the baton and firearms. Recruits are also taught how to respond to burglaries, robberies, homicides, and traffic accidents. In order to meet public demands for more service-oriented police, academies have recently added sections dealing with cultural sensitivity, gangs, community service, and "verbal judo," also known as tactical communication.

## WHAT OUR OFFICERS THOUGHT OF THEIR TRAINING

In the remainder of this chapter, we examine the officers' perceptions of their training experiences. We asked them to reveal aspects of their academy instruction they appreciated and those they disliked. We also asked them, if they were to design an academy program, what would they emphasize or de-emphasize for new recruits. These questions were formulated to ascertain which facets of their training the officers believed had job relevancy.

The officers we interviewed did not all have the same academy experience. Some had gone through training more than 20 years earlier, while others had only recently completed the schooling. In addition, they had attended different academies. These variations in their experiences were reflected in their answers. Despite these discrepancies, several issues formed a core around which the officers' answers swirled.

One thing is very clear from the officers' praise and criticisms of academy training: they do not know the purpose of much that they do while they are at the academy. They later develop explanations for situations they experienced, and their opinions differ as to the value of those situations.

## STRESS TRAINING

It is not surprising that stress training was the most often mentioned memory for our officers. As recruits, they were heckled by trainers for minor mistakes or because of their status. Supervisors scolded them for having dirty shoes or teased them because their future assignments were with departments in upper-middle-class neighborhoods or simply because they were women. Exercises, such as push-ups or running laps, were used as immediate punishments for incorrect actions. In general, the training pushed the recruits to physical and mental exhaustion.

Stress training is a litmus test. Our officers had survived the experience. Many do not. It takes a certain amount of self-confidence to overcome the psychological intimidation. Other recruits may have decided that the occupation was not worth the experience. Middle-class individuals may not have previously experienced such activities and may not react well to it. For some of the officers we interviewed, this was the value of the stress training. It weeded out those who were not serious. "It was such a commitment," one told us. For him, continued attendance at the academy was proof of his aspiration. "If I didn't want it as much as I did," he concluded, "I would have quit."

Recent weakening of stress training, we were told, had resulted in "wishy-washy" rookies who, after leaving the academy, still had not decided "whether they wanted to be cops or not." A longtime veteran put a slightly different spin on the same argument. He believed that those who made it through high-stress training were a higher "caliber of people." Lowering stress, he and others believed, was a means for cities to save money.

> From what I've heard, it is more of an economic reason. A city will invest a certain amount of money for each person, and if a new person is dumped, then all the money invested goes right down the tubes. It seems like they are just letting people slide through instead of the money being lost.

The result, he argued, was fewer good officers.

Officers with military experience (who were more likely to be men) had an easier time with stress training because they had gone through the ordeal in boot camp. One officer suggested that military experience would help women withstand the academy pressure. He remembered "two women in the military who handled stress much better than the men." Some male officers also mentioned that the experience of participating in team sports enabled them to deal with academy stress.

Not all officers had experienced the same stress training. Different academies had treated the matter differently. Training conducted on college campuses, from what the officers told us, likely involved less belittling than training conducted at other sites. Officers who had undergone the experience 15 years previously probably endured more anxiety-producing situations than recent recruits, which affected how they perceived the training. Veterans who had survived "full stress," as many referred to it, seemed more likely to believe that it had value and that perceived weaknesses in newer officers were directly related to a de-emphasis on this aspect of the academy experience. A homicide detective with 15 years' police background was typical. He posited that recruits should

> go through full stress so that once they come out of the academy they can handle any situation on the street. Because of different federal decisions

and the way a lot of administrations are going, people are passing the academy and they really can't cope with the situations on the street. I would go back to the full stress and tough them up. We don't have that now. I am beginning to see a lot of agencies—not just ours—where recruits come in and they just cannot handle the situation; the cities should see that because you get a lot of the young guys leaving because of stress and [charges of] brutality. I think if they went back to the full stress academy, they would know when to use force and when not to use it.

For these veterans, the strain of stress training gave them the ability to remain calm when the situation around them was chaotic.

A female officer called it "psychological training" and counted it as "most important." She echoed the sentiments of a plurality of individuals who told us it prepared recruits

because no matter what happens, if you have your head, things will work out okay; you will think of other options. But if you panic, you have lost everything and no matter how strong you are, no matter how many degrees you have, no matter if you are a guy or a gal or whatever, if you lose your head, you have lost it all.

She views her occupation as potentially dangerous and stress training as a means to lower the chances of death or injury. As one of the male officers in her department put it, "You don't want anyone that is going to fold, bend, or break under stressful situations because any given second could be the last one."

Stress, it was argued, also taught the recruits to follow orders, an item at least one officer tied to the "dangerousness" of the occupation. He asserted:

Stress does play a major role. I can give you a good example. Say, for instance, you're out there doing drills and [academy instructors] tell you to get down. There are reasons for that. When you don't get down fast enough, it's going to reflect on what happens out in the field. . . . If you get shot at, you are still going to be standing, looking around to see what's going on, instead of doing exactly what you were trained to do in the academy.

Several officers, however, pointed to less lethal circumstances that they routinely handled for which they believed the "in your face" training helped. According to one 20-year veteran, "half of the people we deal with on the street are going to be spitting on you, kicking you, biting you, and calling you and your family all kinds of names." A 27-year-old woman added, "You always are going to come across somebody that's not happy, and it's so easy to sit back now and just listen to it and it doesn't bother me. I figure it's their stress level if they want to scream, yell, and rant and rave." She argued that the academy should be full stress because "If you can't take it at that level, when you get out on the streets, you're lost."

Most of the officers who commented on stress training did not appear to recognize that one of its major goals is to establish teamwork. Officers who are not team players may cause trouble for other officers and their departments. They may try to do too much on their own and in the process place police and citizens at risk. As one woman told us, learning teamwork in the academy is important because "these are the people who are going to back you up."

The military uses stress training to break down individuals' self-identities so that they may become part of the whole. It is a degradation ceremony in which the self is destroyed so that a new image can be assumed.[63] Stress training in the academy is the same. It is devastating to the recruits' self-images. They are unable to master the duties that the trainers daily heave their way. It is not long before students bond with the other cadets at least in partial opposition to their instructors—the result of the relentless discipline they daily inflict upon the recruits. In the end, the individual is assimilated into the whole.

Our sample of officers' nonrecognition of teamwork as an important lesson to be gleaned from the training reflects a weakness in academy instruction. As university professors, we often instruct our teaching assistants that it is important to first tell the students the purpose of the material that one is about to present, then to present it, and when finished, to remind students why they were told the information. From what a handful of officers related, this is far from the case in the academy. Twenty years later, one of our informants remembered, "When I was in the academy they wanted us to act as a unit, to act as one. But they never told us that." Another longtime veteran found the psychological game-playing particularly irksome. She remembered a class where the instructors

> sent one set of instructions out to half the class and another set of instructions to the other half of the class. . . . They never did come back and say "This is why we did this." They did a whole bunch of things like that, psychological game-playing that was fine and would have taught everybody a really good lesson had they explained what lesson they were teaching after they had taught it. And they never did that. That's one of the big changes that I'd make. I would explain what I was doing through-out the training process. Somewhere along the line, they should sit down and just explain one or two things at a time. "Remember when we did this? This is why we did it." And then they can go and scream and yell at you again for other stuff, and later on you know that some explanation is going to come instead of just being yelled at for three months. The recruits would learn something from it, rather than just thinking to themselves that "this is maybe what they're doing" or "maybe they were designed to scream and yell."

These officers believed that if they and other recruits had known the purpose of the training, they would have better dealt with the experience and learned more from it. One officer's comment provided support for this view. She recalled:

> Before I went to the academy, I had somebody sit down and talk to me, and he gave me some good advice. "Everything they yell at you about has a meaning. There's something they're trying to teach you. They yell at you if your shoes look cruddy, but they're trying to teach you some-thing." He said, "Always look for the message for whatever they're doing," and it made it so much easier.

Less than a handful of officers had attended academies that did not have stress as a major component. These officers were unlikely to see the utility of such training. Also, a few officers felt that stress training could be counterproductive. They argued it made learning difficult and stifled independent thought. Rather than unduly stressing recruits, a 15-year veteran told us, he "would emphasize independent thinking so that they could make a decision without being taught that if 'A' happens than you do 'B'. I think they should be encouraged to express their opinions and not have to rely on a supervisor every time it isn't clear."

An additional handful of officers warily reproached trainers for going too far with stress training, suggesting that the instructors abused their power and singled out particular types of individuals for harsher treatment. The critics made their comments cautiously. In the past they may have had their concerns rebuked by other officers who were more in line with the majority view and might have labeled the critics as "whiners" who needed to be "weeded out." Perhaps because of the potential for conflict, the critics phrased their comments within the prevailing ideology. Illustrative was a woman who pointed out that merely being able to listen to people yelling at you might not be sufficient or advisable. She told us:

> I've noticed a lot of people go through the academy and a lot of what they get is being yelled at. That's wonderful; I mean, you have to yell at people to discipline them. The way that they do it, quasi-military, works. But they don't teach people how to talk to people, and we have a lot of officers that get in fights, that have complaints against them from the public, because they're not taught to talk to people.

## COMMUNICATION SKILLS

Concern that the academy failed to teach communication skills was one of the most common complaints voiced by those we interviewed. For these officers, "the ability to talk is the most important tool you have because you can talk to people and de-escalate the situation." A female officer with eight years experience believed that communication skills needed to be taught so that officers could "show a little more understanding." She told us that "a lot of officers tend to get cocky or not personable" and they needed to learn that such behavior was counterproductive. She echoed the sentiments of other officers: "It's your mouth that gets you where you've got to go in this business. You can talk yourself right into a fight or you can talk yourself right out of one."

The officers who recognized the advantages of communication may well have regarded their occupation in a much different light than did the officers who believed that the best way to handle irate citizens was to

ignore them. The former had excellent verbal skills and probably made
good use of them on the streets. Illustrative are the words of a detective
with nearly 20 years on the job. He explained:

> When you're dealing with people, you are not there to take them to jail,
> but you're there to help solve some of the problems. . . . You have to know
> how to talk to people. If you can't talk to people, it is not a business for
> you. The academy doesn't teach you that. It doesn't teach you how to han-
> dle disturbances. It doesn't teach you how to relate to people, to sit down,
> look them in the eye and talk to them and try to help solve the problems.

Tied to communication was the need, expressed by some officers, for the
academy to teach cultural understanding. These officers were dispropor-
tionately ethnic/racial minority members from departments located in
cities with diverse populations. They recognized, as we were told by an
African-American community affairs officer with more than 15 years in
policing, that the meaning of an "action in our culture may be totally
different in another." "One needs to be aware of those types of things,"
he concluded.

The purpose, however, for understanding various cultures differs
among officers and reflects at least two distinct policing philosophies. A
white, veteran officer's reasoning parallels community policing ideology.
He believed that, as "the result of the Rodney King incident," police officials had been reminded that

> we are a part of the community, rather than apart from it. We need to
> work and live with the community and they need to work and live with
> us. . . . We cannot function without the community being our eyes and
> ears. If we alienate the public, we might as well pack it up and go home
> because we will not survive.

A more Machiavellian view of cultural awareness also exists. An
African-American officer at the same department as the previous quoted
officer also reflected on the beating of Rodney King. The 18-year veteran's comments mirror his allegiance to bureaucratic policing and the pervasive "us versus them" conviction. He told us:

> Social awareness is becoming an issue now with things in the media. A
> lot of people are carrying around video cameras and they are videotaping
> everything we do. If you're making an ass out of yourself, it is reflecting

on the department. You can get yourself and the department wrapped up in a lawsuit. You need to learn how to talk to people of different origins and creeds so as not to offend them and start a fight with them.

## FIELD PROBLEMS

Officers from all the departments spoke about the need for more chances to practice simulated police encounters. In the academy, recruits participate in mock scenarios, called "field problems" or "practicals," created to simulate real police situations. Volunteers portray the suspects, victims, and citizens, while the recruits assume the role of patrol officers. The field problems depict calls such as traffic accidents, domestic violence, robberies-in-progress, and drunk drivers. Recruits apply their classroom knowledge and are evaluated based on their ability to bring about a solution. As in actual police work, the problems have more than one acceptable outcome. Field problems introduce recruits to police work, giving them the opportunity to make mistakes and learn in a safe environment. They are told that once on the street, they will be handling real situations where mistakes can be fatal.

Many officers felt that field problems enabled recruits to learn how to apply criminal laws and enhanced their skill of talking to people. Once cadets learned criminal law and procedures, they still needed to master the application of the knowledge. Field problems, we were told, provided recruits with an arena where they could practice the use of discretionary powers and learn how to "think on their feet." Officers judged it a good idea to extend the use of field problems to cover all aspects of a patrol officer's day.

## MUNICIPAL EFFECTS

Our interviewees' reflections on the benefits and shortcomings of their academy stays probably were affected by their current departmental employment. In particular, officers working in an upper-middle-class area criticized the extensiveness of the physical training they received in their academy and believed they would have been better served by spending more time on academics—learning the penal code and report writing, for the most part. The philosophy of the officers from this city is most likely a reflection of their department's ideology. The community has very little recorded crime; Uniform Crime Report data place it among one of the safest cities in the nation. Murders almost never occur, and it is unlikely that the city's police officers would find themselves in physical confrontations with felony suspects. Neophyte officers within the department can get themselves into trouble if they do not take these matters into consideration. An officer from the community told us:

> One of my fellow recruits was extended in his [field training] program because he did everything by the book. He'd get a call to a burglary alarm and he'd find subjects in the building. They were obviously janitors because they had keys to the building, but he would do a felony stop. He treated every call like the big one, and you can't do that; you have to relax. Sure, you have to be on guard in case it is the big one, but you can't treat every call like that. He was just overly aggressive on everything, and that is from the academy.

Trained side by side with individuals who were on their way to cities with high crime rates, the officers from this well-to-do community, as recruits, were judged against the policies of departments that stressed crime control. Once on the job, they realized that the measures used to evaluate them at the academy were inappropriate given their actual assignments. Their current contacts with the middle-class community members are often connected to traffic matters. The individuals they stop are well educated and more aware of their civil rights than citizens of other communities, and these facts are mirrored in the answers we received from the officers working in well-to-do neighborhoods. Officers in such areas can expect to have citizens challenge their authority for stopping them. Knowledge of the legal basis for actions under such circumstance is preeminent. One officer reflected:

> They could have spent more time on the academics. There are so many laws that we work with that they didn't give us in the academy, especially vehicle codes. That's your bible, your p.c. [probable cause] for stopping people. They didn't cover nearly as much as we needed.

These officers had little use for the physical training but stressed the need for more education in the activities that made up extensive portions of their workday. "We spend most of our time on the job writing reports," we were informed, and "this should be emphasized." The officers (in particular, the women we interviewed from the well-to-do community) thought physical aspects of the academy were "too much" and that they were "used as punishments" or as "a form of stress." Rather, as one argued, "I would emphasize report writing, and if [the recruits] couldn't do it they would be gone. Academics and report writing are the most important, and a lot of people had problems with them, but were allowed to graduate."

The need for more training in report writing was a common concern of officers from most departments. They realized that good paperwork was necessary in order to make a good arrest. In this regard, a 15-year veteran in an urban department noted, "Every time we arrest someone, it could go all the way up to the Supreme Court." In this regard, report writing fit within the law enforcement ideology of policing; it was necessary to send the bad guy to prison.

Officers from ethnically diverse communities, working in order-maintenance departments, offered answers that were in sharp contrast to those provided by the middle-class community officers. They felt that they had not received enough physical training at their academies. Their answers reflected the belief that law enforcement activities were the preeminent part of the job and that one needed to be prepared to use force in carrying out the occupation. As far as they were concerned,

> The classroom experience is designed to give only a basic understanding, which is all you really need at that point anyway. I think I would do a little more hand-to-hand type combat, such as control holds—if you are involved in a struggle, how to deal with someone without your weapons and without your baton. A lot of times you can't get to that and a lot of times you don't need it to avoid an altercation and excessive use of force.

These officers did not uniformly reject the academic portion of their educations; many felt report writing and legal codes were very important. Rather, they emphasized crime control, probably because it was the part of the job they enjoyed. For example, an eight-year veteran told us she found "the arrest and control" training very useful because "it just got you in the right frame of mind more than the classroom stuff." Being a police officer to her meant arresting the bad guy, and one did not accomplish that task with textbooks.

The officers' comments about the physical component of their academy training revealed that they were unsure as to its purpose. In this regard, their remarks were similar to those they made about stress training. Some individuals, for example, thought the physical exertion was directly related to occupational activities. They believed that the training got them "in condition to deal with the physical needs and demands of the job." Those who were not in good condition were not to be trusted "when something happens out there." Their criticisms of some of their academy training reflected the view that something in the physical activities was necessary to the occupation. A 25-year-old woman told us:

> Now in the training they have set different levels for the physical parts. The slower runners are in a separate group than the faster runners. Since everybody is going to be out there doing the same job, I think that they should throw everybody into one big group.

Women in the academy, according to what we were told by our informants about their experiences, had suffered the most from this view. Their inability to perform at the same level as the men was proof for some that they could not do the job.

A few officers, less than a handful, recognized that physical exercise might have other purposes. One woman noted that it established a certain measure of confidence in oneself. She remembered:

> I just had a baby and I started running again. I finally realized I am never going to get rest, so I said, "Forget it; I am going to have to start working out." So I am running again, and because I know what I used to be able to do, I can get out there and strive for that again.

Another officer, with 20 years' experience on the job, felt that the benefits of long-term physical exercise included the ability to withstand the everyday stress and strains of the occupation. He told us:

> I wouldn't stress as much physical as they do, like 18-inch arms or neck, but you have to be physically fit—in good condition, not 50 pounds overweight—because of the rotating shifts, the stress, the adrenaline

going up and down. That's why some cops don't live 10 years past their retirement. They don't take care of themselves. As far as new recruits, I don't think it's in my top five. Sure, be in shape but not to run the 4-minute mile.

## DISCUSSION

Overall, it appears that academy training has changed little during the past half-century. Instructors continue to reject service ideals and place a great deal of emphasis on crime control activities.

In general, our sample of officers agreed that learning the law and learning how to write reports were useful parts of their academy schooling and that these components should be maintained or extended. Their experiences since leaving the academies had taught them the value of this information, even though they might not have seen it when they were in school. The officers were split on other matters. Policing middle-class individuals, for example, does not require great physical ability and officers working in such neighborhoods rejected the usefulness of physical training, while officers working in areas with street crime and social disorganization wanted more of it. Officers were also split over the usefulness of stress training. Some thought it prepared them for life on the streets, while others felt it prevented learning. In general, no differences were noted between the answers of male and female officers.

It is apparent from the answers the 80 officers gave us that, as recruits, their instructors had failed to make clear the purpose of much of their education. Perhaps the instructors themselves were in disagreement as to the specific reason any material is taught. The physical component is illustrative. Many officers, including academy teachers, probably believe that slower or weaker recruits are less able to do the job. They believe that officers need a strong physical presence to deter violence or to be able to handle it if it erupts. Research, however, has shown that this is not necessarily the case.[64] Size and strength do not have an effect on most aspects of an officer's job. Even in volatile situations, an officer is better off using verbal skills to diffuse the circumstance or a drawn weapon to prevent physical attack. Instructors are in a quandary; their beliefs are in conflict with the evidence. Under such circumstances, it is predictable that recruits would not receive a clear message as to the purpose of some of their education.

Much of what today constitutes police training may be based on unchallenged tradition. Stress training, for example, may be a relic left over from when academies first came into being. Most likely the early instructors were former military men who had undergone this type of education during their boot camp days. Now it is a rite of passage, delivered from one generation of police officers to the next. We need to be concerned as to whether this type of training "weeds out" individuals who could probably handle most other aspects of police work. It may also fail to teach officers to effectively deal with citizens; ignoring their complaints does not seem the best way to handle such matters. In addition, officers may be learning unintended lessons from the "in your face" education. Once on the street, officers may emulate instructors; they may find that threats and bullying are effective ways to handle disgruntled individuals. Attempts by citizens to discuss matters with the officers may only result in threats of arrest.

Other means to educate officers are worthy of consideration. Medical school provides a good example. Physicians, in general, face many more life-and-death situations than police officers. They must deal with upset patients and their families, who may be inclined to take out their frustrations on their doctors. Stress is a common component of a physician's life. Long hours, unpredictable schedules, and extended time away from family are all stress producers with which doctors must deal. Yet no one argues that medical teachers should get "in the face" of their students to prepare them for such situations. Rather, the need to learn imposing amounts of material, extensive hours spent with other medical students, and calm rebukes from their instructors result in the trainees' bonding together and learning to deal with occupational stress.[65] It seems likely that the same measures might work with police.

# CHAPTER SIX

## On the Street

In some ways, what police like about their jobs has changed little during the last 100 years. At the beginning of the 20th century, officers patrolled neighborhoods that were both ethnically and socioeconomically homogeneous. Their daily activities were varied and differed from one neighborhood to another.[1] One officer, strolling the downtown area, would stop and talk with shopkeepers. A dozen blocks away, another officer might visit with residents in a working-class neighborhood. In cities, people lived close together and distances between home and work were minimal. Police officers patrolled on foot and enjoyed a great amount of autonomy in performing their duties. Headquarters and other officers were rarely close by, and the men needed the support of the community in order to perform their job. Accordingly, officers' decisions fit within the prevailing ideology of the area's citizens, an ideology that they probably shared anyway. To do otherwise would be to risk losing the community's support. The men, for example, might immediately punish wrongdoers that they caught on the streets. (Officers and the citizens they served agreed that judges were too lenient.) The penalties they delivered to the miscreants needed to be deemed acceptable by the community.[2]

Police at the beginning of the 20th century probably saw law enforcement as their primary activity. For them, crime prevention meant that "criminals must be caught promptly, sent to jail without delay, and kept there indefinitely."[3] They were irked when arrests and proof of guilt netted acquittals and bothered by legal rules that seemed to them to favor crooks.[4]

Women's early entrance into policing probably solidified the men's view that their job was to arrest and punish. The men had normally carried out social work activities while on patrol; to name a few, they might have settled a dispute between neighbors, fetched a nurse, or gotten youngsters to repair a fence they had broken. But after the "fair sex" entered the force, such activities were "women's work" and to be impugned. Stigmatizing the women required denigrating their work as well.

Changes in the 1920s and 1930s further influenced what officers liked and disliked about the occupation and the formation of an enduring police culture. Technology increasingly separates us from contact with others, and it was no different early in the 20th century. The automobile provided people with mobility previously unknown, and old neighborhoods began to change as newer immigrants supplanted established ones. The automobile also made the police more mobile, and its use in place of foot patrols removed officers from contact with the community. The daily passing of information and salutations between officer and citizen ceased. Previously, when problems occurred, officers asked the combatants to control themselves or turned for assistance to the friends and relatives of the misbehaving individuals. But officers in cars were unable to establish local goodwill and neighborhood contacts, and they were more likely to try to control behavior by legal threats. "Stop, or go to jail," was the general theme. Community members had been part of the police's strength. Now, according to a writer during Prohibition, the public, "afraid to become involved in gang vengeance, turns the other way and does not assist the police."[5]

Prohibition and bureaucratic policing played symbiotic roles in changing the police culture. Prohibition mobsters used automobiles and trucks in their business, and the police felt compelled to use them to equalize the battleground. More importantly, Prohibition created scandal for the police. Officers received bribes in exchange for ignoring illegal alcohol sales and other vices that were being carried on around them. The police already had a poor image among reformers, and newspaper accounts of payoffs intensified the calls for change.

Bureaucratic policing was seen as the answer to the problems. Citizens who wanted police help called headquarters, and orders were issued by radio to the patrol cars. Officers increasingly saw citizens only during crises.

The bureaucratic model strengthened the hold of the law enforcement component on policing. Bureaucratic organizations rely on measures to judge their effectiveness. Police, led by J. Edgar Hoover, urged
that they were responsible for crime control and should be evaluated
based on their handling of it. "Arrests" became one of the accepted
measures of police performance, and apprehending felons was "coin in
the bank so far as the police department's institutional transaction with
the community" was concerned.[6]

As the 1930s ended, the public seemed willing to accept the notion
that a bureaucratic police force could effectively battle crime.[7] By the
time World War II began, the police culture as it exists today was firmly
established. Economic security and the opportunity for "red-blooded,
open-air adventure and action" were favored points by those doing the
job.[8] Big-city police officers regarded themselves as combatants in a
war to protect the community against crime; victory could best be won
by making arrests and sending criminals to prison, and police leaders
urged society to grant them greater freedom in quelling the enemy.
They believed they were unfairly hamstrung by constitutional guaran-
tees that favored the lawless, who were shielded by "shysters" and weak
judges. They saw criminals as less than human and not worthy of such
protection.[9] From what our interviewees told us, very little has changed
in the last 60 years.

## WHAT THE OFFICERS SAID

Two statements can be made about the police based on our interviews.
First, officers are different from each other. Because one says certain things
and acts in certain ways does not mean that others will act exactly the
same; because one officer beats suspects does not mean they all do. The
second point, however, is a proviso: the actions officers do take must fit
within a culture that is in many ways stronger than any religion.
Individuals who share core police values are isolated from much of the rest
of society and find easiest the companionship of those like themselves.

Officers' enculturation begins with their selection by hiring boards
and is continued during their academy training. It is after graduation,
however, as many officers told us, that the most meaningful part of their

education begins. "You can't just sit in the classroom and learn how to," one of their number told us; "you have to do it."

Freshly graduated recruits are placed in field training programs under the careful supervision of veteran officers, who introduce them to the streets and to departmental policies. These programs are divided into phases in which the academy graduates are taught, tested, and continuously evaluated. They learn by following the examples of their trainers and by listening to their talk and stories. They are taught by the older officers that some of their academy training has little relevance to patrolling the streets.[10] "Through the eyes" of the field training officer (FTO), rookies learn "what kinds of behavior are appropriate and expected of a patrolman."[11] It is during this apprenticeship that the neophytes' acceptance of the culture is solidified. A police expert commented: "This traditional feature of police work—patrolmen training patrolmen—insures continuity from class to class of police officers regardless of the content of the academy instruction. In large measure, the flow of influence from one generation to another accounts for the remarkable stability of the pattern of police behavior."[12]

## VARIETY

One of the most enduring aspects of the police culture is its favor for activities that are neither routine nor mundane.[13] Humans may have a psychological need to experience new situations and achieve competence in them.[14] In general, one's occupation contributes to an individual's sense of identity and self-worth, and work is satisfying when it "challenges an individual's skills and requires ingenuity."[15] In this regard, the police occupational fondness for variety differs little from that of the larger culture. Western thought, to a certain extent, favors excitement, the ups and downs of life. Our fictional stories, for example, require a crisis for the hero to overcome. In contrast, Native American stories are linear and do not require the main character to overcome some obstacle.[16]

One lesson we should all have learned is that much of life is routine, but we nevertheless desire variety. It is the rare individual who might say that the best part of his or her job is that it never requires innovation, and so it was with our interviewees. There was the exception—the former military police marine who enjoyed "the routine calls"—but all other officers prized variety. A number of different factors, we were told, create variety within the police occupation, including unexpected activities, the opportunity for officers to have various types of contacts with citizens, an expectation of the unexpected, changes in assignments, and autonomy from supervision.

## THE UNEXPECTED

Officers enjoy the unexpected nature of their work. Although much of what they do is predictable, there is always the potential for exciting, adrenaline-producing activity. "I was addicted to the adrenaline," a woman with 13 years' police experience told us. It's not unusual for officers to refer to themselves as adrenaline "junkies."[17] Exiting the occupation leaves them craving this aspect of the job. "When you are away from it, you go through withdrawal," we were advised.

Other work offers the potential for adrenaline-producing situations—doctors in emergency rooms, lawyers handling high-profile cases, business executives battling deadlines and hostile takeovers—but most of these occupations are unavailable to individuals who become police officers, and the need for firefighters and paramedics, positions that officers might fill, is limited. Officers may get the rare chance to participate in similar operations—delivering a baby or using first-aid skills to revive an unconscious heart attack victim—but for the most part, the adrenaline rush they desire is associated with law enforcement actions and is not substantially different from the thrill obtained by their criminal prey. A high-speed chase excites both the hunter and the hunted. The motivation for some individuals to commit crimes may not be that different from the motivation of others to become police officers: they do it for the thrill. Police work, however, is safer in this regard than the road chosen by the crook, who faces stiff penalties if caught.

Adrenaline-producing situations, referred to as "hot" or "heavy" calls, contain circumstances that may result in trouble. For officers, they represent the type of situation for which they have prepared, and rookies' execution of such calls are severely scrutinized.[18] An FTO commented that she enjoyed most "the adrenaline rush to the emergency calls; knowing at any moment you can screw it up. You can learn from your mistakes. You can do better." From the perspective of the veterans, successful performance on a hot call transforms a recruit into a police officer.[19]

Officers probably would not like nonstop excitement. We were told that it is the promise of such activity that inspires them. "The biggest thing that I like is that there is always the potential for the big one," an officer explained. "You never know what is going to happen on each call. I anticipate the hot calls for my adrenaline to start pumping." Whereas many of us might find such circumstances stressful and anxiety producing, officers, we were told, found them "challenging and rewarding."

Officers spend most of their time on activities other than chasing crooks, and hot calls are rare. One study, for example, estimated that a patrolling officer might hope to catch a burglar in the act, on average, only once every 3 months and a robber once every 14 years.[20] A former officer commented:

> Eight hours of driving up and down streets broken only by routine reports and many coffee breaks, five days a week, year in and year out is very tiresome. Any call which promises action is welcomed. The possibility of physical conflict is looked forward to with anticipation. Action of any sort is welcomed to the beat man.[21]

To create adrenaline-producing situations, patrol officers often engage in "games of cops and robbers."[22] Such contests include high-speed chases, fighting, and attempts to catch individuals consuming illegal drugs or engaged in public sex. As one woman, reflecting on her habit of looking for drunk drivers, told us, "It was fun. It was like a game. The hunt was on."

By participating in the games, officers are able to vary their activities from day to day and increase the potential for adrenaline-producing situations. A female patrol officer explained:

> I like knowing that I can go to work every day and I can decide "Okay, today I can concentrate on the prostitutes that work on the street" or "Today maybe I will concentrate on a really bad populated area and the problem is cocaine." I can stop cocaine addicts on the street and I can

decide what I want to do. Whatever mood I am in I can decide what I want to do that day. I'm not limited.

Participation in police games by officers is not necessarily a seeking of dangerous situations. Officers are well aware that their chosen occupation is tinged with the potential for serious harm and it is not something they like.[23] In one study, occupational hazards, such as the danger and tension inherent in making arrests, were the items that officers least liked about their job.[24] One of our officers, a member of a SWAT (Special Weapons and Tactics) team, commented, "There is always that threat of deadly force, but it is rare. I don't let it bother me." More common comments with respect to danger came from officers who noted that they had picked the city where they currently work because it was safer than other places.

## ASSIGNMENTS

Departmental choice was important with respect to occupational variety because some cities provided the opportunity to move from one type of assignment to another. A narcotics officer with nearly 15 years' experience explained to us this aspect of the job:

> I became a patrol cop first and I worked hard to master it. I got a handle on it, then I wanted something different so I became a foot cop. After 4-1/2 years it became the same old, same old. Then I became a canine cop for 3 years. Then I trained rookies for a couple of years. . . . After 10 years in uniform I decided I wanted to be in narcotics. . . . I can leave narcotics and become a sergeant or go to motorcycles or go to juvenile or go to homicide. Not that I'd ever do any of those things, but there's a chance to really expand as far as not doing the same thing over and over, day in and day out.

Large departments in high-crime areas were prized by officers because, among other factors, they presented the possibility for service in different units. A minority officer, for example, told us that she had "wanted to work for a big city that has problems . . . that has all the major crimes represented. In [the city where she previously worked], most of the crimes were property crimes, burglary, whereas here you get a taste of everything." A smorgasbord of criminal activity translated into a variety of unit assignments and actions—a condition the officers appreciated. A woman explained to us the relationship:

> I lateraled over from another department and worked there for three years, and it was very, very boring. Not that I ever wanted a shooting or anything like that, but I just needed more of a challenge. It was very slow and it was a basic PR [public relations] department. I lived in that city, 12,000 people. Crime hardly ever goes on there. This department presented more of a challenge, to handle more of the type of crimes and situations that you get into the job for.

## AUTONOMY

For a small but substantial group of officers, variety hinged on the autonomy or self-direction the job afforded them. They recognized that an office and desk constrained one's activities and made supervision easier. But, we were told, "in your car, you have supervisors, but you can pretty much do what you want to do." The lack of management surveillance allowed officers to participate in their favorite activities. The just-quoted officer added, "If you just want to take calls, then that's it; or if you want to go out and write tickets, or get out and walk the street. Whatever your specialty is, every officer has something they like to do."

Another officer likened the experience of "being out in a car and making my own decisions" to being self-employed. She was not the only officer to compare police work to "running your own business" or "being your own boss"—perhaps the analogy stems from a desire to one day own a business or the level of responsibility they feel is required of the occupation.

Officers who enjoyed the freedom of the job linked the ability to choose how to handle their daily activities to a level of trust and status. A woman with five years' police experience noted that she enjoyed calls because "it's my responsibility and even if the calls are similar, every call is different because the people involved are different." A male colleague at the same department provided a concrete example, noting that an officer may only be "22 years old but have to go out and solve marital disputes that have been going on for 10 years."[25]

For officers who enjoyed the autonomy aspect, job satisfaction did not require a law enforcement component or adrenaline-producing activities. These officers may have appreciated such opportunities, but they were not necessarily the part of police work they enjoyed the most. A detective with a decade of service explained to us that "the most satisfaction is you get to deal with, basically, society in general. You deal with crooks; you deal with lots of kids; every aspect of society you deal with—good guys, bad guys, people that need your help." Another officer added that he liked "the chance to go out there and think on my feet. It's like a crossword puzzle, and I'm the kind of guy who likes to figure them out. It's just a constant challenge and every situation is different."

At a certain level, autonomy equals power. At the individual tier, it means the power to do what one wants, to be master of the situation. The sentiment was clearly expressed to us by a 20-year veteran reflecting on his earlier years. His example portrays the close connection for police officers between variety, autonomy, and power. We asked him, "What do you like best about being a cop?" and he replied:

> The most satisfaction I got was being a police motor officer. I wanted to ride the motorcycle. I just thoroughly enjoyed it. Once my neighbor called in to complain to my supervisor that I sit on that motorcycle like King Kong. I was proud to sit on that bike. I spent six hours a week cleaning that bike and I would still be on it today if I wasn't promoted.

We asked if it was just the bike he liked or if it was the police aspect. He added:

> There is a difference between a civilian and a police bike. The civilian gets on the bike and goes from point A to point B, continuously looking ahead. On a police motorcycle, you are the center of attention for the most part. For 10 hours of the day you are out there; you really have nowhere to go. In this department, you are totally free; you are not confined to a particular area. Also, you can take a motor accident scene; you can reconstruct it; you can draw whatever you need to. A person will tell you one thing and you can say, "No, this is what really happened."

The importance of autonomy to the officers came across more clearly when officers discussed factors that inhibited their choices. The officers' disdain for the bureaucratic model also shows in these complaints. It begins with paperwork, a staple of the bureaucratic organization. Most officers probably spend at least half their active workday completing paperwork.[26] Police superiors require reports and logs so that they may control the activities of officers. Patrol logs are tedious and can include

> details of when they went on duty, the weather conditions, their assigned radio calls, the pedestrian and traffic stops they initiated, the miles driven during their shift and the times of their lunch breaks. . . . In addition to the patrol log, officers must fill out reports on all activities during the course of their shift. For example, when an officer handles a theft, burglary, or traffic accident, he or she must complete the relevant report. If involved in a traffic accident that damages the vehicle, a high-speed pursuit or other chase, the use of force to control an offender or the discharge of a weapon, the officer must complete a special report detailing the circumstances of the incident.[27]

Although often mentioned in other studies,[28] complaints about paperwork were rare from our officers, perhaps because they recognized the need for it in a litigious society. Those few who complained did so because they found excessive the extent of documentation requested from them.

Some officers at every department had something negative to say about rules and supervision—two other cornerstones of the bureaucratic model. A 14-year veteran, working in narcotics, complained bitterly about departmental castigation for what he perceived as petty indiscretions. He told us, with some indignation, that "I don't like coming in here and because I was two minutes late or my hair's too long or . . . because I was driving five miles over the speed limit, they yell at me about that or some . . . ludicrous rule like that." Another officer was a little more eloquent. He related:

> We just had an awards dinner and the sheriff told a story about a little puppy that got out the gate and he was running out in the streets. He was just scared to death because the big bad wolf was out there. He finally found his way back home and was so happy to be back home where it's safe and all his master could do is scold him for leaving the yard. A lot of times that's how it is here. You get out there in the streets and you're

scared. There's a lot out there. And when you come back, there's the administrator saying, "Well, you did this wrong or another rule here, another rule there."

Regulations are used within a bureaucratic organization to control the office holder; the more rules, the stricter the supervision. A professional, in contrast, is granted great discretion in how to accomplish his or her job; a bureaucrat is strictly controlled. Officers, from the answers we were supplied, consider important the autonomy of a professional. Their treatment as bureaucrats by superiors is frustrating to them, and they lash out at those who attempt to control them. A veteran patrol officer provided us a cynical comment on his superiors and rule making: "They design these policies to make our job better, but they may only do it to make themselves look better." He added, "We are not little kids, we are men who do a job and can do the job." His criticism makes clear his distaste of supervision and belief in his own ability. It is a rejection of bureaucratic policing and a statement in favor of officers' professionalization.

The loss of autonomy is clearly associated with a loss of personal power. Officers have long-established beliefs and ways of working. Outside influences tend to undercut these and challenge officers' authority. Officers dislike their autonomy being infringed upon by individuals who they perceive as nonexperts. Indeed, bureaucratization was an effort by police administrators to establish themselves as the experts on crime control and remove policing from under the thumb of local politicians. Departmental budgets, however, are decided by municipal officials, and most police chiefs serve at the discretion of locally elected politicians. These items result in police paying more attention to complaints that originate with mayors, city council members, and other local officials. A longtime veteran, for example, complained to us that "Priority items are set aside simply because some politician's relative is involved or they claim to be the victim. So we have to stop what we are doing. We are like puppets."

Changes in the way the job is done substantiate for officers that they and their departments are no longer granted carte blanche with respect to crime control. A homicide detective targeted "special interest groups" as the problem. He argued that they were "more interested in obtaining their goals than getting justice." We asked him to give us an example. He told us:

> All kinds of special interest groups are affecting the political and legal arena, nothing specific. But where race is not an issue, suddenly it becomes an issue. . . . I've been accused of arresting a person because he was black, and it had nothing to do with that. It never even crossed my mind, but yet it is popular to call policemen racist. I'm not. We are biased by certain types of people. For example, I think that after being in the department for a while, you get used to certain kinds of people that you have contact with. And just as you learn to read body language, you learn to make an estimation of what this person is doing or who they are. It's an inherent part of many jobs. To policemen, it's a very important part of the job. You are constantly contacting people. Within moments you have to size this person up. There are certain traits that you begin to associate with certain types of people. If a guy's got tattoos that are very obviously from prison, you can make certain conclusions about his experiences with law enforcement, and those are fair conclusions. It's frustrating when special interest groups take a nonissue and make it an issue. The truth of the matter is that race has a lot less to do with it than the public is led to believe. If anything, we bend over backwards so that we don't appear to be racist.

This officer assured us that he is not prejudiced against anyone based upon their race, but he quickly added that he does prejudge people based upon other characteristics. Unfortunately, some of the characteristics used to evaluate individuals are also associated with race. For example, some officers may be suspicious of individuals based upon what they perceive of as "gang dress," loose-fitting clothes being the most recent example.[29] Dress, however, is a matter of style and not gang affiliation. Millions of youngsters donned such outfits; only a small percentage were outlaws. The use of stereotypes to conduct police business, however, ignores such differences. One individual is treated as anyone else who falls within the stereotypical group—no better, no worse. People, however, demand to be treated as individuals, and when they are not, it should come as no surprise that they may complain to city and departmental officials. Such complaints lead to greater supervision. In the end, officials usually blame somebody for the problem—the "bad apple" who if left unattended, the argument goes, will spoil the police barrel. As we were told by one of our officers, "someone will be a scapegoat." As for the officers, we were advised, "It makes for terrible morale."

## CULTURAL FAVORITISM

The influence the police culture has on officers differs from individual to individual. However, certain beliefs are universally held. The strongest of these is officers' certainty that the most important part of their job is to catch criminals in order to protect the public. Officers daily help citizens in a number of ways. They may give directions to lost individuals, direct traffic, assist during health emergencies and traffic accidents, or find lost children. Such activities, however, are not viewed as "real police work," and officers are more likely to complain about such duties. One, for example, said he disliked dealing with drunks because they didn't appreciate that he was trying to help them. Another officer complained about having to make traffic stops when the weather was poor, while a third told us that he hated "cleaning up other people's garbage." These matters are often associated with the city in which one works. A 15-year veteran griped:

> Here most of the matters are petty and the feeling is negative—not a lot of satisfaction in working patrol in this city. It is a very dissatisfying environment, as far as a nuts-and-bolts police department, compared to what I was weaned on at [names of cities]. This is a very traffic-oriented police department because of the large volume of accidents. There is big pressure to write tickets. So you may write someone up that you would normally just advise. This affects the officer's ability to use discretion. This impacts me because I have to go to night court, and it's a waste of my time and a waste of payroll. I don't like to give tickets to good citizens who are good drivers and just make a simple mistake. I had a woman the other day, never got a ticket. She made a U-turn across a double-double yellow line. She cried and pleaded with me not to write her up. I didn't want to tell her the only reason she was getting a ticket was because the city was imposing an illegal quota system, which they don't. But it affects my job and my paycheck, so she gets a ticket.

In contrast, this officer and almost all others prized situations in which there was a victim and an offender. This was "real police work": an innocent individual hurt by a criminal, who preys on the weak, who is thwarted by the efforts of the police. Typical of such stories was the chance occurrence related to us by a 15-year veteran who spotted someone walking in a residential neighborhood carrying a videocassette recorder. "I called over the radio, 'Has anyone had a burglary tonight with a missing VCR?'" he told us. The officer recovered the stolen item. "The victim was a Hispanic man who had saved for a couple of years for this, and there was just the satisfaction of seeing the look on his face of happiness."

The tales the officers recounted to us indicated that three components of victim-offender situations provided them fulfillment. The first was halting the victimization by the use of police skills. Ending physical violence was at the top of the list. "When I see someone hurting someone else, I feel good if I can jump in and stop it, protect the victim, be the big brother."

An expression of appreciation by victims to the officers was the second component of victim-offender incidents that provided the officers we interviewed with satisfaction. They didn't expect people to make a big deal out of what they had done, but like anybody they longed for signs of gratitude. Officers reported that "sometimes people will write or call and thank me," and this lets them know that "somebody does appreciate it." Recognition could also be less direct. Friendly conversation might suffice. "It is nice to work graveyard and see a lady out walking her dog by herself because she feels comfortable in this neighborhood," a patrol officer related. "You feel like you're part of it; you can stop and they like to talk to you."

The third element of the victim-offender situation that provided officers with fulfillment was putting criminals behind bars. As one described it, "The bottom line, putting the bad guy in handcuffs and taking him to jail." Of course, the process does not end with arrest; seeing a case through to, in their eyes, a successful completion increased officers' satisfaction. A detective with more than 20 years' experience exclaimed: "You can't imagine the 'high' that you get when you're sitting in the courtroom and the jury comes back with a guilty verdict. That to me is satisfaction: putting the bad people away, the people that prey on the innocent. That is the ultimate high." This component was also the most difficult to achieve, and officers clearly recognized this. Patrol officers were at a particular disadvantage in this regard. A homicide detective explained:

> On patrol, you initiate something and then you don't often see the end result. In [my job], you often get the end result on the day it occurs, and you carry it through the court process to completion and sometimes to the appellate division. You get completeness out of this aspect here. I don't know about on patrol.

As a result, patrol officers perhaps placed more importance on expressions of victims' appreciation. Exemplary was a patrol officer who liked "putting the bad guys behind bars." But he added:

> I've been doing this for six years now and you see the crime victim, the child that gets raped, the person that gets robbed at gunpoint; you see the fear in their eyes. You tell someone that you caught the guy who did it and you see the smile come over their face. Whether they end up going to court or they end up dropping the case, at least you get that satisfaction.

Officers were most pleased with criminal cases in which the offender was convicted and imprisoned. As a result, individuals and circumstances that prevented such conclusions frustrated them. Judges received the most condemnation, but district attorneys (DA) were not immune from censure. The prosecuting attorneys were criticized for failing to take cases to trial. A 15-year veteran, for example, told us, "It's really disheartening to see new officers coming on and making some really dynamite arrests, really good, thought-out arrests, and having the district attorneys not file it." The DAs were also viewed as part of a court system that allowed defendants to escape full punishment for their misdeeds by pleading guilty.

The officers we interviewed seemed unaware of the obstacles district attorneys might face in court trying to prove guilt beyond a reasonable doubt. (The outcome of the criminal trial of O. J. Simpson illustrated such difficulties for the public.) Rarely were the constraints of rules of evidence mentioned, and when they were, they were viewed as impossible restrictions upon officers' ability to do their trade. "If you do the job, no matter how well you do it," we were instructed, "someone can always make a complaint and the judge will say, 'Yeah, you did wrong.'"

Our interviewees also ignored other items that might compel district attorneys to act judiciously. Jail overcrowding, for example, an important determining factor for DAs trying to assess which defendants most deserve incarceration, was barely mentioned. Also left unsaid were limitations such as fixed staff, public sentiment, and sympathetic defendants (who are hard to convict).

Judges were the main lightning rod for police officers' disfavor with the court system. California's judges hand out the most severe sentences in the world, and they jail as high a percentage of the guilty as judges in other jurisdictions.[30] Despite these facts, as one officer put it, "the dirt bags are mollycoddled by the court, and they don't get what they have coming to them." This officer and others were expressing their frustrations at being blocked from their goal of putting criminals in prison. Another added:

> You waste all this time and when you get down to it, they end up getting probation. I think that's frustrating because you've worked so hard on a case and you walk into the courtroom and you testify and the . . . jury finds him guilty or they plead guilty and they end up with no time. There's no punishment meted out, and maybe my problem is with the justice system. The punishment they're getting doesn't go with the crime. I think that's the frustrating part of it. It's supposed to be the culmination of all the hard work that you've done, of your hard work, the detectives' hard work, the ID technicians' hard work, the sergeants that were there, and you cumulate that together and you get down to the very end and you're not getting anything out of it. It's very frustrating and you end up leaving and saying, "Why am I doing this; why am I bothering to arrest these people?"

The release of defendants from custody also undercut the satisfaction officers obtained from expressions of the public's appreciation. Citizens expect that policing follows a process in which they report offenses, police arrest perpetrators, and offenders are convicted and punished.[31] Variations from this pattern discredit the police and the court system in some individuals' eyes. Some officers believe that the brunt of citizens' ire is aimed at them, when, in their view, it should be leveled at the courts. Illustrative, a 14-year veteran described the court system as frustrating. She explained:

> We take all the repercussions from it. The victims call us and are angry with the police department because the same person who has victimized them is still out walking the street. And they don't realize that it's not us.
>
> We do everything we can to put them in jail, but we don't let them go.

Another veteran painted even a darker picture, suggesting that officers would be held responsible by the public for violence predicated on the release of criminals. "My job is only to arrest this person and then the courts have to do theirs, but we have to answer to the public," he griped. He quickly added, "The victims, the witnesses, we can't protect them 24 hours a day. The suspect is out there." The officer is grim. From his perspective, the court is the ally of criminals, releasing them so that they may once again prey on the innocents.

Officers had one more shot to take at the courts. They were immensely irritated that the courts infringed on their time off. Police officers often must testify in court. "It gets old real fast," one officer told us. Another added, "The rest of the world is awake during the day. I've been up all night and they expect you to be there in court." These officers, mostly women, disliked the fact that they were not free to plan their personal time as they saw fit. In this regard, the courts undercut another of the items most cherished by our interviewees: their autonomy.

## POLITICS

Individuals in every department had difficulties with what they defined as departmental politics. For the most part, these were issues associated with promotion.

Police departments usually have little room for upward mobility. As in most bureaucracies, their organizational structure is in the shape of a pyramid; there are few leaders at the top and an increasing number of individuals at each lower level. Promotion becomes more difficult as one climbs higher in the occupation and finds fewer open positions above. Small departments offer few chances for advancement, while larger departments with numerous units present ambitious officers the best opportunity for promotion and a reason to stay on the job. An officer told us:

> I definitely have aspirations to move up and I do plan on staying. I'm going to stick it out because I love it. I'm going to be here until I retire. I work in Detectives, specifically in the Crimes against Persons Division. I came from Burglaries to Crimes against Persons. There will soon be an opening in Homicides, and I'm thinking of stepping into that division. There's plenty of movement up here.

In contrast, other officers complained about the lack of movement in their departments, and for some, this was a reason to leave the occupation. An FTO with 7 years' experience, for example, said she planned to go back to school to prepare herself for other employment. She cited the lack of movement as the reason for her decision, adding, "I don't want to be in patrol forever." Another officer explained:

> Two years ago, I went for lieutenant and was sort of disappointed at the fact that no matter what your work product was or how much you produced or what level of quality it was, when it came down to the end, with the entire list of prospective lieutenants, it was based on seniority and education. I don't have seniority and everybody had education at parity, so promotions were all pretty much based on seniority. They promoted people at the top of that list that obviously can't do the job, but they had the seniority and they passed all the little hurdles, and so they became lieutenants. I don't try anymore.

Conflict between officers is created because of the competition for a limited number of positions, which undermines the officers' view that they are a family. A 15-year veteran complained, "We don't have a department of brethren. We have a department of individuals here. There is competition: he got that ticket, he got that arrest; now I have to go out and do it." Another officer added:

> A lot of people say cops are a real tight group and all that. Yes and no— not everybody likes everybody. A lot of people twist things and there's a real

undercurrent of rumors. It's phenomenal. You could make soap operas at the police department. *General Hospital* is boring in comparison.

The criteria upon which promotions are based are unclear to officers, and they tend to believe that personal associations play a stronger role than ability. Such ideas are not new or exclusive to police departments. "Old-boy networks," as they have been known, excluded outsiders and preferred to hire and promote friends. Equal opportunity laws were designed in large part to remove such favoritism and allow minorities and women the chance to obtain equal footing on the occupational pyramid. From what we were told, favoritism continues to exist. Although mentioned by men and women, minority and white, the following officer's comments were arguably the most bitter. The 18-year veteran's words indicate that the bias undercuts the solidarity of the police culture. He complained about his department and told us that there are people "in police work, in my department, that I feel shouldn't be there. They make it bad for everyone." We asked him, "What do these people do that they shouldn't be in the department?" He replied:

The backstabbing, the cheating while they are in the department. Me being a black man, I have been the brunt of some of this. Some things are unfair. Some in the department are treated like children and some are treated like stepchildren, and I have a problem with this. Some of the people in this department have proven to me that they don't deserve trust. . . . It is not just the administration, it goes all the way down to the patrolman. It is like a bad seed got into here and spread like a cancer. Everybody comes in with their prejudices, but I don't get caught up in that. I just come in and do my job and leave to go home. I don't associate with these officers after work. I hang out with other friends.

This officer blames all levels of police officers for the injustices he perceives. Other officers, for the most part, tended to blame supervisors. For example, we were told that assignments were based on "a lot of brown-nosing. . . . So if you piss one supervisor off one time and he gets that detail, you pretty much have to say, 'I'll just have to wait until they change supervisors.'"

## THE PUBLIC

Officers chafe at the public scrutiny they receive. It is a limit on their ability to work as they please. In many ways it is similar to the public treatment that all high-profile occupations and individuals receive. Doctors, lawyers, and sports stars can expect both praise and ridicule for what they do, and the activities of the police are no different. People do not possess a single set of attitudes about the police; they have both positive and negative concerns about their paid protectors.[32] Two well-known police experts wrote:

> Policemen live in an environment of attitudes which appears quixotic and uncertain. They long to know the rules for winning approbation and seek them in vain. At one moment they are applauded for the important job they are doing; at another they are criticized intemperately for not doing enough, for doing too much, for being too tough, for being too lenient, for being too community conscious, for not being community conscious enough.[33]

Police feel put upon. More than in other high-profile groups, the actions of some malefactors are hoisted onto the group. Perhaps their uniforms and bureaucratic coldness make it easy for the public to lump them together; "They look and sound alike," the thought may run, "so they must act alike." It is ironic that the police would damn stereotyping— something officers told us they used in their job—when it is wielded against them. "There seems to be a myth that policemen are supposed to be [a certain] type of individual, and we're not. We're as different as any other group of people," a longtime veteran told us. He complained that he did not like "the stereotypes and the prejudice that are currently applied to policemen. It's not fair and it's inaccurate."

Many officers felt unappreciated by the public. The good deeds they thought they did were overwhelmed by public perceptions. "It's a real negative job," one commented.

> You don't get a lot of praise; you don't get a lot of people saying "thank you." People expect that of you because that's your job. They don't understand that it's a basic human need to be praised every now and then. I don't think there is near enough of that going on. It just seems like

there is always some kind of controversy going on. One person does something wrong and they get what's coming to them, but then the whole job in general is tarnished and everybody thinks because that's what happened, all of us are that way.

Officers believe that the public doesn't understand their job.[34] From their perspective, media presentations are biased and their critics are uninformed. "Here are a bunch of people who are passing judgment and haven't even been in a patrol car," an officer griped. "People who are going to make policies should know what we go through," he reckoned. He suggested, "We should let the public go on ride-alongs, come out with us, go on a family disturbance call and see what it is like. They would say, 'Wow, these people are jerks to you. How can you deal with this?'"

It is not easy for officers to adjust to the public abuse they may periodically receive. A sizable minority of officers view their job as "thankless." Our officers argued that the public misunderstood their actions. A detective explained:

> You try to do something for somebody; they don't see it as help. They see it as harassment and they see us as overstepping our bounds, being badge heavy, gun heavy, etc. I'm doing something for them, and they're belittling me, berating me, threatening me. Why are they doing this? And this is really discouraging, especially when you're driving down the street and maybe you wave to someone, the little kid and the parent flips you off. That's discouraging. One time, a little kid was saying hi to me, and his older brother slapped him on the head and said, "Don't you wave to that pig," and that kind of hurts.

Such actions must take a psychological toll on some officers. A 20-year veteran surmised that

> most police officers adjust; some don't. Some get to the point where they think everybody is a bad guy. It takes a hell of a lot to be positive and keep a good attitude. That's what I used to tell my trainees, and even today I have a good attitude. I come to work with a good attitude and usually maintain it—unless somebody spits in my face.

Some officers we interviewed recognized the continued association between public perceptions of the police and the extent of supervision they received. A 15-year veteran, who was working in homicide when we spoke with him, illuminated the connection:

> I don't like the microscope that we are kept under from both the public and the administration. The scrutiny by the public is probably why the administration scrutinizes us too. A policeman is a human being just like anybody else. But if he happens to be at a party and overindulges in alcohol, people think, "Oh, he's a cop. He can't do that!" If a policeman happens to miss a payment on a credit card, you don't have a credit card company calling a trash collection agency saying, "Hey, your man missed a payment," but yet they call the police department. And I don't like that. If you work hard and happen to have a brand new car, then a lot of people look at you like, "What assignment is he working; is he taking any money; is he taking graft?"

In the end, public criticism of the police leads to greater supervision of officer behavior by departmental leaders and further undermines officer morale.

## Discussion

Officers see themselves as autonomous members of a team who perform an exciting and useful job. Certain types of activities are favored. Exhilarating action, which results in the arrest of an offender, is looked forward to. For most officers, such opportunities represent the type of calls that had originally attracted them to police work. They are, however, rare. The more common situations that confront officers daily are often disliked. Officers find particularly distasteful calls that seemingly involve social work tasks.

Officers enjoy the freedom their occupation offers. Most days they can pick among an extended menu of possible options, and they prefer to emphasize this aspect of their daily activities. They do have more power and freedom than most individuals. At their discretion, they can arrest or ignore similar behaviors. Moreover, no other peacetime occupation allows its employees to choose to kill others under certain circumstances.

Despite their self-image as powerful individuals, officers complain bitterly about rules, regulations, and departmental politics that constrain their activities. The district attorney's office and the courts further undermine the officers' view of themselves and their jobs. From the officers' viewpoint, these members of the criminal justice system release the guilty to once again victimize the innocent.

Officers feel like an oppressed minority. The rest of the criminal justice system undoes their good work and criticizes them for how they do the job. The public is no better. Citizens complain about crime and chastise the police for activities that officers feel are acceptable. Only other officers seem to understand their plight. Unable to satisfy the demands of exogenous pressures, officers attempt to meet the norms of the police culture, a society in which they are understood and appreciated. In the next chapter, we examine how our officers responded to the isolating aspects of the police world.

# Chapter Seven

## Responding to the Culture

Officers have different mechanisms for adjusting to the isolating influences of the job. Sizable segments withdraw to the companionship of other officers or their families, and a measurable group sticks to the fellowship of old friends. From what our respondents related, it is the rare officer who establishes new friendships with a variety of individuals.

Arguably, the most common reaction to the isolating influences of police work is for officers to withdraw to a world of police friends, where they are better able to combat the psychological strain caused by their position. Their comrades understand the difficulties of the occupation.

New members of any group probably have a psychological craving for acceptance by veterans of the occupation. Such need may be particularly pronounced in police recruits. Their academy education emphasizes teamwork and attempts to create solidarity among the neophytes. Upon entering their field training, the recruits look for signs that they have been accepted into the larger group. Invitations by older members to participate in informal social activities are a common gesture of acceptance in most assemblages. Among police officers, one of the more common of such activities is drinking after work, and officers long remember their initiations. "I worked graveyards," a 14-year veteran remembered, "and that was a very, very strong clique. After the first couple of days they asked me to [go drinking] with them and I felt accepted. It was great."

In rapidly expanding Southern California, officers are often not from the neighborhoods they patrol and may have few ties to the area. Today's society, in general, includes individuals who are far removed from family and childhood friends. People are more mobile and distances and places that once seemed far away are increasingly being considered home. For officers in this situation, the lure of occupational friendships may be overwhelming. One of our informants, for example, after his discharge from the Marines, "was isolated," he told us, because "my whole family is back on the East Coast. I had no friends except for the people I knew in this department or in the Marine Corps at Twenty-nine Palms." Under such conditions, it was easy for him to rely on his new friendships with other people in law enforcement.

Some officers who do have local ties may find it convenient to cut them as they come to see their old acquaintances as nuisances. "Every time I see them they ask for legal advice or they tell me about negative encounters," an officer complained. Another echoed the sentiment: "At a party there is always someone that wants to complain about some traffic ticket that they got."

The inability of old friends to share the police perspective was for some officers the cause of their small sphere of confidants. One officer recounted that "friends drift away because they don't know where you're coming from." This officer and others found a growing abyss between themselves and their old companions, who were critical of the police occupation. The experience led the just-quoted officer to comment:

> I think that's kind of the general public attitude: "You do all that stuff you need to do as long as we don't have to know about it." People don't like to deal with the problems we deal with and they don't like the way we deal with them, but they definitely want something done about the problems.

These officers have become prisoners within the police culture. Their identities have intermingled with their occupation, intensifying the "us versus them" attitude normally associated with the occupation. Each publicized misdeed becomes a reflection upon themselves and probably further isolates them within the world of police officers. A veteran patrol officer, reacting to a series of highly publicized police misdeeds, told us she hated "what is going on right now in the media. I won't even turn on the news." During her police career, she recognized that she changed until all of her friends were cops. She concluded about her previous buddies, "They are the same; I am not."

## ESCAPING THE POLICE CULTURE

Retreating into family life was one way for officers to avoid capture by the police culture. Occasionally, the police world would take a heavy toll on the family life of officers—"It cost me my first marriage," a now wiser individual told us—but usually, from what our interviewees said, home and hearth were safe havens. They still faced the same concerns that had driven colleagues deep into the culture, but these officers had an escape—their families. A 15-year senior patrol officer explained that he has

> a warped, demented view of life because of this job. I'm vulnerable; I can't afford to maintain friends who are involved in questionable activities. I am very introverted because of my job. I don't socialize with others here—just my significant other and my family.

These officers do their best to separate their work from home activities. As a result, they are better able to escape the police culture. "I am just a mom, and when I get home, I am a mom, not a police officer. I leave police work behind," we were told. "My friends and I don't talk about police work," this officer continued. "We talk about things that are happening at the time, like love life, friends, motherhood."

Motherhood has a strong cultural, if not biological, attraction for women, and its fulfillment keeps some female officers from giving themselves unconditionally to the police world. An officer with less than five years' experience revealed that when she was in patrol, she talked about the job at home. "It was a way of venting," she explained. But now she is able to mentally divide her worlds. "My family tends to be number one the minute I'm off-duty," she concluded. We asked her if she had children:

> Yes, quite a few of them. I have one son of my own, and then I have two stepchildren. They take up a large amount of our time for after-school and weekend activities. I spend a lot of time doing things with them, doing things with my husband, who's not a cop, which is wonderful.

Police work does come up, but I tend to be the type of person that likes to leave it at the office. I don't watch cop shows; I don't want to have anything to do with it.

Men also benefited from family life, and they did not differ from women in their belief that it was important. One told us, "I got married when I was really young. . . . I don't hang out with the guys. I have a couple of friends. My family life is important." And another officer informed us that his "wife wouldn't tolerate me just hanging out with cops."

Women more often supplied us with details of their home life, perhaps testaments that women, even working police officers, continue to do the majority of the domestic duties. Or the difference may simply be the result of cultural norms; men may be fairly mute on home life. A single father, for example, mentioned nothing more on the matter than he did not like shift work. "If I wasn't in my present [daytime] assignment, it would be a problem, not just a dislike," he concluded. His silence concerning his domestic life can best be attributed to a desire to not share his personal activities with total strangers.

Maintaining old friendships was also a buffer against the seductive nature of the police culture. A community affairs officer with 17 years of police service told us:

Personally, I don't socialize with police officers when I get off duty. I leave the job behind me when I step out the door. I may have occasion to socialize with police officers, but what I try to look at is that I am a human being. I have a life, just like anyone else. I try to maintain my friends that I have known all along, and I have some very old friends that have been with me throughout the years. This job should have no effect on who you are or what you are. Initially, you do hang out with cops because you look for that acceptance. You go along with it for a while, then you begin to see that you do have a life. And you think, "I am not going to let this job interfere with my life." If you let it interfere, then you have gotten into the badge-heavy concept because you want to go along with the program. As the very unfortunate incident of the King beating shows, one thing you want to stay away from is being a part of the group. It happens in everyday life. It's not unique to police work.

A 14-year veteran remembered:

That was one thing that they did stress in the academy: "You had these friends before, so keep them. Don't get locked into the situation that everybody you see and do things with are other cops, because then you never get away from it." So when I go away from here, my friends are my friends from 15 years ago and people that I meet through them. They found out what I did and it was no big thing because I don't talk about it.

I want to be away from it because it gives me an out.

These officers felt the same pressures as officers who withdrew into the police culture. New acquaintances were uneasy around them and old friends questioned them about publicized incidents of police misconduct. "It's tough because you get tired of talking about it," one complained. The camaraderie of established friendships, however, undercut the necessity of relying on police companions. The just-quoted officer told us that he keeps his "friends outside of work because I like to get away from it." He believed that some cops intertwine their personalities with the job, and that creates problems. "It transcends into their lives and they end up getting divorced or even going to jail."

Shift work presented a problem for officers attempting to establish new relationships. Newer officers rarely get to work during the day shift and have their evenings and weekends free to socialize. Rather, they are working when their outside friends are sleeping. It is often easier in such circumstances to spend time with other officers, family, or old friends. But even here, shift work got in the way. An officer explained, "It's really hard to call up my old friend, my best friend, and say 'Hey, it's two o'clock. How would you like to go running with me? It's a gorgeous night.' She'd think I was brain-dead."

Despite the sizable difficulties of making and maintaining friendships outside of police work, many officers are willing to overcome the barriers because of the perceived benefits. Friendships outside of the occupation provided officers with other interests, diversions from the law enforcement world. An officer told us that when he was in his 20s, he would

go to cop parties, hang around with cops off-duty, drink with cops after work. That was bad. It got to be too much for me. I recognized it as such so I took up hobbies. I rodeo and I have a lot of civilian friends who are cowboys. They have nothing to do with law enforcement. I went back into the Marine reserves and met a lot of kids who were college students.

So now I have a great variety of civilian friends mixed into my world as well as police officers. I don't socialize with cops hardly at all anymore. The cops I do socialize with, they rodeo with me. My two roommates are police officers, but the only common denominator we have as friends is we all rodeo together. That was a good decision on my part to get out of the police mentality. It has helped me a great deal with my outlook. I don't look at things like we're the only ones who are right and everybody else are assholes. I don't like cops who have that mentality.

In order to make new friends that were not in law enforcement, some officers chose to keep their occupation secret from new acquaintances. They had discovered through experience that if they did so, people were more likely to accept them. A field training officer with a decade of police service remembered that when he first joined the police department, he had "a supercop concept" of himself. "People don't want to associate with you," he told us. "But as you get some experience, you don't emphasize what your job is so much when you first meet someone." Laughing, he told us, "You don't say, 'I am a police officer.'"

Officers with "hidden identities" waited until friendships were established before telling others their occupation. "They say, 'I never realized you were a policeman,'" a homicide detective told us. In this fashion, they were able to establish new relationships.

Departmental assignment may also assist a small number of officers to escape the police culture. Among our sample, DARE (Drug Abuse Resistance Education) and community service assignments helped. Working with children as a DARE officer or with community groups is not as isolating as other assignments. Illustrative was a DARE officer who commented that the assignment had provided her with new friends outside the occupation. It may be the case, however, that individuals assigned to these units are different from other officers. Some minority officers, for example, may have found it easier to work as community officers within neighborhoods in which they had been raised. One such officer discussed with us how his background had affected his dealings with community members. He told us:

I grew up here, went to school here, still live here. I bought a house here. I couldn't see policing in another city when I live here. I don't consider myself a warrior of the community, but if I'm going to take care of problems, I want to take care of problems in the community where I live. I don't want to commute an hour to take care of somebody else's community. I spent four and a half years on foot patrol in the housing projects, which are about 85 percent Hispanic, 10 percent black, and 5 percent Samoan and other nonwhites. I started a Boy Scout troop in the projects, which was comprised mostly of Hispanic kids. There were some black kids and other gypsy kids. I started a black-white youth group. I was really involved and recognized in the Hispanic community as a COP [community-oriented policing] law enforcement liaison. I was also assigned a community position as a liaison officer even though I was still a foot beat cop because I knew everybody in the community.

Another minority officer, working within his childhood community, told us:

A lot of my friends here felt that they were not getting a fair shake from the police. But when I became a police officer, they had someone to iden- tify with, and they were more likely to ask for help. I feel good about this trust that they put in me. They look beyond the badge and at the person. It feels good when people trust me. You can help people resolve their problems and you feel good about that.

There was a direct relationship between this officer's friendships with people in the community and his ability to help the neighborhood. They supported him and he helped them. Together they formed a bond that allowed the 20-year veteran to avoid becoming ensnared in the police culture.

## Female Officers

Female officers' immersion in the police culture was affected by their unique status within the occupation. Entrance into any culture requires acceptance by its members, and women have had difficulty gaining approval in many male-dominated occupations, including law enforce- ment. Obtaining a position within a department does not mean accept- ance for female officers. A 15-year veteran told us, "I wonder how old I have to be and how long I have to work here before I stop getting rude statements from either male officers or the public."

Some departments, according to officers with whom we spoke, have unwritten rules barring females, while other policing agencies have "a very poor track record with female officers. They have very low retention of female officers; they will sexually discriminate; they are very hard on their women." Illustrative, an officer told us she had switched agencies "because in the department where I worked prior to this one, I was the only female officer—first one they've ever hired—and there was a lot of bullshit and I got tired of it."

To be accepted into the law enforcement world, women must exhibit behaviors and language that are consistent with the belief system: they must, in the vernacular, "walk the walk and talk the talk." They may, however, "initially lack the inside knowledge, the trade secrets which can be helpful" in gaining approval.[1] Field training officers normally introduce neophytes to culturally accepted street behaviors, but in the past this period has been problematic for female recruits. They had no women as role models to teach them how to do their job. There were "not even any female figures in the films used for in-service training."[2] A patrol officer with more than 15 years' police experience explained to us the importance of a woman learning the job from another woman:

> Women would benefit from seeing other women in police work. I think that a female recruit should at least ride with another female, or have at least one female staff or one female FTO, because we do things a little differently. We all get to the same end result, but getting there is a little different. We use our mouth instead of our brawn. We have to search differently because we are a little smaller. Upper-body strength is lacking, so we may have to go to our baton a little faster. The way we handle ourselves is different. I went on a ride-along with a woman who was really short, and it helped me a lot to see how she did things.

Lacking female trainers and partners, women must learn the basics of police work and its culture from male officers. Women attempting to do the job in the same fashion as the men may make some mistakes, but errors committed by women may have more negative consequences than lapses by men. Women are a minority group within policing and because they are few in number, they are unable to blend in with the much larger majority. They are easily identified and stigmatized as a group that, as far as many men and a sizable portion of the public feel, cannot do the job. A mistake by any member of the stigmatized group adds to the evidence that its members are unworthy of the occupation. As a result, women recruits who succeed do so in the face of added adversity. A female FTO explained:

> A woman has to try 10 times harder and do 10 times better. If a female makes a mistake, it's all the females. If a male makes a mistake, no one pays attention. The quality of females as a group is probably better than the males. I am not just saying that because I am female, but the females do have to try much harder. The female standard has to be much higher than the male standard. You can have some men that are not good police officers and they make it. But women have to make good arrests, write good reports.

Mistakes by males or females delay their acceptance into the police culture. Blunders indicate that the individual may be unable to support another officer during a crisis situation. All officers are suspect until they perform some activity that transforms them into a cop in the eyes of their colleagues. An officer remembered:

> When any recruits come out [into the field], they have to prove themselves before you want them to back you up. It was not harassment, but when I called for backup, they wouldn't come and when I said I would back someone up, another officer would say he was closer. After I got into a couple of altercations, it all went away and it hasn't been a problem since then.

Getting into brawls was a way for the women to show that they had the "right stuff" to be members of the police culture. As another female officer told us she had problems in the beginning, but they disappeared after she got "into a couple of fights just to prove myself."

New female officers faced another barrier to entering the law enforcement world that their brethren did not. Men slid into the culture during after-work drinking sessions and other social activities with other male officers. Such rendezvous, however, were not freely open to women. The female officers did not feel as if they were being discriminated against. Rather, they saw the gender separation as a normal consequence of our society. One reason was that there were not many women with whom to associate. One woman, for example, had transferred into her current department from one that had a sizable number of women with whom she spent time. She missed the camaraderie of the women's locker room. She was the only woman assigned to her current shift and "had to dress in a shoebox." She felt isolated because she had no one to turn to for advice or to confide in. She felt awkward about participating in other officers' activities, for example, eating breakfast together. She told us:

> Female support is important to making it as a police officer. Everyone needs to talk about their stress and problems. There was no one I could talk to because I didn't know if they would say, "It's typical she would feel that way. All women feel that way." I was afraid of what I would say. I didn't know if they would judge me as a person or as a female. Actually, they did both all along.

A female narcotics officer with 8 years' experience felt that some of the other 18 officers in her unit, all of whom were men, were her "close friends," but she didn't do anything with them outside of work. She explained, "That's because I'm a female. . . . It's not that I'm excluded; it's just that their interest is in their wives or their girlfriends or their male friends. We have a common interest here [inside the unit] but really not outside work."

It may take a special type of woman to survive in policing without a female support system. Those women who needed one may have been less likely to endure long enough to become part of our sample. Several of the female officers who had persisted told us that they believed they were different. We extensively quote one of their number here because her words clearly illustrate the women's position. We asked her if she felt a need for a female support group. She replied:

> I personally have never been in need of it. In all honesty, most of my girlfriends that started out as police officers have dropped out or had a more difficult time with it. I personally get dragged down when I hear a lot of "woe is me" stories. I have overcome it. The more you draw attention to yourself as being different, the more people will look at you as being different. In this job and in any other male dominated profession, you have to get used to the fact that men work differently than women do. Men talk to each other and relate differently than women do, and

you have to accept the differences in the sexes and not let it bother you too much. I prefer working with men to working with women. They are more enjoyable. Maybe because it is simpler—the emotions aren't as involved; their personal lives don't get involved with their jobs as much.

It is possible that this woman and others were using excuses to convince themselves that the situation they found themselves in was preferable. Another officer with a similar viewpoint, for example, denied the need for a female support system, but within seconds she provided us with an example of the benefits of such friendships. She began by telling us:

My best friends are the male officers. I don't think female support is nec-essary. I don't like the female/male thing, the female versus male. I never had as many problems as I have seen other women have. Some women come in tough, trying to act like the men, and the men resent it. It just wouldn't work for me. I don't act tough. I don't like to fight; I would if I had to. I'd jump right in, but I'd rather not if I can avoid it.

But she immediately added that she could "help other women by giving them little tricks to being successful in police work. For example, if you go to court wearing a skirt or dress instead of a uniform, you don't win as many cases."

Female officers are in an odd position. They want to be accepted into the police world and yet find structural barriers, such as the limited number of female officers, in their way. As the male officers do, the women rely on old friends and family for companionship. But they probably find their old relationships strained because they are women participating in a male-dominated occupation. One of the female offi-cers, for example, divorced after 10 years of marriage, blamed the breakup on her "spouse's inability to deal with the job. It was very intim-idating to him. I think he was threatened by it."

Unmarried women found dating difficult. Shift work played a role, but probably of more importance, the men they met were often "put off" by the women's occupation. Female officers found it easier to date and marry police officers. Such men understood the world of law enforcement and were accepting of their wives' occupation. Moreover, as spouses of police officers, the women were accepted into the male officers' social world. Weekend outings with other police families guaranteed them acceptance into the police world. A woman whose marriage to a civilian ended in divorce told us about police, "We consider ourselves a family. We have our own world and the outside world doesn't understand what it's like to go to work and deal with some of the things we deal with."

Some female officers made an effort to make and keep outside companions. A DARE officer was happy because her assignment had given her new friends outside of policing. "I have women friends again," she exclaimed. And as the men did, the women found it convenient at times to keep their occupation hidden. A 15-year veteran, for example, didn't tell the other women in her craft classes that she was a police officer (nor did she tell other police about the craft classes).

Despite all the barriers to women's absorption into the police culture, a sizable segment of the females were deeply immersed. A seven-year veteran, for example, had increasingly become isolated from the general society but had not been able to establish police friends. She had, however, accepted the police culture's view of "us versus them." She told us:

> Police work has limited my relationships. You start to doubt people and unless you work on going out and meeting people, you become more withdrawn because you get so wrapped up in what you are doing on the job that you start doing that on the outside, too. I never was into hanging out drinking with the officers. Since I have been a police officer, I have been more focused on the job than a social life.

The job had become her family, a reference made by other female officers. Rather than turning their attention to the public, these officers withdrew into the comfort of the police culture, a culture that only partially accepted them. Still, the attraction was strong. A female patrol officer conjectured, "In very few other professions do you go to work and put your life in the hands of the person you're working with. I think that just bonds you together."

The officers provided us with statements that indicated the situation for women might be slowly changing. Women may find integration into policing easier as their numbers within departments grow. An officer from a department that had a good reputation for its treatment of women told us:

> We have a new chief that's been here about 2 years. I get the impression that he's very profemale, that he wants females to move up within this department and he's doing what he can to promote them as well as get them motivated. . . . When I first came on board they had just hired a whole slew of females. Up until then, they only had 6 or 7, and now it's 25 or 30. . . . We are starting to see some change.

A transformation in attitudes among male officers may also facilitate women's entrance into the police culture. Newer officers were raised in an era of expanded opportunities for women, and such men may be more likely to perceive women as deserving of a police job. Indicative were the words of one of our officers, who felt that

> The men over 40 are the ones that make it hard. Sometimes I say, "Good morning," to an officer in the hall and he doesn't respond but looks at me as if to say, "What the hell are you doing in a uniform?" The guys that are 20 and 30, they accept you. Sometimes they even forget you are a female.

Veteran female officers may also lessen the extent of torment new women officers receive. Abuse flourishes when left unattended, and new officers may lack the gumption to say anything about their ill treatment. Experienced officers are more likely to speak out. One told us that harassment "is a lot less now than when I was younger." She remembered, "When I was brand new or in my 20s, I tolerated it a lot more than I do now. Now I wouldn't hesitate to put someone personally on notice or go to a supervisor, which I wouldn't have done 10 years ago. I have become a little more vocal about women's rights." Her frankness with male officers probably lessens the extent of abuse directed against female recruits.

## CONCLUSION AND DISCUSSION

A majority of both the male and female officers we interviewed adjusted to the isolating influences of the police occupation by withdrawing to the companionship of other officers. The women, however, had a harder time doing this because they were not readily accepted by male officers. For the women, dating or marrying another officer was one way to gain acceptance into the police culture.

A minority of officers were able to escape entrenchment in the culture by withdrawing to their families. Another small group of officers accomplished the same task by keeping old friends, while another handful of officers escaped the culture by making new friends outside the occupation. They keep their occupation hidden from new acquaintances for fear that, once known, they will be shunned.

Overall, however, it appears that once one enters the policing occupation, one is separated from the attitudes of the general population. The viewpoints heard are those of other officers. In such an environment, the tenets of the police philosophy are rarely questioned. In the next two chapters we illustrate the culture's impact on police officers' handling of specific calls.

# CHAPTER EIGHT

## *Domestic Disputes*

In this and the next chapter, we describe how the cultural favoritism toward certain activities affects officers' handling of common incidents. We focus on domestic disputes and vandalism by juveniles and present a detailed history of their handling by police. Policewomen had carved out their niche by presumably handling such situations more appropriately, and women's more recent integration into patrol was partially predicated on the belief that they would bring a different style of policing to these calls. We selected these tasks on which to focus because we anticipated that if men and women did their jobs differently, any variations would show up here. The answers provided by the officers, however, indicate that, for the most part, men and women perceive these situations similarly and probably do the jobs in the same fashion. Any distinctions we did note were between officers from different departments.

## RESULTS OF PREVIOUS STUDIES

Quarrels between husbands and wives and other family members result in a large proportion of murders in the United States each year, and the police have been roundly criticized for their handling of the combatants. Generally, the complaint has been that the police fail to act when there are obvious signs of violence. A notable study in Kansas City revealed that the police, in response to fights couples were having, had visited the homes of 85 percent of the domestic homicides between men and women prior to the murders. In about half the homicides, the police had been to the homes at least five times.[1] Such evidence did not reflect well on the police handling of family violence.

## THE FIRST HUNDRED YEARS

A century ago, it is unlikely that arguments between intimates were a major component of a patrolman's job. Officers could not be easily summoned to break up quarrels. No telephones were at hand, and the whereabouts of the officer on the beat might not always be predictable. Besides, nearby family and friends were much more suited to the task. One member of a disgruntled couple, for example, might leave the home and spend a night or more with family. Additionally, a physically abusive husband risked receiving a severe beating from his wife's relatives, who might not feel constrained by legal considerations.

But one hundred years ago, the forces that would lead police to regularly deal with domestic disputes were also in motion. The great migration to major United States cities from all over the world was a principal element. The industrial revolution had created jobs, and there were not enough U.S. workers to fill them. Immigrants flowed into the country from eastern Europe, while the children of U.S. farmers began their exodus to the growing urban centers. For one of the first times in history, millions of children were being born who might never meet their grandparents.

The transient population undermined many of the previous informal social control networks that were based on extended family and lifelong friends. Without these, there was no one to effectively defuse domestic disputes. It was into this vacuum that officers were drawn. They did not oppose the additional duty, probably because they still did not have much to handle. At the beginning of the 20th century, easy summoning of the police was still decades away. In addition, the newly instated policewomen promised to handle such situations. Policemen, however, did not long escape dealing with family quarrels.

Fifteen years into the 20th century, New York City police were being coached on how to handle domestic disputes. Their commissioner, who was once a schoolmaster, urged his officers to consider methods other than arrest. An officer might detain a husband if his wife claimed that he was beating her in an attempt to kill. Such charges were a felony, and officers had the authority to make an arrest. If the situation was less serious, officers might advise the woman to obtain an arrest warrant from a judge. The police were unable to detain potential misdemeanants unless officers had witnessed the offense. It was normally up to victims to effect an arrest. In New York, a 1915 *Harper's Weekly* article stated that a woman would first go to the local police station to summon help. An officer

> will accompany the woman to her home, see whether there are any children, whether the man is dangerously intoxicated, whether there is but one side to the quarrel. If the conditions seem not to be intolerable, he may say to the wife: "You arrest him. I will appear as a witness."[2]

The police knew well that "Even the wife who has been mistreated thinks twice before she arrests her husband." But they also believed that an abusive husband would think "twice over the fact, before this not known to him, that his wife, or any passerby, has the authority to arrest him."[3]

In general, during the first decades of the 1900s, a new view of the proper role of police was being promulgated by reformers, who urged the police to take action in areas that had previously been considered private. Society was entreated to "stop regarding policemen as mere keepers of order" and to "enlarge our view of their duties far beyond the arrests of criminals."[4] Some social architects recognized the weakening of old control mechanisms and believed that the police might be able to stimulate self-control "by the pressure of neighborhood opinion and crowd self-respect."

The foot patrolman at the beginning of the 20th century, because of his position within the community, was viewed as the vehicle by which new social control networks might be established. Foot patrol officers of the period daily stopped and talked with the inhabitants of their beats. They probably had grown up in the area and knew many of the locals from childhood. Recent additions became known to the patrolman as they settled in the area. In this fashion, the beat officer became aware of the informal social control networks that existed in his community.

When a situation necessitated their invocation, he could call upon his stored up goodwill to get the members of the networks to act.[5]

Bureaucratization and the use of patrol cars made it more difficult for officers to utilize the new networks. Fear that officers would be corrupted if they were in contact with one neighborhood too long caused patrolmen to be rotated through assignments under the bureaucratic model. The automobile further isolated the roving officers from the communities on which they were supposed to keep a watchful eye. Under such circumstances, the patrolmen knew less about the members of the neighborhood and the social control networks to which they belonged.

Patrol cars were ordered to domestic dispute scenes by dispatchers who did not know the circumstances that officers would face upon their arrival. Officers did not know the families nor their problems unless they had previously been summoned to the same addresses. They were unaware as to how a couple might respond to officers entering the house and intruding upon the argument, and once inside the house, they were unaware of the location of potential dangers, such as belligerent family members or weapons.[6]

As strangers to the domestic altercations, police officers were rarely able to do much to help the combatants. They might arrest one of the participants, but administrators and prosecutors frowned on such cases and did not reward officers who chose this action.[7] Officers found family quarrels to be frustrating and, as a response to a situation in which there was no achievable goal, began to dodge such summons[8] or, at the very least, respond to such duties "in a deliberate manner with the hope that the problem . . . would be settled prior to their arrival."[9]

## NEUTRALIZATIONS

By the 1960s, the opinion that arguments between husbands and wives were not police business was firmly entrenched into the police culture. As with any cultural belief, this conviction shaped how the officers perceived circumstances associated with domestic disputes. In particular, officers cultivated "neutralizations" for their inactivity in such matters. Gresham Sykes and David Matza developed the concept of neutralizations in a classic sociological work on juvenile delinquents.[10] They concluded that young criminals "neutralize" the negative definitions that they know "respectable" people apply to their delinquent behaviors. By learning these neutralization techniques in delinquent subcultures, juveniles can render social controls inoperative and be free to engage in delinquency without serious harm to their self-images. Delinquents can remain committed to law-abiding norms but can also "qualify" them in order to make violations excusable, if not altogether "right." Similarly, the officers we interviewed learned the police culture's neutralizations for inactivity in instances of domestic violence. They asserted the appropriateness of their inaction, basing their arguments on the store of knowledge they had accumulated through their previous experience with such incidents.

Several matters formed the core of officers' neutralizations with respect to domestic squabbles. For one matter, officers believed that members of a "fighting family will make up tomorrow, and arrest would be unjust."[11] In addition, they posited that there were no positive results when they did make some effort to assist combatants. The officers reflected that within weeks, they were once again summoned to the same address.[12]

Arrests, the officers held, might easily make matters worse for the antagonists. Calls often came from homes in which the man did not have a job nor any real skills or education that might help him get one. In general, officers argued that the home life they found when attending a family fight was far from desirable.[13] An arrest would only make it more difficult for the man to support his family, and in instances where children were in the house, arrests of both adults could be effected only after the police officer had determined what would happen to the youngsters while their guardians were in jail.[14] In such circumstances, the police argued, "arrests could backfire and cause more serious violence as soon as the couple was reunited."[15]

The police culture also established neutralizations for inaction in situations in which a woman was beaten. A police expert who studied officers' behavior in the 1970s wrote:

> [T]he police generally believe the complainant in these cases is unlikely to make a formal complaint no matter what they do, and that if she does, the case is likely to be dismissed in court anyway because of her own failure to

appear as the complaining witness. They also anticipate that even if the offender were to be convicted, a jail or a prison sentence would be extremely unlikely. Such beliefs, moreover, are probably supported by the facts.[16]

Another neutralization employed within the police culture to avoid action in the handling of domestic fights asserted that the situations were dangerous to police. Stories told to recruits at the academy and in the field illustrated that attempts to arrest in a domestic situation may lead to more emotional outbursts.[17] Combatants may turn against officers with deadly outcomes. Domestic disputes, then and now, do account for a sizable proportion of police deaths, but they are also a large portion of an officer's job. Police officers' arguments that arrests in domestic disputes were to be avoided because they may increase the danger to officers was a direct reflection of the police culture's preference for avoiding such calls. High-speed chases, which are probably more deadly, are by contrast sought-after police activities.

The excuses officers offered for doing little about domestic disputes probably allowed them to avoid becoming frustrated by the squabbles but did nothing to assist the potential victims. It is worthwhile to repeat that a large portion of murders in this country have been direct outgrowths of family fights. The failure of officers to take any actions in nonlethal incidents probably left participants believing that the police did not care. Anecdotes, in fact, indicated that officers might prefer a deadly outcome in contrast to returning to the same address week after week. One former officer reported that he and his partner responded to a family fight, and when they arrived,

> the story was a usual one: the husband had awakened and found that his wife was trying to stab him with a pocket knife. The usual disposition in such a case would be to talk the incident out and when everyone seemed cooled off, to leave. In this particular case, however, I knew that just 16 days before the man's wife had slashed open the back of his head while he was sitting at the dinner table, because I had participated in her arrest for "assault with a deadly weapon." Such being the case, we convinced the husband that he should leave the house for the night, or he might be killed, and my partner made the knife "disappear."[18]

The partner dropped the knife in a bush at the next assignment. The potential homicide hardly seems of interest to the officers according to the story reported. The partner

> later commented that the solution to that particular family's problems might not be far away. He said that if one shot the other then we could take the body to the morgue, the killer to jail, and the kids to the welfare department and the problem would be solved.[19]

Officers' avoidance of domestic disputes left victims unprotected. A woman who was beaten might be asked by police to file charges, but the potential for a retaliatory beating from her husband often prevented such action.[20] The physically abused, after receiving no assistance from the police, had to rely on their own resources.[21] For example, a woman who had been forcibly evicted from her home by her husband would be told that the incident was a civil matter and that she should contact an attorney. For the night, she should find some other place to stay.[22] Such advice might have been appropriate if given to someone of upper socio-economic status, but it hardly seems helpful to a woman of limited resources. By default, the officers sided with the physically stronger husband. It is understandable that women often did not bother to summon the police when crises arose; they had no confidence that the police would do anything about their problems.[23]

## SOCIAL WORK

During the 1960s and early 1970s, another approach to domestic squabbles gained favor. Arrest was still considered to not be in the interest of the family or the state, but doing nothing would only be a continuation of the existing police policy.[24] Rather, the new police effort utilized social workers and specialists trained in the handling of domestic disputes, who employed mediation, counseling, and referrals to other specialists and agencies to handle the family crises.[25]

The new police units did not lack for calls, and their use gained some popularity and success.[26] The employment of social workers, however, met with criticism from police officers. They disliked handling the squabbles but were unwilling to grant that anyone might do it better. From the officers' perspective, the social workers were unavailable dur-

ing the hours when domestic fights erupted, did not do anything special, and, if there was violence, waited until the officers had handled
the worst of the problem before taking any action.[27] Despite public
support for the new programs, in many ways they differed little from
previous police handling of violent domestic situations. Police continued to ignore the potential for grave consequences and refrained from
making arrests.

## LEGAL CHANGES

During the 1970s, members of the women's movement called attention
to the lack of police action in domestic disputes. Most notable, however,
was a civil suit against the New York City Police Department for its officers' failures to make arrests in situations of ongoing brutalization of
domestic partners.[28] The department settled the case with the plaintiffs
by agreeing to arrest in all situations in which there was evidence that
the husband had committed a felony by beating his wife.[29] As an outgrowth of the lawsuit and settlement, numerous jurisdictions began to
consider adopting policies for their departments that would mandate
officers to arrest in instances of physical violence.

Matters were moved along in 1984 as the result of a federal district
court's finding that a department's nonarrest policy in domestic violence
cases was unconstitutional.[30] The victim in this case, who had her neck
broken and who was stabbed repeatedly in the presence of a police officer,
ultimately received $1.9 million for her permanent injuries.[31] The out-
come of the lawsuits and pressure from political groups shoved many
police departments to review their policies concerning domestic disputes.

Political efforts to compel police departments to arrest in situations
involving domestic violence were fueled in 1986 by the results of an academic study scrutinizing the effect of arrest on men involved in misdemeanor spousal abuse. The Minneapolis Domestic Violence
Experiment, which indicated that arrest did reduce the likelihood of
future violations,[32] was quickly endorsed by the U.S. Attorney General's
Task Force on Family Violence.[33] Under political pressure, many police
departments did not wait for replication studies to validate the results of

the Minneapolis experiment, but rather, many jurisdictions rushed to adopt "must arrest" policies in misdemeanor spousal abuse cases. A series of replications have since reached conflicting results—some consistent with the Minneapolis research[34] and some that did not support it.[35]

By 1986, 47 urban police agencies had adopted mandatory arrest policies for family fights involving physical violence.[36] In California, the spousal abuse law allowed for greater arrest powers, and many departments adopted a "must arrest" practice for when injuries were present. The objective of the new strategy was to take the decision to press charges away from women, who for one reason or another might be unwilling to take such action on their own. Despite the changes in law and departmental policy, there is evidence that officers have not changed their practices and attitudes with respect to domestic violence; they continue to not arrest in the belief that family squabbles are none of their business.[37]

## What We Did

We asked the officers how they liked to handle a domestic dispute. To the lay reader, this question probably appears too broad. One might speculate that the officers would each perceive a different situation in their minds, but this is not how officers see the world. Rather, police tend to stereotype people and situations.[38] A police expert called the process "normalization":[39]

> Normalization is the process whereby an officer establishes that a particular encounter is representative of the hundreds or thousands of similar encounters experienced in the past. Normalization is important to an officer for at least two reasons.
>
> First, it allows an officer to reliably predict citizen behavior during the course of an encounter. If an officer can establish that a particular husband-wife dispute is similar to other husband-wife disputes, the officer can expect both parties to be agitated and generally equally responsible for the particular incident. The officer also can predict that the wife will claim to be the victim and ask or demand that the husband be seen as the violator.

Additionally, normalization permits utilization of the decision-making guidelines or "recipes for actions" used in normal encounters. If an encounter can be normalized, the officer can be relatively confident of the general nature of the interaction and ultimate resolution of the problem.[40]

For our purposes, normalization was an advantage. The interviewees fit our domestic dispute question into a single category involving a man and a woman. Occasionally, officers offered anecdotes that strayed slightly from the single vision, but for the most part, they were in agreement about what we meant by a domestic dispute.

## HOW OFFICERS HANDLE A DOMESTIC DISPUTE

The plurality of officers' answers to us were consistent with the training they had probably received while in the academy and the guidelines they would have read in departmental manuals. They recognized the dangers involved in domestic dispute calls and used tactical strategies to keep themselves safe. Their answers revealed that many officers utilized communication skills in their handling of such situations, occasionally trying to counsel couples. But they also used neutralizations to ignore violence and not arrest batterers. Generally, the men and women answered our questions similarly, although more than a handful of female officers were very critical of women victims. A difference did appear between the answers provided by a substantial portion of the officers from the well-to-do community and the rest of those we interviewed. The former were more likely to say that they would follow the mandatory arrest rules and take a suspected batterer into custody.

### DANGER

The officers' answers reflected the police belief that domestic disputes are dangerous situations. The primary item that illustrates this belief is the officers' favor for handling family quarrels in pairs; single officers, we were advised, waited until backup arrived before entering a domicile. An officer told us:

Those calls are the most dangerous, so when you go on those calls you never know what to expect. You can side with one, and then that person will turn against you because her husband [is in trouble]. A lot of people just fight and that's their way. Maybe the neighbors called and you are interfering. They turn on you and they get violent. You never know if they are drunk or under the influence of something. They can be calm and then they'll snap. That's why I always ask if there are guns in the house, knives; you never know what to expect. At least when you go to a robbery or other kinds of problems, you know what to expect. On these it's like a surprise when the door opens. That's why I tell the other cops, "Don't ever go thinking that you don't need another officer there."

The use of two officers also facilitated the handling of the fights, according to what was reported to us. The first step officers wanted to take was separate the combatants; otherwise, they would continue to argue with each other. A 17-year veteran told us his approach: "What I prefer is to separate the two but keep them in close proximity, back to back, with my partner with one of them and me with the other." The strategy was designed to handle the immediate situation. A typical comment was provided by a 14-year officer, who instructed us, "The thing is to solve the immediate problem; that's basically by separating them so they both cool down and come to their senses."

Occasionally, officers handled domestic disputes without backup. This was not their preference, but circumstances necessitated it. An officer told us that it happened "quite a bit." She explained, "It's because there's no beat partner to go with you that day, or the person's coming from a long way away and it's not really an explosive situation."

Officers managing family disputes without a partner had established strategies for dealing with a situation. The most notable technique was based on the cultural characteristics of the couple. A 15-year veteran informed us, "It really depends on the culture of the house you go to. If it is Hispanic or Vietnamese, you always talk to the man first. You do not talk to the female first. With the whites, it doesn't matter." Another officer explained: "They take that as a respect thing. If you tell him to 'stand over there and wait; I'd like to talk to her,' he's going to get mad. She's used to having to wait a minute anyway." A female officer indicated that her gender directed her decision to whom to talk first.

I usually generally talk to the man first because so often people go straight to the woman and she says, "He did this, he did that," and he gets defensive. He's already defensive because you're there as a female. He's the man of the house. Usually they're arguing because he doesn't feel he's the man of the house about something—whether it's financial decisions or whatever. So if I went to her, he'd be saying, "Here's a woman, she's talking to her first, she's going to side with her." He's getting defensive and when I try to talk to him, he doesn't want to talk. So generally, I'll talk to him first.

Lacking cultural considerations, other items were used to determine with whom to talk first. One officer said he talked "to whomever is most upset," while a longtime veteran contacted the wife first, since, as he put it, "usually she is the victim."

The female officers, in situations where they were paired with a man, commonly indicated that they spoke with the male combatants while their partners spoke with the women. This relationship stands in sharp contrast to women's entrance into policing at the beginning of the 20th century, when female officers were hired to deal with other women. Today's female police officer is much different from her predecessor. A woman with 15 years' experience, who had worked in juvenile and child abuse units, told us that she thought female police officers

tend to be a little more critical of women who are victims of abuse. Contrary to popular belief, most female police officers are strong-personality women that I don't think would ever tolerate a man emotionally or physically abusing them, and you look at someone else and say, "Why the heck are you tolerating that?"

The female officers didn't show much sympathy for female victims and often did little to support them. They seemed to prefer talking with the male combatants, and this had its advantages. For one, the men probably cooled down more quickly when speaking with a woman. One of the female officers, for example, remembered that at several calls, "the guys have told me, 'If you were a man, I would have punched you.' But I'm a female, and a lot of guys won't hit females." Because female officers, in her view, were less likely to agitate the male combatants, they were better at managing domestic disputes.

Calming the couple was officers' first priority, and we were often informed about methods to accomplish this task. A veteran of 20 years warned that officers needed to choose their words carefully in order to not provoke the situation:

> Rather than saying, "What is your problem?" I would say, "Excuse me, could you please tell me what is going on?" Because really when you say, "What is your problem?" all the person actually hears is, "What is your problem, asshole?"

Another veteran instructed us as to a common method for getting disputants to talk calmly. She said:

> I like to start out getting their names and what we call their "horsepower": their address, work phone, all that kind of stuff. It gives them a chance to calm down. Now they aren't thinking, "Harry beat me in the face." They're thinking, "Gee, my name is Susan and I live here." We can't solve their 15-year marital problems in 15 minutes. What we need to do is solve the crisis right now and to diffuse it for now.

Having separated the feuding factions and calmed the situation a bit, the officers had various strategies for handling the dispute. A sizable group of officers told us that listening was probably the best service they could provide the disputants, "because that's what people really want is just for you to listen." The couple's problems were unlikely to have just surfaced, the officers felt, and there was little they could do to help.

The majority of officers preferred not to utilize the criminal justice system and turned to other means in attempts to get the couple to behave. A sizable group attempted to persuade the individuals to utilize self-control. This was certainly the case when the disputants were immigrants. The officers had no access to the social networks to which the couple belonged and had to hope that the antagonists might respond to fairly simple suggestions. For example, a 15-year veteran told us:

> When you talk to a Hispanic, you have to tell him that this is the U.S.; it is not Mexico or El Salvador. You can't just come home drunk and beat the wife. There are laws against this in the United States.

The officer hopes that once the individual is told that his behavior is unacceptable in the United States, self-control will exert itself and the beatings will stop.

Officers commonly believed that satisfactory solutions to couples' problems could be achieved only by the combatants, and they defined as counseling their attempts to get the duos to control their own behavior. Although rare, a few officers, from what they told us, were willing to spend some time accomplishing this task. A 17-year veteran, for example, explained:

> I am not going to dictate for them a solution. I am going to help them work their own solution out. What would make you happy? What could you have done to perhaps not have gotten into this? This may take 15 minutes or 45 minutes. . . . If they come up with a solution, as opposed to me dictating one, it may last.

Counseling was perceived as an alternative to arrest. Officers neutralized any misgivings they had about their failure to use legal mechanisms by claiming that arrests have no impact on the combatants. A 16-year veteran, for example, told us that she avoided detaining anyone. Rather,

> I try to counsel. "You loved each other when you first got married," so there must be something they like about each other. I don't like to arrest because it only solves the problem for the next five minutes. We bring them to the station and they are released five minutes later.

Another officer stretched counseling to include explaining to participants the downside of having a spouse arrested. He would ask victims how they wanted to handle the situations, but if they wanted to arrest, he would "present a plain and realistic picture of what will happen."

Extensive violence in family disputes, some officers suggested, required the use of professional counseling. Perhaps they recognized that the situations were beyond a stage when appeals to self-control were appropriate. Continued violence was their evidence for such a supposition. The officers lacked access to secondary social networks—family, coworkers, neighbors—that might have exerted some control over the participants. Increasingly, as people move from year to year, such networks cease to exist. The officers, almost out of necessity, turned to other control mechanisms. Professional counseling was favored over arrest because officers neutralized legal action as ineffective or counterproductive. For example, an officer told us that she would suggest counseling because she was "opposed to taking the male to jail and then once he gets out, he will come back and beat her up again." This officer assuages any guilt she may feel at leaving the woman with her batterer by claiming she is doing it to help the victim.

It was not uncommon for officers in their answers to blame the women for contributing to the violence by failing to take action against the men. Such officers avoided making arrests by asking the woman what she wanted to do. As one told us, "The option is hers regarding arrest. If she wants an arrest, she gets an arrest. . . . About 90 percent of them don't want them arrested." By blaming the woman for not making the arrest, such officers were able to escape personal condemnation for failing to remove the man to jail, although they could have taken such action.

The felony spouse abuse law allows an officer to make an arrest in a dispute when there is physical evidence that a battery occurred. A red mark on the woman's face, for example, is evidence that she was slapped and is sufficient for an officer to make an arrest. Officers in their answers to us, however, routinely expanded the extent of damages needed to make an arrest. By blaming the women and requiring extensive injuries before making an arrest on their own, the officers effectively neutralized their behavior. The following quote from a 15-year patrol supervisor illustrates many of these points. The officer begins by differentiating "between somebody who has a fight and the cops come and the other situation of somebody who has been constantly beaten or mentally abused and they won't or can't do anything about it." He does not arrest in either situation. Rather, he blames the victim for the lack of criminal justice action:

> It would be really nice if we could force the victim, which is most of the time the woman, to initiate some action because they're not in the position to know what's good for them. . . . We have all these things available to them and we say, "You can do this and you can do that and if you did file charges on him, the DA will make him go to counseling classes." But they won't do it. . . . And it's just so frustrating because you can't do anything for the victim unless the victim will do something for themselves. And if we can force something on them, it would help. But it doesn't work this way. A lot of times, we're just beating our heads against the wall, going back and forth until somebody kills somebody.

The officer tells us that he is unable to do anything until the situation turns lethal, which is far from the truth.

Some interviewees also blamed district attorneys for officers' failure to make arrests. District attorneys are often considered the most powerful players in the criminal justice system. They decide who will be charged and with what crimes. In effect, they establish the parameters of the law in their jurisdictions. It is possible, for example, that when officers misquote the felony spouse law, they are accurately stating local district attorneys' filing requirements. Such information is crucial to officers with respect to their arrest decisions. The fact that district attorneys do not file charges against all those arrested in domestic disputes allows the officers to neutralize any feelings of wrongdoing on their part for failing to detain offenders. An officer explained:

> With the new law, if we go out there and reasonably believe that the abuse is not going to stop, we can always arrest them, but they're only going to stay in jail for 48 hours. Then the DA has to file charges against them, and if the victim won't cooperate, then 98 percent of the time the DA will not file charges. The DA will not put any money in the trial if there's no hope of winning.

Inaction by district attorneys irritated a few officers, largely because, as a longtime veteran explained, "the law says that if she has evidence of injury, he goes to jail, whether she wants to prosecute or not. That causes a problem in that we're required to arrest but the DA is not required to prosecute and often doesn't."

For the most part, the answers of officers who avoided making arrests contained a similar theme: domestic disputes are problematic and officers can do little about them; they are best handled by defusing the immediate conflict and leaving as quickly as possible. This focus forms the core of the police culture's belief that family fights are not police business. As a result, officers favored actions that minimized time spent on such disputes. Report taking, for example, was to be avoided; checking a box on a form was preferred. And, although officers commonly mentioned counseling the antagonists as a component of how to handle domestic disputes, such efforts were probably constrained by officers' perceptions of the amount of time these cases deserved. A 14-year veteran explained:

I can't sit there and say, "Tell me all your problems. Okay, now you tell me your problems." Then the cop has spent forty-five to fifty minutes on a fight. That's not our place. Our place is to take care of the immediate problem. If I can't get one or the other to leave, then I say, "Okay, stay and fight." I don't make arrests just to solve a problem since it's just wasting everybody's time because no one will file it. The thing is to solve the immediate problem, basically by separating the two people from each other so they both cool down and come to their senses.

Generally, getting one of the couple to leave the home handles the immediate problem for the disputants and the officers' self-image. At least the officers know the battered individual is temporarily safe. The action also avoids employing the criminal justice system as a solution to the couples' problems and allows the combatants to regain self-control and seek the assistance of members of their informal social networks: friends, neighbors, and the like. An officer with only one year of service provided a common answer:

I usually recommend that one of them go to another place for the evening, either a hotel or a friend's. Just stay someplace else until things cool down. Tension is high at that time; it's not going to resolve a situation if alcohol or tension is involved. By them separating and coming back the next day when things are calm, it seems to work out. Then they can make the determination of what are they going to do.

Officers convinced themselves that by not arresting, they were fulfilling the victims' desires. It also allowed them to ignore direct requests from victims for law enforcement action. A 14-year veteran, for example, told us that she preferred separating the people for the evening so that they might calm down. She did not arrest even when women requested it because the officer believed that "all she wants is him out of the house." The officer's evidence for the belief was "if the female arrests her husband on a citizen's arrest, invariably she calls within two days and drops the charges." This officer and others faced one difficulty in the implementation of their strategy. As we were told, "You can't make someone legally leave their own home." The solution to the problem is ironic given the efforts the officers told us they made to avoid arrests. An officer with nearly 20 years' experience explained: "A police officer cannot force the husband to leave his own house. An officer can suggest that he leave, and I am persuasive about this. If the husband doesn't want to leave, then I can just tell him I will have to arrest him."

Officers who normally avoided arrests would under certain circumstances take an abuser into custody. One told us he would not arrest merely because the woman was slapped, "but if she has a righteous injury, maybe she's bleeding, I'll take him whether she wants it or not." But his reason is not to protect the woman from further violence. He arrests, he told us, because "that protects me." Other officers acted similarly. They arrested because legal constraints required them to do so. They, however, also felt good about the action. We were told, "If I have to arrest, I do it. It makes me feel better. Plus it avoids a lawsuit for not doing my job."

## MANDATORY ARREST

The introduction of mandatory arrest policy in cases of domestic violence probably altered the way a minority of our subjects dealt with family fights. Officers who told us they did arrest when there was evidence of a battery seemed to fall into two groups. The first consisted of officers for whom the law may have had a moralizing effect. Prior to the new pronouncement, they probably were able to neutralize any misgivings they had about not arresting. The change, for them, made it clear that such neutralizations were inappropriate. These few officers made comparisons for us between the way they used to handle the cases and their current manner for disposition. A longtime veteran, now working homicide, explained that when he was on patrol,

> It was a time when they said to the woman, "What are you going to do if we put him in jail?" We asked her, "Who's going to pay the bills? Who's going to take care of the kids? Who's going to buy the groceries?" All that kind of stuff while he went to jail, and that's how it was handled. And then you'd end up having it go around and around and around. So I prefer it going this way, as opposed to the old way, because we were constantly out at the same house over and over again until something seriously violent happened. We didn't do anything often.

This officer and several others liked the fact, at least from their perspective, that the decision to arrest was "out of the officers' hands." They may never have been comfortable with domestic violence situations and may have been relieved to get some direction.

The second group of officers who said that they were likely to arrest did so because they believed it protected victims. While learning the new law, officers were apprised of research suggesting that arrest was more effective at preventing domestic violence, and more than a handful of officers latched on to these studies as evidence in support of putting the batterer behind bars. The largest portion of these officers was from the wealthiest city in our sample. About half of the interviewees from this department stated that they preferred to arrest whenever possible. The officers considered their department professional; they obviously received training on the new law and were more aware of its details, although they "bent them" in their descriptions to us. Typical of officers from this department were the comments of a patrol officer, who posited:

> When a husband has been beating his wife. . . . I want to arrest this person and get him out of there so he can get whatever help he needs and she can get whatever help she needs. I don't like to see people intimidated by other people. I like to take a hard-line approach. You can't just try to pacify the situation and hope it goes away.

These officers were inclined to see domestic disputes as proper police business and taking somebody into custody as a means of protecting the household. "I am being paid to do the job," we were told. Several officers added that failing to take action could result in dire outcomes. Rather than focusing on incidents where the couple reunited, they noted that officers who don't arrest "come back to a battered woman, a shot spouse."

## GENDER DIFFERENCES

Overall, there was no discernible difference between the way male and female officers preferred to handle domestic disputes. Women were supposed to change police attitudes about family fights, but that does not appear to have happened. Rather, for the most part, females' values parallel those of their male colleagues and do not differ that much from the attitudes of officers of past decades. The answers the officers gave us indicate that both groups mistrusted battered women to follow through on prosecuting their male partners, and in instances where immigrants were involved, men and women officers seemed to ignore the plight of female victims in order not to offend the "man of the house."

One male officer's answer might indicate a certain misogyny. He believed that women were willing to risk severe beatings in order to use the criminal justice system to punish their mates. This officer, who admitted he was a chauvinist on these matters, told us:

> There is a spousal abuse law in California, which really ties the officer's hands. A lot of women are becoming more educated about the law so they will get into the male's face until he raises a hand and hits her ever so slightly; it forces the officer's hand that they have to arrest, and that's not right. The women manipulate the situation. There are legitimate cases and I see the necessity for the law, but I think officers should have a little bit more leeway. The officer has to do it by the book; they have no choice. . . . You take a lady who is five-foot-two, 105 pounds. Well, she slaps a six-foot-five male and tells him, "Get out of my way." He takes his hand and pushes her out of the way. She bruises, he doesn't. She runs to the police. . . . The police are obligated to do something, yet they don't know the whole circumstance and this poor man gets an arrest record. And before this happens they should examine the situation, but they can't. The law says, "You shall take them to jail." Something definitely has to be done about this.

A handful of female officers indicated in their answers that they were far from prowomen when it came to domestic disputes and that, in truth, they felt negative about female victims. We were told that females involved in domestic fights believed that the female officers would be on their side, but the officers did not relate to their gender's marriage problems. The lack of sympathy shown battered women by female officers may result in the women's complaints being treated lightly. Further, the victims may be seen as undeserving of police protection. "Sometimes I can understand why the guy has hit the girl. I mean she is just a bitch," one female officer told us. The worst response in this regard, if actually practiced, left female victims of domestic battering open to more physical abuse. A police woman with eight years' experience said she tries to con the couple. She told us:

> I'd probably tell him, "Yeah, I know, she probably deserved being hit, but tell me what happened." Because once they think you're on their side, they'll tell you more. It's a game. I'll say stuff whether I believe them or not just to get what I want to hear. Then I'll talk to her and tell her something completely different. She's probably the victim, and I'll see how it happened. I'm not going to sit there and say, "Well, you deserved it." But I may let him think that's what I tell her.

We must believe that, if the officer's performance is convincing, the man feels that the female officer does not disapprove of his behavior. Why this particular officer thinks this is a good strategy is a mystery.

## CONCLUSIONS

A sizable majority of the officers we interviewed were opposed to arresting offenders in domestic disputes, even when they observed physical signs of violence. They had established a number of neutralizations for their actions, all of which supported the police culture's view that family fights were not proper police business. For the most part, officers told us that they minimize the amount of time they spend at such calls. They might counsel the antagonists, but such efforts were kept short.

At the dawn of the new millennium, women may be no better at handling domestic disputes than men. Male and female officers did not differ much on the way they wanted to handle the situations, with one exception. As a group, the women appeared to be more critical of female victims, ironic in that 90 years ago, women were hired into the occupation to deal with females who came in contact with the criminal justice system.

The similarity between the way men and women answered our question appears to be the result of the police culture's impact on both genders. Any differences that might exist between the genders in the general population with respect to police handling of domestic disputes disappear following a selection process, training, and fieldwork that tends to homogenize officers' attitudes.

One difference between departments was noted. About half of the officers from the wealthy community favored the mandatory arrest law. The department and city are different from the others in the sample. At a minimum, for example, officers must have a four-year college degree to be hired. In addition, the department was the only one of the seven from which we drew our sample that proclaimed it utilized a service style of policing. These matters are reflective of the overall wealth of the community. Rough treatment at the hands of police officers would be unacceptable to its citizens. The difference in the overall answers provided by the officers from this city compared to the others indicates that the police culture is not present in uniform strength in all departments. People who seek police employment in this city may have different motivations for entering the occupation. Certainly, the officers in this department were selected for different reasons than those employed in other cities and, from the answers we were provided, they do the job differently. But there is a dark side to the difference. It provides evidence that one type of policing is deemed appropriate for wealthy communities, while a different form is applied in poorer neighborhoods.

In the next chapter, we focus on police handling of juveniles, another area believed to be better handled by women. But, as in the handling of domestic disputes, we will show that the police culture has a much stronger influence on police behavior than does any difference between the genders.

# CHAPTER NINE

## *Juveniles*

Our concern with how officers might handle a situation involving juveniles is similar to our interest in domestic disputes: women's early entrance into policing was predicated on the belief that they would be better able to deflect children from criminal careers. Their nurturing position within the family was to be transferred to police agencies, where the women were to reform and rehabilitate miscreant youth. As recently as the 1970s, every female officer was assigned to a department's juvenile division at some point in her career.[1] In recent history, women officers have been more likely to be assigned to nonpatrol positions,[2] and they continue to be assigned to juvenile divisions, such as DARE programs.

Officers' dealings with youngsters are important because mishandling may push the youth into criminal activities that otherwise might have been avoided. In lay terms, the argument is that labeling children as bad will result in them behaving badly and involve them in long-term criminal careers. The police, in general, have trouble with situations involving juveniles, and officers have ranked dealings with congregating teenagers as second only to domestic disputes in terms of the difficulties they present.[3]

The main dilemma facing officers when confronted with situations involving youngsters stems from the conflict between the law enforcement role—the tenets of which call for the arrest and punishment of juvenile law violators—and the crime prevention role, in which officers should be concerned with assisting juveniles and should function primarily as social workers. Officers, according to this view, should seek to protect and rehabilitate juveniles who have committed a minor offense or who seem likely to commit a violation. The crime prevention role stresses handling juveniles through informal means: Counseling is preferable to arrest. Arrest should be used only as a last resort and in cases of serious offenses.[4]

The crime prevention function, from the view of members of the police culture, is social work and disdained by officers as detracting from their catching of crooks.[5] Historically, however, police have managed juvenile cases by means other than arrest. This is partly attributable to a "general recognition that it is both necessary and desirable for police to handle a large number of juvenile cases at the police level without referring them to the courts, an assumption less common with respect to adults."[6] Although felonies will usually result in arrest, the handling of less serious acts is unclear. Most juvenile lawbreaking has been considered as trivial by officers, and they did not feel compelled to place misbehaving youngsters in custody. They were more likely to counsel the individuals and release them.

## THE SCENARIO

As with the domestic dispute situation, we wanted a scenario in which officers' judgments might have some variation. We decided to ask officers how they liked to handle youngsters they catch spray-painting gang slogans. We tried other plots, such as juveniles making too much noise, but they produced little information about officers' handling of juvenile crime. Most officers, we surmised, view such juvenile offenses—including riding a bicycle without a helmet, skateboarding in a prohibited area, or being truant from school—as low-priority law enforcement concerns, and as a result, all the respondents would answer the call alike. We also concluded that officers would respond similarly to serious felony offenses—for example, assaults with a deadly weapon or auto theft—due to the gravity of the crimes and laws mandating arrest in such situations. The scenario involving spray-painting gang slogans, initial interviews suggested, would not have such clear-cut dispositions.

Our use of "gang slogans" in our question was on purpose. The police feel that, as a group, gang members are "out to get them" and that the youngsters are a crime problem.[7] Illustrative, when Los Angeles police chief Daryl Gates ordered gang sweeps, he told the community that his purpose was to "put gang members where they belong, in jail."[8]

Officers' attitudes toward gangs are probably a reflection of society's view. The term "gang" carries with it negative connotations of delinquency and criminal behavior. Two experts in the field commented, "Delinquency is a social creation of relatively recent times. It is a concept designed to focus our attention on forms of youthful behavior that, though they have been common throughout history, have become of increasing concern in recent centuries."[9]

Early in the 20th century an influential anthropologist, Margaret Mead, contended that gangs come to exist in a community because of the society's structure, how it treats its young people, and how the youth transition into adulthood.[10] She argued that their presence was a natural manifestation and not necessarily pathological or evil, a conclusion in which she was not alone. The author of a major study of gangs in Chicago during the 1920s determined that gang membership represented a normal and reasonable response to prevailing conditions in society.[11]

Gangs have usually been associated with lower-class youth and generally separated along ethnic and racial lines—for example, Italian, Puerto Rican, African-American, and Hispanic gangs. For some who lived in American ghetto areas, membership in gangs served as a means of protection and identification for individuals. Most fighting and bloodshed between rival groups was a result of territorial claims. In the past, these conflicts rarely involved the police and were frequently settled with fistfights.

More recently, criminal gangs' use of sophisticated weapons, as well as involvement in higher-stake drug deals, escalated the threat to police, even during minor encounters.[12] At one time, some gang members carried chains and knives as their weapons of choice; now they may carry handguns, shotguns, automatic assault rifles, and explosives.[13] Newspapers have been filled with stories of gang savagery, including tragic accounts of innocent people being caught in the cross fire. In one grievous incident, a 3-year-old girl was killed when her family mistakenly drove down a street and was fired upon by gang members who had erroneously identified the car as belonging to a rival gang member. In yet another occurrence, an

11-year old girl seated outside on the porch in a Halloween costume was killed in a drive-by shooting when her home was riddled with bullets. Police no longer take lightly any activity associated with gangs.

The truth of the matter, however, is that most youth, including gang members, are not involved in violent criminal activity. Boys and girls do commonly congregate and "hang around" in groups. Describing a group as a gang has come to mean to the police and the public that criminal activity is involved. Juveniles associated with a gang are automatically classified as delinquents. In California, gang membership automatically makes offenders eligible for more severe punishments.

Youths gather and become involved in lawbreaking as a social event. Peer pressure and camaraderie are strong motivators for youngsters to conform their behavior to the group's, and they look to each other for approval. When they decide to involve themselves in criminal activity, they do so as a group. Lone juvenile offenders are somewhat rare.[14]

Graffiti is one particular activity associated with gangs. For the youngsters, the police are "a handy group to test one's manhood against."[15] They are likely to bask in the glory of their acts and enjoy the chase. They trivialize, or are unaware of, the endless trouble their minor misdeeds may cause them.[16]

We recognized that including the idea of "graffiti" in the scenario would affect the answers we received. How society views graffiti has changed during the last hundred years. Mark Twain, describing a visit to Yellowstone in the 19th century, noted that his fellow tourists, all upper-class individuals, had etched their names into the geyser basins. In the Wild West, cowboys put their names, marks, and often a date next to wall art of American Indians. During World War II, U.S. soldiers were infamous for writing "Kilroy was here!" throughout Western Europe. The Berlin Wall, before its demise, was covered with graffiti. Such activities, accepted in their time and place, would be unacceptable in today's middle-class U.S. society.

Some of today's graffiti is the work of taggers and graffiti artists, not necessarily that of gangs. Taggers are usually not affiliated with a gang. One infamous tagger, Chaka, gained worldwide recognition after receiving a stiff prison sentence for tagging across the United States. How famous the name "Chaka" became was demonstrated in an episode of *In Living Color*, a television comedy show, in which a character was tagged across his bottom by Chaka.

In some locales, graffiti has become an accepted art form, especially among young people. It is used as backdrops in music and workout videos. It is commonly integrated into fabric pattern designs and in the interior decoration of public gathering places, such as coffeehouses and dance bars. And recently, graffiti artists have achieved a modicum of commercial success.

Despite signs of acceptance, most people do not want to find their property defaced with inscriptions. Unwanted markings on buildings and walls are associated with lower property values. Many believe that graffiti attracts crime, that broken windows, graffiti, and other signs of urban decay tell criminals that no one cares about the neighborhood.[17] Community policing efforts to help residents clean their streets and homes are meant to combat that image. Most efforts target the graffiti itself, but behind these endeavors to restore and protect property is the larger goal of preventing crime.

Large portions of tax dollars are spent on prevention and removal of graffiti. Additional money is spent on technological innovations, such as paint that cannot be written on or that can be easily washed, or on barbed wire erected around freeway signs and chain-link fences to replace cinder-block walls. Cleanup crews hired to paint over graffiti do so without regard to aesthetics, whitewashing any color wall to cover the eyesore.

Two recent incidents epitomized the public's general sentiment concerning graffiti. One incident involved a vigilante who shot and killed a tagger who was spray-painting a wall.[18] The tagger had suddenly turned on the man and was shot. Public sentiment favored the shooter, and he eventually received a suspended sentence for carrying a gun. Civil rights groups were incensed by the light punishment and by the public's reaction. In another circumstance, a truckload of teenagers accidentally drove off a freeway overpass and were killed. Sympathetic outpourings ceased when the media announced that the teenagers had been out tagging that night. Friends and families of the victims were shocked after being informed that people felt no sorrow over the loss of "taggers."

How police view tagging or graffiti has not been studied as a separate research interest; however, the public's attitude has been adequately portrayed in newspaper articles and other sources. It is likely that police officers, who are also members of society, possess similar perceptions about these matters. As a result, we believed that participants in the study would regard juveniles spray-painting gang slogans on a wall as more than a minor offense.

## RESULTS

All but one of the officers we interviewed had stumbled across graffiti writers, although not as often as they had dealt with domestic fights. The answers the officers provided about their handling of the juveniles stand in direct juxtaposition to their responses to the domestic dispute scenario. In their dealings with volatile couples, they told us they avoided arrests and they provided us with numerous justifications for this policing strategy. When it came to graffiti, however, the majority of the officers preferred to take the youngsters into custody, either to punish the youth, establish a criminal record, or deter them from future criminal behavior. A sizable minority, however, told us that they might not arrest the youngsters if they believed that other methods might turn the juveniles away from criminal behavior. For the most part, these officers chose to rely on the youngsters' parents to correct the misbehaving. But a few officers told us that they counsel the youth, and at least some of these individuals provided us with detailed accounts of such actions.

### TO COUNSEL OR ARREST?

About 25 percent of our officers leaned toward counseling the apprehended misdemeanant graffiti writers. Officers who took this position used their discretion in determinations about how to handle the youngsters. They did not feel compelled to arrest but would under certain circumstances. They made judgments about the youngsters during talks they had with them.

The officers used several factors to conclude whether to counsel and release youngsters or to take them into custody. It is difficult to argue that one factor was more important than another in their decision making. But it appears that one important determining consideration was officers' perceptions of the youngsters' involvement with gangs. Illustrative were the comments of a woman assigned to work in the juvenile unit. She told us that it "kind of depends on the kids . . . if they are righteous. . . . gangbangers rather than some little kids that just happened along with their dad's spray can and are writing their names on the wall; they'll be handled differently."

One form of treatment was appropriate for innocents and another for gang members. "Kindness is seen as a weakness with the hard-core gang member," we were instructed, "whereas the young juvenile 'wannabe' can be alienated by the heavy-handed approach."

Determining whether one is a gang member or not may be difficult.[19] Records are kept about such matters, and officers might consult them in their decision making. The records, however, are established during street interrogations of youngsters. Numerous stops by the police may be interpreted as active gang involvement and make the individual worthy, from the officer's perspective, of tough treatment. The difference in strategy was meaningful. One officer's approach is illustrative. We were told that "while he is still impressionable I want to steer him towards me and away from the gang. If it is a hard-core [gang member] it will be black and white, right down the line—arrest." The difference in treatment, however, may not be nearly as substantial as it first seems. Overcrowded jails combined with a lack of prosecution by assistant district attorneys means that graffiti writers rarely spend any time in jail. The just-quoted 15-year veteran explained, "If I decided to arrest, it would just be a cite and release, logged as a ticket."

The answers of officers who chose to counsel the youngsters seemed to reflect a feeling that there was little positive that they could do on their own to help the misbehaving graffiti writers. They hoped, we were told, that they might

> break through to one or all of them. In a group of three you may have
> one or two hard-liners and maybe one that is just hanging with them.
> You might be able to get through to him. I try to get out of him what is

happening in his life. I like to spend some time talking to them, unless they are real turds. I usually think, "I like this kid." I usually try to get some counseling for them. I write up a petition and hope something will get done for them.

Youngsters' attitudes, as the just-quoted officer intimates, are important. Almost all studies on the matter conclude that the demeanor of juveniles is a major determinant in the disposition of youth, who have committed misdemeanors. Deference to the officers will keep juveniles out of custody.[20] Deference is shown by a "good" attitude:

A good attitude is demonstrated by a polite, concerned, tractable manner where the offender shows remorse for his transgression, indicates that he feels guilty or sorry for it, implies that he considers the officer's actions correct and justified and indicates that, realizing what he has done, he will not do it again. All of the elements need not be present for the officer to assume that the citizen has a good attitude; politeness and a calm, repentant manner may be enough.[21]

In contrast, juveniles demonstrate a bad attitude when they are, "cool, contemptuous, unconcerned or unrepentant."[22]

Such matters may have a cultural basis.[23] In particular, young members of groups that have a history of negative contacts with the police may have a storehouse of antagonism toward officers and find it difficult to control their emotions when confronted by legal authorities. Cultural characteristics, however, may also work in favor of deference. "Those little shits," a female officer began. "You don't want to segregate, but Mexican gang kids are pretty damn honest. I'd walk up and say, 'Hey, somebody saw you doing this. What's going on here?' They tell you, 'Yeah, we did it.'" The youngsters' honesty got them more lenient treatment.

Another area of concern relevant to police decisions to arrest juveniles is officers' judgments about the type of families they believe the juveniles are from. Patrol officers probably lack actual knowledge about the youngsters' home lives, as they may not have visited them there, but they make guesses based upon what they know of the neighborhoods and the youths' attitudes. A good demeanor reflects well upon a child's ability to control his or her own behavior and the values of the family.

Cooperative juveniles might be given a citation and then released to the custody of their parents, according to a handful of officers. Regarding uncooperative juveniles, one officer commented, "I take them to jail and they are arrested." A few officers, however, felt such action to be wasted. A veteran explained that "if you take them to jail, juvenile hall, they turn around and release them. This generally wastes my time, so I think their parents can do more." Such decisions might be made after the officer spoke with the parents. During such conversations, a 15-year patrol veteran told us that one could "find out about the juvenile: does he belong to a gang? For how long? Talk to his parents. Is he doing it to be cool, or is he an actual gang member?" If this officer determined that the parents could manage the situation, he told us, "then there is no need for me to arrest or to cite him."

Parents were important to the officers. A 50-year-old officer explained to us her strategy for strengthening the parent-child relationship in order to give the family a better chance to succeed:

> If they are under 14, with their parents' permission I put handcuffs on
> them, take their picture, let them sit in a cell, let them see what it is
> like—scares them a bit. I talk mean to them. Then I bring their parents
> in, make it seem like the parents are talking me into releasing them, and
> I try to strengthen the relationship between the parents and the child and
> make me out to be the bad guy.

Juveniles who are from families who have siblings or parents in legal custody are more likely to be arrested. The officers assume that such families are unable to supervise the youngsters and that tertiary controls are necessary.[24]

For some officers, the youngsters' involvement with graffiti was enough to discredit the parents. "I have a hard time taking their spray paint and releasing them to their parents," one officer complained. "Because if the kids are doing that, their parents must not be controlling them to begin with," he concluded.

Most of the individuals who contended they would counsel the youth provided us with minimal information about their techniques. Perhaps they did not believe the incident worthy of much attention or they did not want to bother with university researchers' questions. Or maybe they had not had much experience with such cases. For whatever reason, their answers were succinct. An officer who had recently completed her first year in the occupation, for example, responded:

> By the time I get there, they are usually gone. If I've caught them and they are spray-painting, it's malicious mischief. Right now, because of the gang slogans, the city wants us to file against them and citing them a ticket is what we do. I cite them a ticket, I take them home, and I find out what's happening at home with their parents' situation. At least they will be documented and let the court system continue on from there.

Only a handful of officers provided us with detailed comments regarding their counseling techniques. Of these officers, most fit within what one police expert, William Muir, entitled the "professional response." Muir wrote:

> people had to be scared enough to force themselves to think things through . . . they had to be sobered by the realization that their trespasses were harmful enough that the damage might never be undone . . . for if fear got people to pay attention, there had to be a worthwhile and accurate lesson to pay attention to. . . . [The professional] talked juveniles into feeling that they were responsible for all the effects of their actions, not just for the desirable consequences they envisioned. That took time: a policeman could never be in "too big a hurry."[25]

The lack of officers who provided us with the "professional response" may indicate that a change in policing has occurred since the cited study was completed in the 1970s. Or it more likely represents a difference between the department Muir studied and the various departments included in our research. Graffiti was probably not a concern for Muir's subjects. A few of our officers, however, did supply us with professional answers. A 17-year veteran told us:

> When I talk to any kid, you want to personalize your relationship. You cannot generalize. You personalize your relationship with that person and you try and help them work out the problem. You show them the positive and negative aspects. I tell them to think of three things that will come out of it if they do the action and three things that will come out of it if they don't do the action. I tell them I can't make the decisions

for them. I say, "The only person that will be with you the rest of your life is you, so you can only depend on you to make your decisions." I look at this job like it is a profession.

If there was a difference between the way male and female officers wanted to handle the scenario, it should have shown up among the officers who seemed to take counseling seriously. But we found only one officer whose answer squarely fit within the expectations of stereotypical "female behavior." She began:

> Some of the kids are hard-core. They're tough to deal with. But I'm a mother and my kids aren't even ten years old, so a lot of times I find myself mothering [the juveniles], sitting them down, lecturing them like a mother would lecture. Most of these kids don't get that. They don't have rules and restrictions put on them, and I found a lot that works with my kids when they do something versus saying "You messed up, you did this, you were wrong." I like to turn around and say that this situation is wrong, "Spray-painting, it looks bad. These people work hard for their money to have this kind of stuff. What can you do to make it right?" Now the shoe's on their foot. They have to make a decision. I had one that stole the other night. They caught him and the store didn't want to prosecute, but I told him, "The prices are high because this happens. What can you do to make this right?" And he, on his own, said, "Well, I guess I could come down and sweep the parking lot for him or maybe dump some trash cans," and it was on his own. He thought of it. If I would have told him, "You come down here and sweep the parking lot," he would have said, "No way; forget you!" But when you put the responsibility on them—these kids don't have responsibility so I like to try and do that, make these kids make a decision—nine times out of ten they make the right one.

Her answer is unusual, almost ironic, because it was the type of answer the historical policewoman might have provided on a regular basis. It is also unusual because the youthful officer suggests that she involves the victim in the solution. Her answer indicates that she takes the situation seriously but avoids the use of arrest by utilizing informal social control; she creates a sense of duty between offender and victim. Her answer also highlights the difference between the officers' strategies with respect to domestic disputes and graffiti writers. Victims, according to the officers, were commonly consulted in family fights, and their wishes were used by the officers as neutralizations for not arresting. But in their responses to the juvenile scenario, only this officer and one other suggested involving the victim. Other officers ignored them. In fact, one officer's response implied that there was no reason to contact the property owners. "We have graffiti alert forms and we fill them out and a guy goes out and sprays over the graffiti, even if no one has complained about it," he told us. The irony of the situation is lost on the officer. The city whitewashes the graffiti but—as an irate resident who was not contacted before the whitewashing related to us—creates a larger problem for the property owner, who must then repaint the entire section of fence as opposed to simply sanding or washing the graffiti off the wall.

Officers who leaned toward counseling the graffiti writers reflect a belief in the potential for rehabilitating the youngsters. The rehabilitative model holds that people remain law-abiding because of moral inhibitions and internalized norms. When they violate the law, "they act out of emotional instability, lack of self-control, or because they have acquired the values of a criminal subculture."[26] The function of criminal law is "to bring into play processes for modifying the personality, and hence the behavior, of people who commit antisocial acts, so that they will not commit them in the future."[27] Counseling the youngsters was the primary rehabilitative "treatment" favored by our officers. Officers who wanted to arrest had other punishment strategies in mind.

## RETRIBUTION

The 1980s saw a resurgence of retributive ideology under the concept of "just deserts" as the basis for sanctioning criminals. Individuals were to be punished because they deserved it.[28] For Emile Durkheim, an early preeminent sociologist, such punishments were a barometer of public sentiment. He reasoned "that harsh punishment was a response to feelings of indignation, horror and the desire for vengeance."[29] Similarly, a more recent expert on the subject, Johannes Andenaes, argued that punishment is a "means of expressing social disapproval."[30]

For many of the officers we interviewed, gangs were morally repre-
hensible and the youngsters in our scenario deserved punishment for
their connection to the reviled groups. These officers saw a need to
arrest the graffiti writers. For the most part, this strategy was based on
the knowledge that the youngsters were spray-painting gang slogans.
For the officers, this meant that these individuals were gang members
and guilty of a wide variety of criminal activities other than merely
defacing a wall. "We aren't talking about kids who are just goofing
around," an officer explained.

> They are writing gang slogans. They are involved in other criminal activ-
> ities besides vandalism. They are not just kids on a playground, pitching
> rocks at each other or pitching rocks at a school or breaking a window.
> We are talking about people that are involved in criminal activity and
> need to be dealt with. If they look like a duck, walk like a duck, talk like
> a duck, then they are a duck. If they dress like a gang member and write
> gang slogans and flash [gang] signs, they are going to get dealt with like a
> gang member.

The symbolic meaning of the youngsters' behavior was a more important factor in the officers' decision making than the acts themselves. The
writing of gang slogans became more than a simple act of vandalism. It
was a symbol, a flag that defied the police. It spoke of what gangs were
about. A homicide detective explained:

> Spray-painting intrinsically is not a big deal. I've colored my parents' wall
> with my crayons, which is essentially the same act. But that's not what is at
> issue. What is at issue is what that represents; that means they are marking
> that territory with their gang and all the violence that goes with it.

More than a handful of officers indicated that they would arrest the graffiti writers because they found the behavior particularly contemptuous.
"I was brought up to take care of other people's stuff like I would take
care of my stuff," an officer explained. For him, "Graffiti is like dogs
marking their territory." Such officers personalized the youngsters'
behavior. They imagined themselves in the position of the victim and
were outraged. The words of an officer from a suburban community are
illustrative:

I cannot stand graffiti. I think it's just absolutely unbecoming. It doesn't do anything for me. . . . I certainly wouldn't want to wake one morning and find it all over my fence or my house. I don't want my friends or family to come down to this city and see it all marked up.

Punishment based on retribution is an attempt to restore balance to society, while establishing proper parameters of behavior. According to retributive theory, we punish criminal offenders to take away any advantages they might have gained from their illegal acts, thus restoring the balance society seeks and satisfying our desire for revenge. (The offender has hurt someone, so we will hurt the offender.) Durkheim roughly divided the sanctions "into two major types: repressive sanctions, which are characteristic of penal law and involve punishments for transgressions and deviance, and restitutory sanctions, which, in contrast, do not rely on punishment but rather on righting of a balance upset by the violation."[31] Repressive punishments

consist essentially in some injury, or at least some disadvantage imposed upon the perpetrator of a crime. Their purpose is to do harm to him through his fortune, his honor, his life, his liberty, or to deprive him of some object whose possession he enjoys. . . . As for the other kinds of sanctions [restitutive], they do not necessarily imply any suffering on the part of the perpetrator, but merely consist in restoring the previous state of affairs, re-establishing relationships that have been disturbed from their normal form. This is done either by forcibly redressing the action impugned, restoring it to the type from which it has deviated, or by annulling it, that is depriving it of all social value.[32]

We heard arguments from a few officers that stressed restitutive punishments, usually in the form of community corrections. They chose to arrest the youngsters so that they would be put into government-operated cleanup crews. These officers believed in punishments that included "an eye for an eye." By having graffiti writers clean up the community, the officers believed that future damage could be averted.

Durkheim noted additional benefits to be obtained from punishing offenders: it places the wrongdoing outside the boundaries of what "good" people do and defines the conduct as intolerable.[33] Officers who emphasized retributive ideals in their answers recognized that their jobs involved setting boundaries and that punishment was necessary to achieve this goal. We were advised:

> This one has to be dealt with by the book. This is not the kind of thing you say, "Hey, you guys knock it off," and drive away. Not something lenient, something that gets results. I would arrest. That way they can be assigned to community service so that they can clean it up. I wouldn't just tell them to clean it up myself. We need to preserve this city the way it is and not let it snowball like other cities.

The officer who said this was a member of a handful from an upper socio-economic city who believed that a severe response to the graffiti writers was necessary to prevent their community from being overrun by gangs. The city's police department, in general, has been criticized for harassing minority youth as a means to prevent "undesirables" from entering the city. The attitude is aptly portrayed in the officers' answers. A 15-year veteran told us that she would "arrest them and throw them in jail." She continued:

> We don't have a gang problem, and I don't want to see one start. I am all for consequences of severe behavior. We do get a lot of gang behavior, stealing cars and graffiti. They come down from [a nearby city with numerous large minority populations].

A colleague from the same department added:

> They're marking their territory, and if one starts, others will follow, and then it goes back and forth and so on. We have a lot of spillover from [nearby city]. They are going to our schools. We generally have some mix: white, Hispanic, Asian—sort of all the misfits got together, but their connections spread all over. As a department we have stepped up our enforcement on stuff like that.

By strictly enforcing antigraffiti laws, these officers believed they were sending a clear message to all concerned that the behavior was not acceptable in their community.

## INCAPACITATION

Gangs were described as violent by a majority of officers who commented on them, and this belief affected the manner in which they would deal with the youngsters. There was always the possibility that the graffiti writers carried knives or guns, we were warned. One should be aware, we were advised, that "It's a potentially dangerous call and you have to worry about your safety." This attitude probably resulted in officers taking actions that made them feel safer about their work, but it diminished the possibility that officers would treat the youngsters as individuals.

In the domestic dispute scenario, officers ignored the letter of the law and avoided arresting in order to keep individuals out of the criminal justice system. Just the opposite was true with respect to the graffiti writers. Officers used arrest to remove, from their perspective, violent individuals from the community. We were instructed that officers put the juvenile "into the system. You get him recognized as a gang member. There are all kinds of benefits from doing what you should do legally." A female officer utilized an example to explain the strategy:

> I brought a couple of kids in, a couple of weeks ago, that were swimming in a swimming pool. A woman called and said, "We've been having problems 'boocoo' [many] with them and something has got to be done." When I got to the pool, some of the kids ran from me, but I managed to catch 6 or 8 of them and they were 12, 13, 14, or something like that. I handcuffed them all together, got the jailer to bring the forms down. I went through the whole routine. . . . I brought them all down here, did those reports, and kicked them out the door right from here. Didn't even take them home. I called all their parents first to verify their addresses and the information they gave me and then kicked them out the door. See, that stuff gets filed. I don't know how far they would go with something like that. It's trespassing. It gets filed here, at least in our station. If they get arrested in six months or a year from now for something else, they can always bring that out and send it to juvenile court as well. [Charges against] juveniles can always be compounded. They don't always prosecute on the first offense, but if you get another one, then they'll bring that first offense too.

The officer adds to the youngsters' criminal records because she knows the more prior offenses they have, the more likely they are to be sentenced to jail.[34] Her design is to prevent gang members from preying on the community by incapacitating the youngsters in juvenile hall, a goal consistent with the police culture.

SPECIFIC DETERRENCE

Incapacitation was not the only framework police offered for arresting the
graffiti writers. Some officers' answers stressed specific or special deterrence
as the motivation for punishment. The ideology considers that the "threat
of the law alone was not sufficient to make him conform previously. If he
is now deterred by the actual experience of punishment, we speak of special deterrence."[35] A handful of those we interviewed urged arrest to deter
the youngsters from future criminal activities. As a youthful officer commented, "Juveniles grow up to be adults, and if they get away with things
as juveniles they would think, 'This was pretty easy.'" The result, they
believed, was future serious criminal behavior. Another officer explained:

> I found that in our court system, these kids can do this, I don't know how
> many times, and get away with it. It takes a kid to murder somebody for
> anybody to do anything about it. Well, it [the murder] is from what
> they've been doing all along. It's from their graffiti; it's from their gang
> association and it's from the little things they've built up from when they
> were 10, 12, 13 years old that lead them to where they are when they're
> 17 and they're killing somebody.

Part of the group's anger was the result of their frustration with the
legal system, which the officers perceived as unable to severely punish
youngsters. Juveniles, it was argued, "take the judicial system very
lightly" and have a "You ain't gonna do nothing to me" attitude. We
were instructed that gang members, for example, "know that if they get
caught and go to jail, nothing is going to happen to them. I know gang
members, if a murder is to be committed, who'll have a juvenile do it
because they know the worst that can happen is that they stay in juvenile hall until the age of 25." Officers argued that one needed to dis-
suade offenders of the belief that no punishment would befall them. A
14-year veteran told us:

> I don't care if it's the first time he's done it or if he's a hard-core banger
> putting his mark on the wall. I'd arrest him, make an impression on him.
> "You want to bang, I'll show you the life of a banger." I'd hook him up
> and I'd take him in. . . . He wants to bang, then treat him like a banger. I
> don't care if they're 11 or 21 or 18.

Involvement in cleaning up the graffiti was seen by a few officers as an appropriate specific deterrent for spray-painters. One, for example, told us that she would "definitely arrest them."

> They are going to jail. I think in addition to that, if I were a judge, I would like to see them go back and repaint the damage that they did on that wall, and part of their probation would be serving community time, painting over other gang members' graffiti—kind of further ingraining in them that they cannot destroy other people's property, whether it be city property or someone's car or whatever. I think the restitution program is good. But I don't know how they are ever going to come up with this money. But even if they were to make payments of $5 a week, I think it's better than them just walking away thinking, "Hey, man, this is no big deal. All I did, I served five days and that's it. I'll just spray another car." I think it's important to make them feel uncomfortable. Now, what I mean by uncomfortable is take their freedom away. Put them in the back of the car; separate them from their friends; make them feel small. I think that's important.

The punishment was with purpose. The youngsters were to be cured of their antisocial behaviors by learning firsthand the cost of their misdeeds. A 15-year veteran told us that she believed:

> If they're old enough to deface property, they're old enough to fix somebody else's property. They don't learn anything by going to the [juvenile] hall or by getting arrested and having to go see a probation officer once a week. But the thing that teaches children what was wrong about what they did was seeing how hard it is to undo it. And if they have to go out there and do a whole bunch of physical labor, and it's punishment, pretty soon they'll be objecting to the fact that people are putting graffiti on the wall that they have to clean off. Especially if they have to come back and clean it over and over again.

The punishment is to make miserable the offenders' lives. It was through such treatment, these officers posited, that juveniles could be deterred from future criminal behavior.

These officers were frustrated because they did not understand the world of the youngsters. "My children would never talk to an adult that way," we were told. Another officer, who also did not comprehend the youngsters' behavior, started by graphically describing how he wanted to handle the graffiti writers: "I would like to take that spray paint and spray their face with it. . . . But realistically, I would like to make them eat the spray paint. But the law says I can't do this." We asked him, "Why would you like to spray-paint their face?" and he replied:

> First of all, I don't think the laws serve as a deterrent for the juveniles to not do it. I think it would be more of a frustration of wanting to dish out street justice instead of this malicious mischief [conviction] being enough of a deterrent. Realistically, some of the stuff in LA is actually artistic.

When questioned, he quickly admits that the artists' behavior may not be that bad and that his desired behavior may be the result of his own frustration. But he also sees the application of "street justice" as a specific deterrent to future criminal acts by the misbehaving youth. He is unable to empathize with the youngsters and is baffled by their behavior. More than a half-dozen officers intimated that they dispensed street justice to make sure that offenders were punished. Most were cautious in their wording of the answers they provided. Presumably, they did not trust us enough to risk their careers by being too open. One remarked, "I am not going to tell you the way I prefer to handle them because I prefer not to do that." But he did tell us the only thing graffiti writers understand is "brute violence." He added a prudent proviso: "I'm not saying this is the way to handle it." But not all officers were cautious in their responses to the graffiti scenario. We were instructed by one officer to "take the little buggers and beat 'em." His response was the outgrowth of his frustration. He told us, "The system will take them to jail, call their parents, and release them. By the time you finish explaining to your supervisor and write your paperwork, they're out and it's not worth it. It's even more reason to take your boot to them." Young children did not escape this officer's wrath. Their behavior, in his view, was deserving of physical punishment. He reasoned that "They want to spit on you; they want to give you an attitude . . . and I'm not talking 15 or 16. I'm talking 8 or 9, so young. So just take your boot to them."

Part of the group's frustration was with the public, whom they perceived as wanting the police to get rid of gangs but being unwilling to severely punish youngsters. Certainly factors other than those we have recounted here go into officers' decisions to arrest misbehaving youths. Individual prejudices probably play some role. But these are idiosyncratic matters and are less likely to be endemic in the police culture.

## DISCUSSION AND CONCLUSIONS

In both the domestic dispute and graffiti scenarios, the officers generally indicated a belief that there was little they could do to alter the situations. Given that, however, a majority of officers chose to handle these matters in opposite fashions. Arrest was to be avoided in family fights because it would create a criminal record for the individual and negate the possibility that the combatants, with the help of friends and family, might work the situation out. In contrast, the majority of officers wanted to arrest the graffiti writers in order to establish a criminal record and because they believed the youngsters were too far down the criminal path to be saved. Youngsters were to be punished to deter them from future criminal behavior, yet a majority of the officers failed to apply the same logic to domestic abusers.

For the officers, domestic disputes were social work and best handled by someone else. Minor batterers were to be ignored, according to most of those we interviewed, because arrest might result in their returning after release to do more damage to their mates. Arresting the taggers, in contrast, was a means to stop their behavior. None of the officers suggested that the youngsters might return after their release to do more damage to the property (although this is a common concern of individuals who might report the spray-painting).

The officers' reasoning is at times confusing. They arrest the youngsters to teach them a lesson but then release them. The youth may be learning something, but it probably is not the lesson the officers want to teach. Rather, they learn that the officers cannot follow through on their threats. Some officers prefer to dispense street punishments in order to avoid this problem, but they probably are teaching the youngsters to further disrespect them. The youngsters may come to see the police as little more than another gang, the members of which will dispense violence to whomever they catch.

One explanation for the contrasting solutions to the two scenarios stems from the status of the offenders. Adults can cause officers numerous legal problems, while minority juveniles are unable to cause officers much official grief.[36] The youngsters may be able to retaliate against officers by harassing them (by calling them names, throwing rocks, or shooting bullets at them) or by damaging their cars, but neither they nor their parents are likely to bring suit against the officers. For one, they lack the money to hire an attorney. In addition, the juveniles' parents, who are of the lower socioeconomic class and may be immigrants, fear retaliation from police if they choose to complain.

Socioeconomic status does play a role in police behavior. Illustrative, the most strikingly different answers were provided by the officers from the wealthiest community. The officers from that city seemed more aware of the arrest policies with respect to domestic disputes and wanted to deter gangs from entering their city.

Female police officers' answers to us indicated that there is little difference between the way they handle calls and the manner in which men accomplish them. If anything, female officers at times provided answers that were more "macho" than their male counterparts. They showed no sentiment for female victims and, with the exception of one officer, wanted to handle the graffiti artists in the same fashion as the men.

Departmental rules appear to have some influence on homogenizing the genders' behaviors; a minority of officers mentioned them as important in their decision making. The police culture, however, emerges as a much stronger influence in determining their actions. That is, the selection and training of officers produce individuals who have ways of working and thinking that are consistent with the prevailing police ideology. Neophytes who differ from the mainstream may find themselves ostracized from the larger group and subject to its penalties. In the face of such adversity, they must either conform or leave the force. In the final chapter, we review our findings and suggest a mechanism for change that may be acceptable to the police culture.

# CHAPTER TEN

## *Final Thoughts*

Most of the studies available on the performance of female officers were done in the 1970s and 1980s. Now that the novelty of female officers has somewhat worn off, we can begin to assess their transition into patrol and their acceptance by other members of the law enforcement community. Women's numbers continue to remain low. Recent lawsuits brought by female officers alleging discrimination and harassment by their departments and fellow officers and tales provided by a few of our subjects indicate that problems continue to exist.

The responses of the female officers differed from societal expectations as to how they would do the job. The women were generally not attracted to police work to "help others." In fact, a higher percentage of their number reported seeking the position for excitement, and several female officers expressed dissatisfaction with abused women, stating that they had "no tolerance for women who could get themselves into that situation."

The women we interviewed may be unlike women outside of law enforcement. A few had recognized the difference in themselves and knew that they could handle the rigors of the job. However, we also received evidence that the female officers had some factors in common with other women. They hid their feminine side while on the job, presumably in order to fit in with other officers and to conform to the public's image of police officers.

Despite organizational changes designed to reform the police, the answers provided to us indicate that officer behavior has probably

changed little during the last 50 years. The 80 individuals we interviewed, for the most part, had sought the job for the excitement it
offered. They valued training that had prepared them for the violent side
of policing. Their friends were commonly other officers, and they felt
isolated from other people. They gained the most satisfaction from their
occupation by arresting "bad people" and they disliked aspects—such as
"petty" calls, departmental politics that resulted in unfair promotional
practices and favoritism in assignment, and paperwork—that take them
away from their conception of what constitutes "real police work."
Domestic dispute calls, for example, were not viewed as legitimate police
business, and officers said they avoided arrests in these situations, utilizing enculturated neutralizations to justify their behavior. In contrast,
they wanted to take a hard-line approach with gang members, whom
they see as violent individuals.

   This research did reveal that officers use a great deal of discretion; they
often have self-serving motives for not making arrests, such as getting
back into service in hopes of getting a "hot call." They disregarded
departmental policies and in many cases circumvented the law to make
their job easier.

## PROVISOS

Perhaps this summary is too simplistic and does not do justice to the
intelligence and capability of the officers interviewed here. This group of
officers was articulate, sincere, and candid in their responses. Their participation in this research indicates a willingness to open up to outsiders,
conceivably in an effort to effect change. It is unfair to pigeonhole the
officers into arbitrary categories without giving them credit for the
responsible and courageous job they are doing and for the function they
perform in society. They are very much a product of a system that was
already in place before they came and a system that will be there after
they are replaced by new officers.

   The police have an extraordinarily difficult job not because the job is
dangerous; there are many occupations in which serious injury and
death are more likely. The cause of officers' calamity is the ambiguous

nature of their job. The public expects them to do something about crime, in part, because the police have urged us to consider them this way. They used the media, starting during the depression, to convince us that they could end crime by catching criminals. Now they are held captive by this image, believing that they are the lonely, unappreciated stalwarts against crime.

## IMPLICATIONS OF THIS RESEARCH

Throughout police history, administrators have attempted to improve law enforcement services to the community. Some leaders have emphasized education and training of their officers, hoping to bring about a professional police force. Other leaders have improved recordkeeping and implemented detailed written policies to guide officers' decision making. Current administrators are responding to community concerns, attempting to create a more problem-oriented and community-sensitive police force.

Police agencies are making a genuine effort to gain public support and approval with the use of community-based programs. Under this model, officers are trained in community relations and cultural sensitivity. For at least the last decade, most community and police leaders have embraced the concept, hoping it will bring about needed changes in police practices. Concerns about the model, however, continue to exist. Most notably, the progenitor of problem-oriented policing pointed out that "many police leaders latch onto the label for the positive images it evokes but do not invest in the concept itself."[1]

We have seen evidence that community policing may go the way of previous reforms. At a recent community policing conference for police chiefs in Orange County, California, one administrator called the meeting somewhat successful but noted one important missing ingredient— the community. Another indication that something was amiss was that most vendor booths at the conference were featuring the latest technology in weapons for police officers.

The major obstacle to implementation of the community policing model is the police culture. Our interviews and past research indicate that officers strongly favor the law enforcement component of the job. Supporters rarely question activities that are consistent with the cultural constraints, while ideas that are outside its ideology are denigrated and those who practice them are punished. Initially, with the introduction of any reform, there are supporters and those who can do the job well. Early on, matters go smoothly. But the true test is when administrators attempt to implement the new model throughout the department. Team policing is a good example. Initially successful, the strategy floundered because it lacked the support of rank-and-file officers.

Many experts have posited that community policing requires a different type individual than those currently existing in departments. Jerome Skolnick and David Bayley, for example, argue that "To be successful at community policing, police must be more than large, physical, and tough; they must be analytic, empathetic, flexible, and communicative."[2] Officers must empathize with the citizenry. Those who adhere to a belief structure that defines law violators as "enemies" cannot be expected to understand miscreants' behavior, and they are unlikely to negotiate with the enemy. Rather, law enforcement personnel are apt to try to impose their will. Illustrative are the words of a New York City community police officer:

> You have to project an image especially if you work alone. So you have a little talk with the knuckleheads, introduce yourself and tell them where you are coming from. You say "I'm Officer Jett. This is my neighborhood. If you mess up and I see you around, I'm going to take care of you."[3]

Experts suggest that as police agencies adopt a philosophy of community policing, "a different kind of officer may be required."[4] Rather than trying to "teach an old dog new tricks," they suggest that it might be more feasible to get some new dogs, ones that are already primed to accept a new approach to policing communities.

The belief that community policing requires different skills and types of individuals than those currently represented in agencies may be true, but the reality of the situation is that this new breed of officer is not likely to be attracted to police work nor chosen by hiring boards. Currently, self-selection and departmental hiring decisions minimize diversity, creating a fairly homogeneous group of officers who see themselves as crimefighters, not community service workers. It is unlikely that an organization made up of members of a powerfully institutionalized subculture will suddenly be able to mass-produce a different kind of police officer. Administrators are left wondering what they can do to change officer behavior, aside from providing ongoing training in community relations, communications, and cultural sensitivity and implementing restrictive policies, such as disciplining or firing officers who fail to meet new standards.

To have any chance of long-term success, reforms must be somewhat consistent with the culture within which they are expected to exist. Keeping this in mind, in the next section we make suggestions that we have drawn from the answers provided by our interviewees.

## An Administrative Model

Autonomy on the job is an important aspect of the policing occupation, according to our informants, and practices that inhibit it were most disliked. For the most part, characteristics of the bureaucratic model caused the most complaints.

Officers who enjoyed the freedom of the job linked the ability to choose how to handle their daily activities to a level of trust and status. At a certain level, autonomy equals power. At the individual tier, it means the power to do what one wants, to be master of the situation. A loss of autonomy is clearly associated with a loss of personal power for many officers. For many of the officers who favored autonomy, exciting situations did not require a law enforcement component or adrenaline-producing activities. A variety of activities and the opportunity to use their problem-solving skills were often enough to make the job enjoyable.

The officers' disdain for the bureaucratic model shows in their complaints about the job. Officers in every department had something negative to say about rules and supervision—cornerstones of the bureaucratic model. Regulations are used within the bureaucratic organization to control the office holder; the more rules, the stricter the supervision. Their treatment as bureaucrats by superiors is frustrating to officers, and they lash out at those who attempt to control them.

Police reforms that occur within the bureaucratic model have less chance for success. This is true in large part because bureaucratic indices cannot accurately measure the quality of the job officers do. Consider the situation with respect to officer promotions.

Picking who will be promoted is difficult in any bureaucracy. The obvious obstacle is selecting the criteria upon which advancement will be based. In certain occupations the measures are clear, but these are rarely bureaucracies. Selection to a starting pitching position on a baseball team, for example, is based on the ability to prevent hitters from scoring runs. Promotion to full professor within an academic unit is often based on publications. But upon what yardstick should we measure the performance of police officers? The police culture seems to suggest that arrests be given priority in the selection of those to be advanced, and they are often part of the mix used in decision making. In middle-class neighborhoods, where arrests are rare, supervisors may rely on traffic tickets as a weak reflection of the cultural icon.

Law enforcement, however, represents only a small portion of the police job, and officers urge that other factors be taken into consideration. A study conducted in Florida in the 1970s still has relevance today. Supervisors' evaluations of officers were biased toward law enforcement. Social service activities were given short shrift by the evaluators. Officers, however, thought that their performance should be based on factors such as their use of discretion or their initiative or their ability to get along with others.[5] These factors, however, are also difficult to measure. As a result, administrators fall back upon easily identifiable criteria to decide promotions; obeying the bureaucratic rules, the extent of one's education, and seniority within the department are common considerations. These, however, often have nothing to do with individuals' ability to do the job, and frequently all officers applying for a position may be comparable on these matters. As a result, officers become frustrated and fail to support any reforms.

What is needed, then, is an administrative style that grants officers autonomy while still maintaining control. We cast around for a model that might be applied to policing and found one close to home: the model of shared governance used at universities, which grants professors great freedom within an institutional framework.

University faculty have three broadly defined job duties: service, teaching, and research. Service sometimes refers to service to the community or the profession, but more often it is reflective of the fact that faculty fill administrative positions within the university. University committees, made up of faculty, normally choose other faculty to fulfill the administrative roles. The selected individuals often continue to teach and undertake research but to a diminished extent. Following a term or two, they return to the ranks of full-time faculty. Some individuals become full-time administrators (for example, the chancellor or president of a university), but these people were once faculty. Some administrative staff members have never been professors, but these individuals are almost always under the supervision of faculty. This model accomplishes two tasks. For one, administrators, as current or former faculty, are sensitive to the profession's value system. In addition, administrators are hesitant to act in a high-handed fashion because they will return to the faculty ranks, where their past behavior may return to haunt them.

Committees consisting of other professors decide faculty promotions and pay raises. Every year or two, each faculty member submits a file to his or her department detailing his or her accomplishments in research, teaching, and service. Evaluations of the faculty's performance may be solicited from individuals outside the professor's institution. But the submitted file is the primary source of information for the department. Once a decision is reached, it is forwarded to another faculty committee for review.

The model could be applied to the police. Officers would be expected to fulfill administrative positions with the knowledge that they will eventually return to the ranks of other officers. They could submit files that describe why they should be promoted. Some control of the process can be exerted by delineating the types of activities that are acceptable. For example, service, teaching, and research are university requirements. Similar categories might well work for the police. Service, for example, might refer to administrative duties. Teaching might refer to efforts to inform the public (for example, meetings with community groups or youngsters in which the officers provide information on how to avoid being a victim or strategies for removing neighborhood eyesores). Research might refer to efforts by officers to develop plans to solve community problems.

The description we have provided here is not meant to be a detailed blueprint for a new administrative model. Rather, it is an outline because we believe that officers must themselves develop the particulars, otherwise, they will not accept its implementation.

## Conclusion

Based on what our officers told us, individuals are attracted to the job because of the law enforcement component and they are hired because their views are consistent with the police culture. During their training, the neophytes further learn acceptable behaviors and attitudes. Past and current reforms have been largely ineffective at changing the occupation because they have been unable to alter these matters.

We have argued that policing is unlikely to change as long as crime control remains the measure of police effectiveness. Officers will fail to alter their behavior because they will likely realize they are being evaluated as they always have been. Unhappily, evidence suggests that departments are continuing to rely on crime statistics as measures of performance and that officers still prefer locking up the bad guy.[6]

For community policing to work, officers and departments need to be evaluated on their ability to keep the peace and build community. The police will change only if criminologists and other interested parties can develop measures that reflect their performance on these matters and de-emphasize crime control, arrests, and warlike actions. Officers are not stupid. Provide them a goal and they will figure out a method to obtain it. They can do more than wage war on segments of the population. They can build community.[7]

We have suggested a different administrative model as a means to implement a new ideology, one that rewards officers for activities other than catching the bad guy. Without such changes, policing in the 21st century may, unfortunately, resemble the mindless robots that movies such as *Star Wars* suggest are around the corner.

# NOTES

## PREFACE

1.  C. Foster, M. A. Siegel, and N. R. Jacobs, eds., "Women's Changing Role," *Information Plus* 18 (1990): 29–37.
2.  P. Hammer-Higgins and V. A. Atwood, "The Management Game: An Educational Intervention for Counseling Women with Nontraditional Career Goals," *The Career Development Quarterly* 38, no. 1 (September 1989): 6–23.
3.  Foster, Siegel, and Jacobs, "Women's Changing Role."
4.  K. McGoldrick, "Gender and Economics," *Journal of American Medical Women's Association* 43 (1988): 103.
5.  D. Allen, "Women in Medical Specialty Societies: An Update," *Journal of the American Medical Association* 262 (1989): 3439–43.
6.  Susan E. Martin, *Breaking and Entering: Policewomen on Patrol* (Berkeley: University Press, 1980).
7.  Carol Gilligan, *In a Different Voice: Psychological Theory and Women's Development* (Cambridge, Mass.: Harvard University Press, 1982).
8.  J. Bernard, *The Sex Game* (Englewood Cliffs, N.J.: Prentice Hall, 1968); M. Betz and L. O'Connell, "Gender and Work: A Look at Sex Differences among Pharmacy Students," *American Journal of Pharmaceutical Education* 51 (1987): 3943; E. Douvan and J. Adelson, *The Adolescent Experience* (New York: John Wiley & Sons, 1966); and W. E. Vinacke, "Sex Roles in Three-Person Game," *Sociometry* 22 (1959): 343–60.

## CHAPTER 1: POLICE ADMINISTRATIVE MODELS

1.  A. Holmes, *New York Times,* 5 April 1991, sec. 1A, p. 22.
2   C. Jones, "Took Drug Money on Sergeant's Orders, Deputy Says," *Los Angeles Times*, 9 November 1990, B1.
3.  Gordon Witkin, "When the Bad Guys Are Cops: While Professionalism Is Increasing, a Vicious New Breed of Rogue Officer Has Experts Worried," *U.S. News & World Report* 119 (11 September 1995): 20.
4.  S. C. Gwynne, "Cops and Robbers (Armed Robbery and Murder Case against Antoinette Frank)," *Time* 145 (20 March 1995): 45.

5.  Witkin, "When the Bad Guys Are Cops," 20.
6.  Scott Glover and Matt Lait, "A Tearful Perez Gets 5 Years," *Los Angeles Times*, 26 February 2000.
7.  Ted Rohrlich, "Scandal Shows Why Innocent Plead Guilty," *Los Angeles Times*, 31 December 1999.
8.  Albert Reiss Jr., *The Police and the Public* (New Haven: Yale University Press, 1971); A. Kinnane, *Policing* (Chicago: Nelson-Hall, 1979); and Martin, *Breaking and Entering: Policewomen on Patrol.*
9.  D. Black, "Police Encounters and Social Organization" (Ph.D. diss., University of Michigan, 1968).
10. Samuel Walker, *The Police in America: An Introduction* (New York: McGraw-Hill, 1983), 6.
11. W. Miller, *Cops and Bobbies: Police Authority in New York and London*, 1830–1870 (Chicago: University of Chicago Press, 1973), 19.
12. Walker, *The Police in America*; and A. Silver, "The Demand for Order in Civil Society: A Review of Some Themes in History of Urban Crime, Police, and Riot," in *The Police: Six Sociological Essays*, ed. D. J. Bordua (New York: John Wiley & Sons, 1967).
13. Miller, *Cops and Bobbies*, 15.
14. Walker, *The Police in America*, 7.
15. Miller, *Cops and Bobbies*, 20; and Mark H. Haller, "Chicago Cops, 1890–1925," *Law and Society Review* 10 (1976): 303–23.
16. Miller, *Cops and Bobbies*.
17. R. Lane, "Urban Police and Crime in Nineteenth-Century America," in Modern Policing, ed. M. Tonry and N. Morris (Chicago: University of Chicago Press, 1992), 1–50.
18. Gene F. Carte and Elaine H. Carte, *Police Reform in the United States: The Era of August Vollmer, 1905–1932* (Berkeley: University of California Press, 1975), 11.
19. Newton D. Baker, "Law, Police, and Social Problems," *Atlantic Monthly* 116 (July 1915): 12–20.
20. W. F. White, *Street Corner Society* (Chicago: University of Chicago Press, 1955), 136; see also Carl Werthman and Irving Piliavin, "Gang Members and the Police" in *The Police: Six Sociological Essays*, ed. D. J. Bordua (New York: John Wiley & Sons, 1967), 66.
21. W. J. Gaynor, "The Lawlessness of the Police in New York," *The North American Review* 176 (January 1903): 10–26.
22. W. A. Purrington, "The Police Power and the Police Force," *The North American Review* 174 (1902): 505–17.
23. Haller, "Chicago Cops."
24. Purrington, "The Police Power and the Police Force," 514–15.
25. F. Moss, "National Danger from Police Corruption," *The North American Review* 173 (1901): 471–72.
26. Ibid., 472.
27. Walker, *The Police in America*, 12.
28. S. W. Cooper, "Abuse of Police Power," *The North American Review* 150 (1890): 658–59.

29. E. Bittner, "The Police Charge," in *Police Behavior: A Sociological Perspective*, ed. R. J. Lundman (New York: Oxford University Press, 1980), 28–41.

30. R. B. Fosdick, *American Police Systems* (New York: The Century Co., 1920), 69.

31. G. F. Carte, "August Vollmer and the Origins of Police Professionalism," Journal of Police Science and Administration 1 (1973): 274–81.

32. Haller, *Chicago Cops*, 305.

33. Miller, *Cops and Bobbies*, 17.

34. Ibid., 152–53.

35. A. Coffey, E. Eldefonso, and W. Hartinger, *Human Relations: Law Enforcement in a Changing Community*, 3d ed. (Englewood Cliffs, N.J.: Prentice Hall, 1982); R. Fogelson, *Big City Police* (Cambridge: Harvard University Press, 1977); and S. Walker, *A Critical History of Police Reform* (Lexington, Mass.: Lexington Books, 1977).

36. E.g., see Purrington, "The Police Power and the Police Force," 515.

37. E. R. Brown, *Rockefeller Medicine Men: Medicine and Capitalism in America* (Berkeley: University of California Press, 1979); and Paul Jesilow, Henry N. Pontell, and Gilbert Geis, *Prescriptions for Profit: How Doctors Defraud Medicaid* (Berkeley: University of California Press, 1993).

38. Arthur Niederhoffer lists the characteristics of a profession as (1) high standards of admission, (2) a special body of knowledge and theory, (3) altruism and dedication to the service ideal, (4) a lengthy period of training for candidates, (5) a code of ethics, (6) licensing of members, (7) autonomous control, (8) pride of the members in their profession, (9) publicly recognized status and prestige (p. 19). Niederhoffer, *Behind the Shield: The Police in Urban Society* (Garden City, N.Y.: Anchor Books, 1969).

39. Baker, "Law, Police, and Social Problems."

40. C. B. Saunders, *Upgrading the American Police: Education and Training* (Washington, D.C.: Brookings Institution, 1970), 32.

41. E.g., see Baker, "Law, Police, and Social Problems,"15–16.

42. Miller, *Cops and Bobbies*, 107.

43. G. F. Carte, "August Vollmer and the Origins of Police Professionalism; N. Douthit, "August Vollmer, Berkeley's First Chief of Police, and the Emergence of Police Professionalism," *California Historical Quarterly* 54 (spring 1975): 101–24; and Walker, *A Critical History of Police Reform*.

44. A. Vollmer and A. Schneider, "The School for Police as Planned at Berkeley," *Journal of the American Institute of Criminal Law and Criminology* 7 (1917): 622–24.

45. Saunders, *Upgrading the American Police*.

46. A. Vollmer, *The Police and Modern Society* (1936; reprint, College Park, Md.: McGrath Publishing Company, 1969), 222–23.

47. G. F. Carte and E. H. Carte, *Police Reform in the United States*, 95.

48. A. Vollmer, "Aims and Ideals of the Police," *Journal of the American Institute of Criminal Law and Criminology* 13 (1922): 126–27.

49. L. D. Upson, *Practice of Municipal Administration* (New York: Century Company, 1926), 321, 324–25.

50. T. A. Reppetto, *The Blue Parade* (New York: Free Press, 1978), 246.

51. Brown, *Rockefeller Medicine Men.*

52. Reppetto, *The Blue Parade*, 244.

53. National Commission on Law Observance and Law Enforcement, *Report on Lawlessness in Law Enforcement* (Washington, D.C.: GPO, 1931).

54. President's Commission on Law-Enforcement and Administration of Justice, Task Force on the Police, Task Force Report: The Police (Washington, D.C.: GPO, 1967), 126.

55. Ibid., 121.

56. Ibid.

57. Raymond E. Clift, "Police Training," *Annals of the American Academy of Political and Social Science* 291 (1954): 113–18.

58. N. Alex, New York *Cops Talk Back: A Study of a Beleaguered Minority* (New York: John Wiley & Sons, 1976), 29.

59. Robert W. Hodge, Paul M. Siegel, and Peter H. Rossi, "Occupation Prestige in the United States, 1925–1963," *American Journal of Sociology* 70 (1964): 290–92.

60. Coffey, Eldefonso, and Hartinger, *Human Relations*, 141.

61. *Brown v Mississippi*, 297 US 278 (1936); and *Tennessee v Garner*, 471 US 1, 105 SCt 1694, 85 LEd2d 1 (1985).

62. *Miller v United States*, 356 F2d 63, 67 (5th Cir 1966); *Mapp v Ohio*, 367 US 643 (1961); and *Chimel v California*, 395 US 752 (1969).

63. *Gideon v Wainwright*, 372 US 335, 83 SCt 792, 9 LEd2d 799 (1963); *Escobedo v Illinois*, 378 US 478, 84 SCt 1758, 12 LEd2d 977 (1964); *Miranda v Arizona*, 384 US 436, 86 SCt 1602, 16 LEd2d 694 (1966); *Rochin v California*, 342 US 165, 72 SCt 205, 96 LEd 183 (1952); *Schmerber v California*, 384 US 757, 86 SCt 1826, 16 LEd2d 908 (1966); *United States v Watson*, 423 US 411, 96 SCt 820, 46 LEd2d 509 (1976); *United States v Ramey*, 602 F Supp 821 (EDNC 1985).

64. Alex, New York Cops Talk Back, 132; Richard H. Ichord, "Lawsuits That Handcuff Our Lawmen," *Nation's Business* 60 (November 1972): 27–29.

65. Albert Reiss Jr., "Professionalization of the Police," in *Police and Community Relations: A Source Book*, ed. A. F. Brandstatter and L. A. Radelet (Beverly Hills: Glencoe Press, 1968), 215–16.

66. Walker, *The Police in America*, 15.

67. Frederick W. Taylor, *Scientific Management* (New York: Harper and Row, 1939) [reprinted in Critical Studies in Organization and Bureaucracy, ed. Frank Fisher and Carmen Sirianni (Philadelphia: Temple University Press, 1984), 68–78]; and Max Weber, *The Theory of Social and Economic Organization* (1925; edited, with an introduction by Talcott Parsons, New York: Oxford University Press, 1947).

68. Frank Fisher and Carmen Sirianni, "Organization Theory and Bureaucracy: A Critical Introduction," in *Critical Studies in Organization and Bureaucracy*, ed. Frank Fisher and Carmen Sirianni (Philadelphia: Temple University Press, 1984), 3–20.

69. Taylor, *Scientific Management*, 69.

70. Ibid., 71.

71. Weber, *The Theory of Social and Economic Organization*, 328.

72. Ibid., 331.

73. Ibid., 332.

74. Ibid., 333–34.

75. James Q. Wilson, "The Police and Their Problems: A Theory," *Public Policy* 12 (1963).

76. R. N. Harris, *The Police Academy: An Inside View* (New York: John Wiley & Sons, 1973), 50.

77. Geoffrey P. Alpert and Roger G. Dunham, *Policing Urban America*, 3d ed. (Prospect Heights, Ill.: Waveland Press, 1992), 76.

78. O. W. Wilson, "Picking and Training Police and Traffic Officers," *The American City* (May 1930), 118.

79. Ibid.

80. Revel Denney, "The Plainest Plain-Clothesman," *The New Republic* (31 January 1955): 14–16.

81. J. Q. Wilson, "The Police and Their Problems."

82. A. Vollmer, "Police Progress in Practice and Theory," *The American City* 43 (September 1930).

83. "G Men Wage Unending War" and "Radio Patrol Most Effective Crime Deterrent," *Literary Digest* (3 August 1935): 18.

84. "Beating the Motorized Criminal with Swifter Motors," *Literary Digest* (12 November 1927): 71–75.

85. Max Weber, *Essays in Sociology*, ed. and trans. H. H. Gerth and C. Wright Mills (New York: Oxford University Press, 1946), 31.

86. A. Vollmer, "Improving Police Methods," *American City* 49 (1934), 13.

87. See A. Vollmer, " Police Progress in Practice and Theory" for new technologies.

88. Illustrative of the point is information from a 1939 magazine (Curtis Billings, "Policing Becomes a Profession," *The Rotarian* [June 1939]) of 48 men joining the Portland, Oregon, police force in the last two years, all were college men, most of them with degrees; that 130 college graduates (including two West Point men) were among the applicants for posts in the Indiana State Police Department recently (p. 27). . . . in 1928 the average Army alpha score for the entire [Wichita, Kansas] department was 79.73. This has risen year by year and now is 131.27. In 1928 the average education of the department was 9.14 years. In 1937 this average had risen to 11.82 (p. 29). Niederhoffer notes, "Of the 300 recruits appointed to the New York City Police Department in June 1940, more than half held college degrees" (Niederhoffer, *Behind the Shield*, 17).

89. Niederhoffer, *Behind the Shield*, 16.

90. Ibid.

91. G. F. Carte, "Changes in Public Attitudes toward the Police: A Comparison of 1938 and 1971 Surveys," *Journal of Police Science and Administration* 1 (1973): 182–200.

92. "Fewer and Better Police through Modern Equipment and Higher Standards," *American City* (November 1949), 17.

93. Chief Kelley of the Kansas City Police Department quoted in Gary M. Chamberlain, "How to Solve the Police Crisis—Part I," *The American City* (1971): 94–95, 98, 101.

94. President's Commission on Law Enforcement and Administration of Justice, *The Challenge of Crime in a Free Society* (New York: Avon Books, 1968), 267.

95. American Bar Association, Advisory Committee on the Police Function, *The Urban Police Function, Project on Standards for Criminal Justice* (Chicago: American Bar Association, 1973), 186–88.

96. Alpert and Dunham, *Policing Urban America*, 36–37.

97. John Harold McNamara, "Role Learning for Police Recruits," (Ph.D. diss. University of California, Los Angeles, 1967), 11.

98. Alpert and Dunham, *Policing Urban America*, 52.

99. J. H. McNamara, "Role Learning for Police Recruits," 258–262.

100. Martin, *Breaking and Entering: Policewomen on Patrol*, 83.

101. President's Commission on Law Enforcement and Administration of Justice, *The Challenge of Crime*, 120.

102. Ibid., 121.

103. Reiss, *The Police and the Public*, 96; Joyce L. Sichel et al., *Women on Patrol: A Pilot Study of Police Performance in New York City* (Washington, D. C.: GPO, 1978); J. Fox and R. Lundman, "Police Patrol Work: A Comparative Perspective," in *Police Behavior: A Sociological Perspective*, ed. R. Lundman (New York: Oxford University Press, 1980), same as "Problems and Strategies in Gaining Research Access in Police Departments," *Criminology* 12 (1974): 52–69; and Donald Black, *The Manners and Customs of the Police* (New York: Academic Press, 1980).

104. John A. Webster, "Police Time and Tasks" in *Thinking about Police: Contemporary Readings*, ed. Carl B. Klockars (New York: McGraw-Hill Book Company, 1983), 232–38.

105. E. Bittner, *The Functions of a Modern Society* (Chevy Chase, Md.: National Institute of Mental Health, 1970), 4.

106. J. Rubin, "Police Identity and the Police Role, in *The Police and the Community*, ed. R. F. Steadman, (Baltimore, Md.: Johns Hopkins University Press, 1972), 12–50.

107. Walker, *The Police in America*, 79.

108. D. Carter, A. Sapp, and D. Stephans, *The State of Police Education: Policy Direction for the 21st Century* (Washington, D.C.: Police Executive Research Reform, 1989), 42–43.

109. President's Commission on Law Enforcement and Administration of Justice, *Task Force Report*.

110. McNamara, "Role Learning for Police Recruits," 40.

111. Reiss, "Professionalization of the Police," 215.

112. Alpert and Dunham, *Policing Urban America*, 78.

113. H. W. More, *Special Topics in Policing* (Cincinnati: Anderson Publishing Company, 1991), 115.

114. Ibid.

115. Walker, *The Police in America*, 13.

116. President's Commission on Law Enforcement and Administration of Justice, *Task Force Report*, 123.

117. President's Commission on Law Enforcement and Administration of Justice, The Challenge of Crime, 261.

118. President's Commission on Law Enforcement and Administration of Justice, *Task Force Report*, 28.

119. Michigan State University, *A National Survey of Police and Community Relations: Report to the President's Commission on Law Enforcement and Administration of Justice, Field Survey V* (Washington, D.C.: GPO, 1967), 86–87.

120. Antony Michael Pate, "Community-Oriented Policing in Baltimore," in *Police and Policing: Contemporary Issues*, ed. Dennis Jay Kenney (New York: Praeger, 1989), 112–35; M. W. Field, "Evaluating Police Services through Citizen Surveys," *Police Chief* 57, no. 10 (1990): 69–72; L. P. Brown, "Violent Crime and Community Involvement: Community Policing," *Vital Speeches* 58, no. 6 (1992): 182–84; C. A. Gruber, "Elgin's Resident Officer Program Makes a Difference," *Police Chief* 60, no. 5 (1993): 30; "New York's Experience," *CQ Researcher* 3 no. 5 (1993): 110; Q. C. Thurman, A. Giacomazzi, and P. Bogen, "Cops, Kids, and Community Policing: An Assessment of a Community Policing Demonstration Project," *Crime and Delinquency* 39, no. 4 (1993): 554–64; H. Idelson, "Community Policing Concept Gets a National Tryout," *Congressional Quarterly Weekly Report* 52, no. 10 (1994), 602; P. Kim, "Specialized Unit Helps Overcome Cultural Barriers," *Police Chief* 61, no. 5 (1994), 50; S. Margolis, "Blythe Street Team Makes an Impact, *Police Chief* 61, no. 10 (1994), 70; and R. Moran and B. Bucqueroux, "Have the Benefits of Community Policing Been Oversold?" *CQ Researcher* 5, no. 44 (1995), 1057.

121. Lisa M. Riechers and Roy R. Roberg, "Community Policing: A Critical Review of Underlying Assumptions," *Journal of Police Science and Administration* 17, no. 2 (1990): 105–14,

122. G. J. Kelling and W. J. Bratton, "Implementing Community Policing: The Administrative Problem," *Perspectives on Policing* (Washington, D.C.: National Institute of Justice, U. S. Department of Justice, 1993); L. Sherman, C. Milton, and T. Kelley, *Team Policing: Seven Case Studies* (Washington, D.C.: Police Foundation, 1973); J. H. Skolnick and D. H. Bayley, *The New Blue Line: Police Innovation In Six American Cities* (New York: Free Press, 1986).

123. Walker, *The Police in America*, 90–92.

124. W. A. Kerstetter, "Patrol Decentralization: An Assessment," *Journal of Police Science and Administration* 9, no. 1 (March 1981): 48–60.

125. Kelling and Bratton, "Implementing Community Policing."

126. Sherman, Milton, and Kelley, *Team Policing*.

127. Antony Pate, "Experimenting with Foot Patrol: The Newark Experience," in *Community Crime Prevention: Does It Work?*, ed. Dennis P. Rosenbaum (Beverly Hills: Sage Publications, 1986): 137–56.

128. Robert Trojanowicz, "Evaluating a Neighborhood Foot Patrol Program: The Flint,

Michigan Project," in *Community Crime Prevention: Does It Work?*, ed. Dennis P. Rosenbaum (Beverly Hills: Sage Publications, 1986): 157–78.

129. Herman Goldstein, "Improving Policing: A Problem-Oriented Approach," *Crime and Delinquency*, (April 1979): 236–58.

130. Dennis P. Rosenbaum and Arthur J. Lurigio, "An Inside Look at Community Policing Reform: Definitions, Organizational Changes, and Evaluation Findings," *Crime and Delinquency* 40 (1994): 299–314.

131. Goldstein, "Improving Policing," 246.

132. H. Goldstein, *The New Policing: Confronting Complexity* (National Institute of Justice, U.S. Department of Justice, 1993), 3.

133. J. Song, "No White-Feathered Crows: Chinese Immigrants' and Vietnamese Refugees' Adaptation to American Legal Institutions," (Ph.D. diss., University of California, Irvine, 1988).

134. President's Commission on Law Enforcement and Administration of Justice, *The Challenge of Crime*, 34.

135. Stephen D. Mastrofski, "Community Policing as Reform: A Cautionary Tale," in *Community Policing: Rhetoric or Reality*, ed. Jack R. Greene and Stephen D. Mastrofski (New York: Praeger, 1988).

136. H. Goldstein, "Police Discretion Not to Invoke the Criminal Process: Low-Visibility Decisions in the Administration of Justice," *Yale Law Journal* 69 (1960).

137. D. Dodson, speech delivered at Michigan State University, in *Proceedings of the Institute of Police-Community Relations*, The School of Police Administration and Public Safety, Michigan State University, East Lansing (15–20 May 1955), cited in Niederhoffer, *Behind the Shield*, 75.

138. P. Jesilow and D. Parsons, "Community Policing as Peacemaking," *Police and Society* 10 (2000): 163–82.

139. J. H. Skolnick and D. H. Bayley, "Theme and Variation in Community Policing," in *Crime in Justice: A Review of Research*, vol. 10, ed. M. Tonry and N. Morris (Chicago: University of Chicago Press, 1990).

140. A. I. Schwartz and N. C. Sumner, *The Cincinnati Team Policing Experiment: A Summary Report* (Washington, D.C.: Police Foundation, 1977), 7.

141. Walker, *The Police in America*, 95.

142. Jesilow and Parsons, "Community Policing as Peacemaking."

143. D. Parsons, "Police Officers' Perceptions: A Comparative Study by Gender and Organization," (Ph.D. diss., University of California, Irvine, 1996).

144. Riechers and Roberg, "Community Policing," 111.

145. M. Banton, *The Policemen in the Community* (London, Tavistock, 1964); M. Cain, *Society and the Policeman's Role* (London: Routledge, 1973); R. Graef, *Talking Blues* (London: Collins, 1989); and W. A. Westley, *Violence and the Police* (Cambridge, Mass.: Massachusetts Institute of Technology Press, 1970).

146. A. Cardarelli, J. McDevitt, and K. Baum, "The Rhetoric and Reality of Community Policing in Small and Median-Sized Cities and Towns," *Policing: An International Journal of Police Strategies and Management* 21, no. 3 (1998): 397–415; and Jack R. Greene and Stephen D. Mastrofski, eds., *Community Policing: Rhetoric or Reality* (New York: Praeger, 1988).

147. P. Jesilow, J. Meyer, D. Parsons, and W. Tegeler, "Evaluating Problem-Oriented Policing: A Quasi-Experiment," *Policing An International Journal of Police Strategies and Management* 21, no. 3 (1998): 449–64; and P. Jesilow, J. Meyer, and N. Namazzi, "Public Attitudes Towards the Police," *American Journal of the Police* 14, no. 2 (1995): 67–88.

148. Jesilow et al, 1996, 1998; and Stephen Mastrofski, Roger B. Parks, and Robert E. Worden, "Community Policing in Action Lessons from an Observation Study," *National Institute of Justice, Research in Progress Seminar Series* (June 1998), 2.

149. D. H. Bayley, *Police for the Future* (New York: Oxford University Press, 1994); D. H. Bayley, *What Works in Policing* (New York: Oxford University Press, 1998); P. Jesilow et al., "Evaluating Problem-Oriented Policing: A Quasi-Experiment," *Policing: An International Journal of Police Strategies and Management*, 21, no. 3 (1998): 449–64; and P. Jesilow, J. Meyer, and N. Namazzi, "Public Attitudes towards the Police," *American Journal of the Police* 19, no. 2 (1995): 67–88.

150. Albert Reiss Jr., for example, found that 58 percent of requests for police service involved criminal behavior according to citizen perceptions. But from the police position, only 17 percent of the calls involved criminal conduct (Reiss, *The Police and the Public*, 73).

151. Reiss, *The Police and the Public*, 77.

152. Jesilow, Meyer, and Namazzi, "Public Attitudes towards the Police."

153. P. Manning, *Police Work* (Cambridge, Mass.: Massachusetts Institute of Technology Press, 1977).

154. G. L. Kelling et al., *The Kansas City Preventive Patrol Experiment: A Summary Report* (Washington, D.C.: Police Foundation, 1974); Antony M. Pate, "Experimenting with Foot Patrol: The Newark Experience" in *Community Crime Prevention: Does It Work?* ed. Dennis P. Rosenbaum (Beverly Hills: Sage Publication, 1986), 137–56; and President's Commission on Law Enforcement and Administration of Justice, *Task Force Report*

155. National Commission on Law Observance and Law Enforcement, *Report on the Police* (Washington, D.C.: GPO, 1931), 19.

## Chapter 2: Women in Policing: A Tale of Cultural Conformity

1. Mary E. Hamilton, *The Policewoman: Her Service and Ideals* (New York: F. A. Stokes, 1924), 5.

2. L. K. Lord, "A Comparison of Male and Female Peace Officers: Stereotypic Perceptions of Women and Women Peace Officers," *Journal of Police Science and Administration*, 14, no. 2 (1986): 83–97.

3. Early writings on women in policing sometimes refer to "policewomen" and sometimes to "police women." We will use the term "policewomen" unless we are quoting.

4. Kerry Segrave, *Policewomen: A History* (Jefferson, N.C.: McFarland and Company, 1995), 24–25.

5. Dorothy Moses Shultz, *From Social Worker to Crimefighters: Women in United States Municipal Policing* (Westport, Conn.: Praeger, 1995), 2.

6. Segrave, *Policewomen*, 25.

7. Mary E. Odem, *Delinquent Daughters* (Chapel Hill, N.C.: University of North Carolina Press, 1995).

8. A. Platt, *The Child Savers: The Invention of Delinquency*, 2d ed. (Chicago: University of Chicago Press, 1977).

9. Segrave, *Policewomen*, 25–26.

10. Max Weber, *The Protestant Ethic and The Spirit of Capitalism*, trans. Talcott Parsons (Hammersmith, London: Harper Collins Academic, 1991).

11. Maudee Miner, "The Police Woman and the Girl Problem," round table held at the National Conference on Social Welfare, in *Proceedings of the National Conference of Social Work*, 46th annual session, Atlantic City (1–8 June 1919): 134–42.

12. Bertha H. Smith, "The Policewoman," *Good Housekeeping* 52 (March 1911): 296–98.

13. Ibid.

14. Alice Stebbens Wells, "Women on the Police Force," *The American City* 8 (April 1913), 401.

15. B. H. Smith, "The Policewoman," 296.

16. Ibid.

17. Ibid., 298.

18. Peter Horne, *Women in Law Enforcement* (Springfield, Ill.: Charles C. Thomas, 1980), 29.

19. Miner, "The Police Woman and the Girl Problem," 134.

20. Ibid., 135.

21. C. Feinman, *Women in the Criminal Justice System* (New York: Praeger, 1980), 72–73.

22. Miner, "The Police Woman and the Girl Problem," 134.

23. E. A. O'Gary, "Policewomen and Their Work," *The American City* (January 1919), 59.

24. Ibid.

25. M. E. Hamilton, *The Policewoman*, 4.

26. E. L. Hutzel, *The Policewomen's Handbook* (New York: Columbia University Press, 1933), 3.

27. H. M. Walbrook, "Women Police and Their Work," *Nineteenth Century and After* 85 (February 1919): 377–82; Mina C. VanWinkle, "The Policewoman as Socializing Agency," *The American City* 34, (February 1926); and "The Police-Woman Is Marching On," *The American City* 9 (November 1914), 403.

28. Mary E. Hamilton, "Woman's Place in the Police Department," *The American City* 32 (February 1925): 194.

29. Walbrook, "Women Police and Their Work," 382.

30. Virginia M. Murray, "Policewomen in Detroit," *The American City* 25, no. 3 (September 1921): 209–210.

31. Louise Brownlow, "Police and the Cause of Crime," *The American City* 36 (June 1927), 797.

32. Moss, "National Danger from Police Corruption," 470–80; and Hamilton, *The Policewoman*, 5.

33. E. D. Graper, *American Police Administration* (New York: Macmillan Company, 1921), 226–33.
34. Ibid., 228–29.
35. Helen D. Pigeon, "Policewomen and Public Recreation," *The American City* (October 1927): 448–50.
36. Miner, "The Police Woman and the Girl Problem," 136.
37. Ibid.
38. Hamilton, *The Policewoman*, 9.
39. Hamilton, "Woman's Place in the Police Department," 194.
40. Walbrook, "Women Police and Their Work." 377.
41. Segrave, *Policewomen*, 20.
42. Shultz, *From Social Worker to Crimefighters*, 80.
43. Ibid.
44. Ibid., 79.
45. Segrave, *Policewomen*, 111–12.
46. Walker, *The Police in America*, 16.
47. Ibid.
48. Martin, *Breaking and Entering: Police Women on Patrol*; and More, *Special Topics in Policing*.
49. "Salaries and Working Conditions in Police Departments," *Monthly Labor Review* 52 (April 1941): 817–26.
50. Margaret M. Boyd, "The Role of the Police Woman," in Police Yearbook: *Proceedings of the 59th Annual Conference of the International Association of Chiefs of Police* (Washington, D.C.: International Association of Chiefs of Police, 1953), 148–150.
51. "More Cities Employ Policewomen," *The American City* (February 1948), 17.
52. President's Commission on Law Enforcement and Administration of Justice, *The Challenge of Crime*, 125.
53. Theresa Melchionne, "Where Policewomen Are Better than Men," *The American City* 75 (April 1960), 161.
54. Ibid.
55. "Women Are Tougher as Traffic Police," *The American City* 69 (May 1954), 183.
56. Ibid.
57. "Girls Make Better Radio Dispatchers," *The American City* 68 (November 1953), 149.
58. President's Commission on Law Enforcement and Administration of Justice, *The Challenge of Crime*, 125.
59. R. L. Warner and D. S. Steel, "Affirmative Action in Times of Fiscal Stress and Changing Value Priorities: The Case of Women in Policing," *Public Personnel Management*, 18, no. 3 (1989): 291–309.
60. Segrave, Policewomen, 116; and Mary Abrecht with Barbara Lang Stern, *The Making of a Woman Cop* (New York: William Morrow and Co., 1976).
61. Marion Morse Wood, "Stress and the Corporate Woman," in *Stress and the Organization*, ed. Richard H. Davis (Los Angeles: University of Southern California Press, 1979), 33–44.

62. E. Durkheim, *The Division of Labor in Society*, trans. W. D. Halls (New York: Free Press, 1984).

63. For evidence of discrimination against female officers, see Martin, *Breaking and Entering: Policewomen on Patrol*; Segrave, *Policewomen*, 117–33; Douglas S. Drummond, "Law Enforcement: The Cultural Impact on an Occupation" (Ph.D. diss., August Vollmer University, 1988); and Connie Fletcher, *Breaking and Entering: Women Cops Talk about Life in the Ultimate Men's Club* (New York: Harper Collins Publishers, 1995).

64. "The Policemen," *Saturday Evening Post* 13, no. 238 (March 1965): 100.

65. Edward F. Murphy, "Men in Blue," *New York Times Magazine* (6 March 1966): 52.

66. "The 'War Against the Police'—Officers Tell Their Story," *U.S. News & World Report* (26 October 1970): 82–86.

67. Louis M. Brown, "When Should You Call the Police?" *Better Homes and Gardens* 50 (March 1972): 78.

68. Alpert and Dunham, *Policing Urban America*; Gerald Caiden, *Police Revitalization* (Lexington, Mass.: Lexington Books, 1977); "The Female Fuzz," *Newsweek* 80 (23 October 1972): 172; and Segrave, *Policewomen*.

69. Illustrative of this view was the beating of Rodney King by officers of the LAPD following a freeway chase. Sergeant Stacey Koon initially took charge of the situation because he believed that Melanie Singer, the California Highway Patrol officer who was the first to confront King, might use the gun she had drawn (Lou Cannon, *Official Negligence: How Rodney King and the Riots Changed Los Angeles and the LAPD* [New York: Times Book, 1997]).

70. The men had tales of women that indicated lack of physical strength. One department in 1957 "had to send back twenty-one snub-nosed .38-caliber pistols it had ordered for its female officers after a trial shoot proved that none of the policewomen was strong enough to pull the trigger" (P. Steiner, "Policeman's Lot," *New York Times Magazine* [September 29, 1957]: 84).

71. "The Female Fuzz," 172.

72. More, *Special Topics in Policing*, 114.

73. Caiden, *Police Revitalization*.

74. Martin, *Breaking and Entering: Policewomen on Patrol*, 92.

75. More, *Special Topics in Policing*, 115.

76. E.g., see P. Bloch and D. Anderson, *Policewomen on Patrol: Final Report* (Washington, D.C.: Police Foundation, 1974); M. T. Charles, "The Performance and Socialization of Female Recruits in the Michigan State Police Training Academy," *Journal of Police Science and Administration* 9 (1981): 209–23; and C. A. Jones, "Predicting the Effectiveness of Police Officers" (master's thesis, San Diego State University, 1987).

77. M. T. Charles, "Women in Policing: The Physical Aspect," *Journal of Police Science and Administration* 10, no. 2 (1982): 194–205; S. Gross, "Women Becoming Cops: Developmental Issues and Solutions," *Police Chief* 51 (1984): 32–35; C. H. Milton, *Women in Policing* (Washington, D.C.: Police Foundation, 1972); and Sichel et al., *Women on Patrol*.

78. Ester Koenig, "An Overview of Attitudes toward Women in Law Enforcement,"

*Public Administrative Review* 38 (1978): 267–75; L. W. Sherman, "An Evaluation of Policewomen on Patrol in a Suburban Police Department," *Journal of Police Science and Administration* 3 (1975): 434–38; and Sichel et al., *Women on Patrol.*

79. *Report of the Independent Commission on the Los Angeles Police Department* (Los Angeles: Independent Commission on the Los Angeles Police Department, 1991).

80. Other possible explanations exist for lower arrest rates among female officers. They may indicate "that women were not taking enough initiative." Alternatively, they might indicate that women handled the situations better than male officers, if the latter caused incidents to escalate into confrontations that resulted in unnecessary arrests. A third explanation is that male veterans, coupled with female rookies, were more likely "to take charge of the situation and take credit for arrests more frequently than with male rookies" (see Susan E. Martin). "Female officers on the Move? A Status Report on Women in Policing," in *Critical Issues in Policing: Contemporary Readings*, ed. Roger G. Dunham and Geoffrey P. Alpert (Prospect Heights, Ill.: Waveland Press, 1989), pp. 312–30.

81. The officers were matched for "length of time on force, patrol experience, and type of precinct" (Sichel et al., *Women on Patrol*, iii).

82. Ibid.

83. Ibid., 53–54.

84. Ibid., 60.

85. Ibid., 61.

86. Ibid., 63.

87. See generally Wood, "Stress and the Corporate Woman."

88. Jessie Bernard, "Models for the Relationship between the World of Women and the World of Men," in *Research in Social Movements, Conflicts and Change*, ed. Lewis Kriesberg (Greenwich, Conn.: J.A.I. Press, 1978): 291–331.

89. T. A. Johnson, G. E. Misner, and L. P. Brown, *The Police and Society: An Environment for Collaboration and Confrontation* (Englewood Cliffs, N.J.: Prentice-Hall, 1981), 240; and Martin, *Breaking and Entering: Policewomen on Patrol*, 86.

90. Martin, *Breaking and Entering: Policewomen on Patrol*, 12; see also M. Young, *An Inside Job* (Oxford: Clarendon Press, 1991), 193. Young argues that women who do "penetrate this masculine world can only ever be partially successful and will often have to subsume 'male characteristics' to achieve even a limited social acceptability."

## CHAPTER 3: HOW THIS STUDY WAS CONDUCTED

1. Sichel et al., *Women on Patrol.*

2. J. A. Davis, "Perspectives of Policewomen in Texas and Oklahoma," *Journal of Police Science and Administration* 12, no. 4 (1984): 395–403; N. K. Grant, C. Garrison, and K. McCormick, "Perceived Utilization, Job Satisfaction and

Advancement of Policewomen," *Public Personnel Management* 19, no. 2 (1990): 147–54; L. K. Lord, "A Comparison of Male and Female Peace Officers"; J. McGeorge and J. A. Wolfe, "A Comparison of Attitudes between Men and Women Police Officers: A Preliminary Analysis," *Criminal Justice Review* 1 (1976): 21–33; M. S. Meagher and N. A. Yentes, "Choosing a Career in Policing: A Comparison of Male and Female Perceptions," *Journal of Police Science and Administration* 14, no. 4 (1986): 320–27; E. D. Poole and M. R. Pogrebin, "Factors Affecting the Decision to Remain in Policing: A Study of Women Officers," *Journal of Police Science and Administration* 16 (1988): 49–55.

3.   N. Alex, *New York Cops Talk Back*; D. S. Drummond, "Law Enforcement"; Fletcher, *Breaking and Entering: Women Cops Talk about Life in the Ultimate Men's Club*; Frances Heidensohn, *Women in Control? The Role of Women in Law Enforcement* (Oxford: Clarendon Press, 1992); Martin, *Breaking and Entering: Policewomen on Patrol*; Milton, *Women in Policing*; William Ker Muir Jr., *Police: Streetcorner Politicians* (Chicago: University of Chicago Press, 1977); and J. G. Wexler and D. D. Logan, "Sources of Stress among Women Police Officers," *Journal of Police Science and Administration* 11 (1983): 46–53.

4.   Dan Weikel, "Two Irvine Female Officers Claim Sexual Harassment and Bias," *Los Angeles Times*, 19 November 1992, A38, col. 5.

5.   "City Offers Women Awards Not to File Sex Harassment Lawsuits," *Los Angeles Times*, 21 January 1993, A30, col. 4.

6.   D. A. Smith, "The Organizational Context of Legal Control," *Criminology* 22 (1984): 19–38.

7.   D. A. Smith, "Crime in Cities: The Effects of Formal and Informal Social Control," in *Communities and Crime*, ed. A. J. Reiss Jr. and M. Tonry (Chicago: University of Chicago Press, 1986): 313–41.

8.   James Q. Wilson, *Varieties of Police Behavior* (Boston: Harvard University Press, 1968).

9.   Ibid., 140.

10.   Ibid.

11.   Ibid.

12.   Ibid., 173.

13.   Ibid., 200.

14.   Female officers, due to their few numbers, were frequently solicited by their superiors to participate. This was done in order to meet our request for a matched number of male and female participants from the same department. All officers were briefed by us that their participation was optional and that they could decline to take part, even in the middle of an interview. It was our original intention to compare the answers of matched groups of male and female officers by assignment and longevity. The small number of female officers, particularly those with higher ranks and extended service, made gaining a matched group impossible.

15.   U.S. Department of Justice, *Bureau of Justice Statistics Source Book* (Washington, D.C.: GPO, 1990).

16. Alpert and Dunham, *Policing Urban America*; H. T. Buckner, "The Police: The Culture of a Social Control Agency," (Ph.D., diss., University of California, Berkeley, 1967); William A. Westley, "The Police: A Sociological Study of Law, Custom and Morality" (Ph.D. diss., University of Chicago, 1951); and Mark Baker, *Cops: Their Lives in Their Own Words* (New York, Simon and Schuster, 1985).

17. M. Baker, *Cops*, 13.

## CHAPTER 4: WHY WOULD ANYONE WANT TO BE A POLICE OFFICER?

1. Brown, *Rockefeller Medicine Men*; and Paul Starr, *The Social Transformation of American Medicine* (New York: Basic Books, 1982).

2. Haller, "Chicago Cops," 3; and Miller, *Cops and Bobbies*, 152–53.

3. Walker, *The Police in America*, 8 (Walker cites Robert K. Merton, *Social Theory and Social Structure* [New York: Free Press, 1968]: 126–36).

4. Ibid., 54; Doris Graber, "Evaluating Crime Fighting Policies: Media Images and Public Perspective," in *Evaluating Alternative Law Enforcement Policies*, ed. Ralph Baker and Fred A. Meyer Jr. (Lexington, Mass.: Lexington Books, 1979): 179–99; John H. Culver and Kenton L. Knight, "Evaluating T.V. Impressions of Law Enforcement Roles," in *Evaluating Alternative Law Enforcement Policies*, ed. Ralph Baker and Fred A. Meyer, Jr. (Lexington, Mass.: Lexington Books, 1979): 201–12; Stephen Arons and Ethan Katsch, "How T.V. Cops Flout the Law," *Saturday Review* (19 March 1977): 13; Bittner, "The Police Charge," 28–41; Timothy N. Oettmeier and Lee P. Brown, "Developing a Neighborhood-Oriented Policing Style," in *Community Policing: Rhetoric or Reality*, ed. Jack R. Greene and Stephen D. Mastrofski (New York: Praeger, 1988): 121–34; and Jay Livingston, "Crime and the Media: Myths and Reality," *USA Today (The United States of Violence: A Special Section)*(May 1994): 40–42.

5. McNamara, "Role Learning for Police Recruits," 283–84.

6. Heidensohn, *Women in Control?* 75.

7. Walker, *The Police in America*, 12.

8. Buckner, "The Police," 248; and W. A. Westley, "The Police: A Sociological Study."

9. Alan W. Benner, "Psychological Screening of Police Applicants," in *Critical Issues in Policing Contemporary Readings*, ed. Roger G. Dunham and Geoffrey P. Alpert (Prospect Heights, Ill.: Waveland Press, 1989), 72–86; and H. T. Buckner, "The Police," 253.

10. Benner, "Psychological Screening of Police Applicants," 77; and Buckner, "The Police," 253.

11. Buckner, "The Police," 253; and Westley, "The Police: A Sociology Study," 187.

12. Buckner, "The Police," 253.

13. Oettmeier and Brown, "Developing a Neighborhood-Oriented Policing Style," 130.

14. Niederhoffer, *Behind the Shield*, 17.
15. O. W. Wilson, "Picking and Training Police and Traffic Officers," 116.
16. Ibid.
17. President's Commission on Law Enforcement and Administration of Justice, *Task Force Report*, 36.
18. During this period, recruitment of officers was particularly problematic. The status of the police was in decline. Their relationship to the urban riots and their handling of antiwar demonstrations reduced their standing among minorities and college students—the very groups from which they wanted to draw members.
19. Marshall Spiegel, "Pros & Cons on Joining the Police," *Mechanix Illustrated* 67 (July 1971): 41–43, 102.
20. See Roger Brown, *Social Psychology* (New York: Free Press, 1965) for a good review of early studies.
21. Benner, "Psychological Screening of Police Applicants."
22. Alpert and Dunham, *Policing Urban America*, 37.
23. Alex, New York Cops Talk Back; and Martin, *Breaking and Entering: Policewomen on Patrol*.
24. McNamara, *Role Learning for Police Recruits*; Niederhoffer, Behind the Shield, 38; D. H. Bayley and H. Mendelsohn, *Minorities and the Police*, 31; Westley, *Violence and the Police*; Harris, *The Police Academy*, 16–17; Alex, New York *Cops Talk Back*, 22; Bittner, "The Police Charge," 39; and John Van Maanen, "Observations on the Making of Policemen," *Human Organization* 32 (1973): 407–18.
25. McNamara, *Role Learning for Police Recruits*, 164; Niederhoffer, *Behind the Shield*, 41. An exception occurred during the depression, when patrolman was an enviable job. Patrolmen earned $3,000 a year and could own houses and automobiles. They were middle class and they were never laid off. (Niederhoffer, *Behind the Shield*, 16.)
26. Alex, *New York Cops Talk Back*, 23–25.
27. U.S. Department of Justice, Bureau of Justice Statistics, *Local Police Departments 1997*, NCJ 173429 (Washington, D.C.: U.S. Department of Justice, 2000), 7, table 10.
28. Heidensohn, *Women in Control?* 126.
29. Abrecht, *The Making of a Woman Cop*, 82–83.
30. Alpert and Dunham, *Policing Urban America*, 40.
31. For example, see Martin, *Breaking and Entering: Policewomen on Patrol*.
32. Shultz, *From Social Worker to Crimefighters*, 5.
33. Martin, *Breaking and Entering: Policewomen on Patrol*, 65; Heidensohn, *Women in Control?* 162; and Shultz, *From Social Worker to Crimefighters*, 5.
34. Larry A. Taylor, "How Your Tax Dollars Support the Boy Scouts of America," *Humanist* 55, no. 5 (September–October 1995): 6–14.
35. To some extent, the figures furnished here are used only to render an idea of the relative size of the categories. Putting officers into one category or another is somewhat misleading. Our interviews allowed officers to elaborate, and they

supplied several explanations. Surveys, perhaps, might better lend themselves to quantitative analyses if officers were forced to pick one reason or another, but we would have lost the richness of their stories.

## CHAPTER 5: TRAINING

1. Silas Bent, "Police Training in New York," *Harper's Weekly* 61 (25 December 1915), 610.
2. "Policing as a Career for Young Women," *Education for Victory*, (1 October 1943), 11.
3. Douthit, "August Vollmer, Berkeley's First Chief of Police," 104.
4. Ibid.
5. Haller, "Chicago Cops," 305.
6. Bent, "Police Training in New York," 610.
7. N. D. Baker, "Law, Police, and Social Problems," 16.
8. O. W. Wilson, "Picking and Training Police and Traffic Officers," 117.
9. Ibid.
10. Curtis Billings, "Policing Becomes a Profession," *The Rotarian* (June 1939): 27–30.
11. Clift, "Police Training," 116.
12. Ibid; "Crime's $20 Billion Calls for More Police," *Public Safety* (1957).
13. President's Commission on Law Enforcement and Administration of Justice, *Task Force Report*, 138.
14. Survey of the International Association of Chiefs of Police, Washington D.C., 1966; President's Commission on Law Enforcement and Administration of Justice, *Task Force Report*, 139.
15. Thomas Shaw, "The Evolution of Police Recruit Training," *FBI Law Enforcement Bulletin* 61 (January 1992): 2–6.
16. President's Commission on Law Enforcement and Administration of Justice, *Task Force Report*.
17. Buckner, "The Police"; and McNamara, *Role Learning for Police Recruits*.
18. Robert Merton, "The Bureaucratic Structure and Personality," *Social Theory and Social Structure* (New York: Free Press of Glencoe, 1957): 195–206; and Howard S. Becker, *Boys in White: Student Culture in Medical School* (Chicago: University of Chicago Press, 1961.
19. McNamara, *Role Learning for Police Recruits*, 11.
20. Harris, *The Police Academy*, 86–87, 91; Van Maanen,"Observations on the Making of Policemen," 391.
21. Van Maaren, "Observations on the Making of Policemen," 390.
22. McNamara, *Role Learning for Police Recruits*, 296.
23. Niederhoffer, *Behind the Shield: The Police in Urban Society*, 46.
24. McNamara, *Role Learning for Police Recruits*, 258–59.
25. Ibid., 262.
26. Van Maanen, "Observations on the Making of Policemen," 392.
27. Ibid. Becker found the same separation between medical school teachers and their students (Becker, *Boys in White*).

28. Durkheim, *The Division of Labor in Society*.

29. Harris, *The Police Academy*; and Abrecht, *The Making of a Woman Cop*, 25.

30. Alpert and Dunham, *Policing Urban America*.

31. Buckner, "The Police," 390.

32. Alex, New York Cops Talk Back.

33. Harris, The Police Academy, 56.

34. Van Maanen, "Observations on the Making of Policemen," 391; and Harris, The Police Academy, 164–65.

35. President's Commission on Law Enforcement and Administration of Justice, Task Force Report, 35.

36. Muir, *Police: Streetcorner Politicians*; and Shaw, "The Evolution of Police Recruit Training," 5.

37. David E. Barlow and Melissa Hickman Barlow, "Cultural Diversity Training in Criminal Justice: A Progressive or Conservative Reform? (Engaging Criminal Justice)," *Social Justice* 20, no. 3–4 (fall–winter 1993): 69; President's Commission on Law Enforcement and Administration of Justice, *Task Force Report*.

38. Barlow and Barlow, "Cultural Diversity Training in Criminal Justice."

39. Michael P. Brown, "Multicultural Training for Police: A National Survey," *Police Chief* 62, no. 11 (November 1995): 44.

40. Glenford J. Shibley, "Teaching Officers to Serve Seniors," *FBI Law Enforcement Bulletin* 64, no. 1 (January 1995): 23.

41. Stephen M. Hennessey, "Achieving Cultural Competence," *Police Chief* 60, no. 8 (August, 1993): 46.

42. Harris, *The Police Academy*, 151.

43. Barlow and Barlow, "Cultural Diversity Training in Criminal Justice."

44. Sabina Leigh Burton, "Cultural Diversity in Law Enforcement: The Effects of Academy and Field Training" (Ph.D. diss., University of California, Irvine, 1996).

45. Ibid., 144–45.

46. Ibid., 139–41.

47. Ibid., 75.

48. Ibid., 156–59.

49. Evelyn B. Schaffer, *Community Policing* (London: Kroom Helm, 1980), 101.

50. Burton, "Cultural Diversity in Law Enforcement," 6.

51. Shaw, "The Evolution of Police Recruit Training," 4.

52. Minority cadets may identify with their own ethnic groups. In one study, recruits from single minority areas favored policing their own; recruits from multicultural neighborhoods did not have an ethnic preference (Burton, *Cultural Diversity in Law Enforcement*, 98, 119–123).

53. Burton, *Cultural Diversity in Law Enforcement*, 125.

54. Schaffer, *Community Policing*, 102.

55. D. H. Bayley, "Community Policing," 225–38.

56. K. D. Codish, "The New Haven Police Academy: Putting a Sacred Cow Out to Pasture," *Police Chief* 63, no. 11 (November 1996): 40.

57. Oettmeier and Brown, "Developing a Neighborhood-Oriented Policing Style."

58. James J. Ness, "The Relevance of Basic Law Enforcement Training—Does the Curriculum Prepare Recruits for Police Work: A Survey Study," *Journal of Criminal Justice* 19, no. 2 (March–April 1991): 181–93; and Shaw, "The Evolution of Police Recruit Training," 5.

59. Rene A. Browett, "Managing Police Basic Training Curriculum," *FBI Law Enforcement Bulletin* 59, no. 3 (March 1990): 19–20.

60. Ibid., 23.

61. Lois Pilant, "Weapons and Accessories Selection," *Police Chief* 62, no. 2 (February 1995): 36.

62. James M. Crotty, "Holster an Empty Weapon—A Routine Command with Potentially Fatal Consequences," *Police Chief* 60, no. 8 (August 1993): 34.

63. Harold Garfinkel, "Conditions of Successful Degradation Ceremonies," *American Journal of Sociology* 61 (1956): 520–24.

64. Bloch and Anderson, *Policewomen on Patrol*; Charles, "The Performance and Socialization of Female Recruits," 209–23; and C. A. Jones, "Predicting the Effectiveness of Police Officers."

65. Becker, *Boys in White*.

## CHAPTER 6: ON THE STREET

1. H. L. Mencken, "Recollections of Notable Cops," in *Thinking about Police: Contemporary Readings*, ed. Carl B. Klockars (New York: McGraw-Hill Book Company, 1983), 8–11.

2. Miller, *Cops and Bobbies*, 148.

3. Vollmer, "Police Progress in Practice and Theory," 112.

4. N. D. Baker, "Law, Police, and Social Problems,"14; and John Barker Waite, "Protection from the Police," *Atlantic Monthly*, 138 (August 1926): 162–67.

5. Ernest Jerome Hopkins, "The Lawless Arm of the Law," *Atlantic Monthly* 148 (1931): 279–87.

6. Buckner, "The Police," 344.

7. G. F. Carte and E. H. Carte, *Police Reform in the United States*.

8. Billings, "Policing Becomes a Profession," 30.

9. Hopkins, "The Lawless Arm of the Law."

10. McNamara, "Role Learning for Police Recruits," xi; and Niederhoffer, Behind the Shield, 53.

11. Van Maanen,"Observations on the Making of Policemen," 392.

12. Ibid., 393.

13. Alpert and Dunham, *Policing Urban America*, 98; Muir, *Police: Streetcorner Politicians*; Rubin, "Police Identity and the Police Role"; Van Maanen, "Observations on the Making of Policemen," 396; Alex, *New York Cops Talk Back*, 11–12; Harris, *The Police Academy*, 134; "Mike Jr.: 'The Bullet Missed My Head by an Inch or Two,'" *Life* 69 no. 13 (1970): 32–37.

14. Herbert Ginsburg, *Piaget's Theory of Intellectual Development*, 2d ed. (Englewood Cliffs, N.J.: Prentice-Hall, 1979).

15 More, *Special Topics in Policing*, 172.

16. J. Bierhorst, *The Mythology of North America* (New York: William Morrow and

Company, 1985). Due to their emphasis on oral history, many Native American stories simply recount an event (especially creation myths) or the gifting of a song or tradition to the people. Of course, there are also stories in which characters either overcome obstacles or fail to do so (hence, the lesson when Coyote lost his eyes due to failing to obey the Medicine Rabbit's order not to send his eyes up onto the treetops more than three times in a given day). These stories serve more as charter stories, however, which contain directions for living. Some Native American stories can be considered "boring" to outsiders, especially those that serve historical or ceremonial purposes. One primary difference might be that Native Americans do not consider their stories to be fictional, even the more fantastic ones. Since they serve more than entertaining functions, they do not have to be exciting for the listener.

17. Skolnick and Bayley, *The New Blue Line*, 14.
18. Van Maanen, "Observations on the Making of Policemen," 394.
19. Heidensohn, *Women in Control?* 142–43.
20. Philip Ennis, "Crime, Victims, and the Police," *Trans-Action* 4 (1967): 36–44.
21. Buckner, "The Police," 207.
22. Ibid., 208.
23. Between 1980 and 1989, about 800 officers were murdered: 328 (41 percent) while making arrests; 132 (16 percent) while responding to disturbances (56 when called to a family disturbance; 76 in other disturbance calls, such as bar fights), 115 (14 percent) while investigating suspicious persons; 108 in traffic pursuits or stops; 70 in ambushes; 34 while handling or transporting prisoners; 13 by mentally deranged suspects; and 1 in a civil disturbance (United States Department of Justice, *Law Enforcement Officers Killed and Assaulted* [Washington D.C.: GPO, 1990]).
24. Bayley and Mendelsohn, *Minorities and the Police*, 52–53.
25. It may or may not be significant that both of these officers worked as FTOs with the department. Their answers may represent an ideology that is being passed to neophytes or, from the view of a cynic, they may be administrative platitudes provided for consumption by outsiders.
26. Alpert and Dunham, *Policing Urban America*, 76.
27. Ibid.
28. Alex, *New York Cops Talk Back*, 56–58.
29. Cherrie Tsai (unpublished student manuscript, University of California, Irvine, 1997).
30. J. Meyer and P. Jesilow, *Doing Justice in the People's Court: Sentencing by Municipal Court Judges* (Albany: State University of New York Press, 1997).
31. Buckner, "The Police."
32. Bayley and Mendelsohn, *Minorities and the Police*; Jesilow, Meyer, and Namazzi, "Public Attitudes towards the Police."
33. Bayley and Mendelsohn, *Minorities and the Police*, 54–55.
34. The belief by police that they are held in poor regard by the public is not new to this generation. Surveys conducted in the 1960s revealed that the view was widespread. Twenty-six percent of the officers in one study considered "rela-

tions with the public" to be the principal problem confronted by police (Jerome H. Skolnick, *Justice without Trial: Law Enforcement in Democratic Society* [New York: John Wiley and Sons, 1966], 50), while more than 70 percent of officers in a big-city department "had an acute sense of citizen hostility or contempt" (James Q. Wilson, "Police Attitudes and Citizen Hostility," quoted in Skolnick, *Justice without Trial*, 62). In a third survey, 22 percent of officers cited public lack of respect as something they most disliked about the police job (Albert J. Reiss Jr., *Police Officer Attitude toward Their Work and Job* [Ann Arbor, University of Michigan, 1966], quoted in The President's Commission on Law Enforcement and Administration of Justice, Task Force on the Police, *Task Force Report*, [(Washington, D.C.: GPO, 1967], 144). Finally, 20 percent of officers in a fourth study responded "public disrespect and understanding" when "[a]sked what things they liked least about being a police officer" (Bayley and Mendelsohn, *Minorities and the Police*, 52–53).

## Chapter 7: Responding to the Culture

1. Heidensohn, *Women in Control?* 167.
2. Ibid., 172.

## Chapter 8: Domestic Disputes

1. Police Foundation, *Domestic Violence and the Police: Studies in Detroit and Kansas City* (Washington, D.C.: Police Foundation, 1977).
2. Bent, "Police Training in New York," 610.
3. Ibid.
4. N. D. Baker, "Law, Police, and Social Problems," 15–16.
5. Buckner, "The Police," 284–85.
6. Walker, *The Police in America*, 127; and Muir, *Police: Streetcorner Politicians*.
7. Buckner, "The Police," 108.
8. Niederhoffer, *Behind the Shield*, 63–64.
9. Richard J. Lundman, "Domestic Police-Citizen Encounters," *Journal of Police Science and Administration* 2 (1974): 25.
10. Gresham Sykes and David Matza, "Techniques of Neutralization: A Theory of Delinquency," *American Sociological Review* 22: 664–70.
11. Buckner, "The Police," 326–27.
12. Ibid., 342; Rubin, "Police Identity and the Police Role," 28; and Walker, *The Police in America*, 128.
13. Muir, *Police: Streetcorner Politicians*, 27.
14. Bayley and Mendelsohn, *Minorities and the Police*, 101.
15. L. W. Sherman, "Police in the Laboratory of Criminal Justice," in *Critical Issues in Policing Contemporary Readings*, ed. Roger G. Dunham and Geoffrey P. Alpert (Prospect Heights, Ill.: Waveland Press, 1989): 48–69.
16. Black, *The Manners and Customs of the Police*, 114–15; see also Gill Hague et al., "Women's Aid: Policing Male Violence in the Home," in *The Boys in Blue:*

*Women's Challenge to the Police*, ed. Christina Dunhill (London: Verago Press, 1989), 23–37.

17. Bayley and Mendelsohn, *Minorities and the Police*, 101; Abrecht, *The Making of a Woman Cop*, 25; Buckner, "The Police"; Harris, *The Police Academy*, 44; McNamara, *Role Learning for Police Recruits*, 89–90; and Walker, *The Police in America*, 304.

18. Buckner, "The Police," 61.

19. Ibid., 62.

20. Joseph Livermore, "Policing," in *Police Behavior: A Sociological Perspective*, ed. Richard J. Lundman (New York: Oxford University Press, 1980), 45–46.

21. Muir, *Police: Streetcorner Politicians*, 88.

22. John P. Kenney and Harry W. More, *Patrol Field Problems and Solutions—476 Field Situations* (Springfield Ill.: Charles C. Thomas, 1986), 17–60.

23. Hague et al., "Women's Aid."

24. Barnard L. Garmire, "The Police Role in an Urban Society," in *The Police and the Community*, ed. Robert F. Steadman (Baltimore: Johns Hopkins University Press, 1972).

25. Walker, *The Police in America*.

26. Muir, *Police: Streetcorner Politicians*, 84; Walker, The Police in America; Morton Bard, *Training Police as Specialists in Family Crisis Intervention* (Washington, D.C.: Law Enforcement Assistance Administration, 1970); and Morton Bard, *The Police and Interpersonal Conflict: Third-Party Intervention Approaches* (Washington, D.C.: Police Foundation, 1976).

27. Schaffer, *Community Policing*, 64; Harvey Treger, *The Police-Social Work Team: A New Model for Interprofessional Cooperation* (Springfield, Ill.: Charles C Thomas, 1974).

28. *Bruno v Codd*, 90 Misc2d 1047, 396 NYS2d 974 1977.

29. Goldstein, "Improving Policing."

30. *Thurman v Torrington*, 595 FSupp 1521 (D-Conn., 1984).

31. H. Eigenberg and L. Moriarty, "Domestic Violence and Local Law Enforcement in Texas," *Journal of Interpersonal Violence* 6, no. 1 (1991): 102–109.

32. L. W. Sherman and R. A. Berk, *The Minneapolis Domestic Violence Experiment* (Washington, D.C.: Police Foundation Reports, 1984).

33. U.S. Department of Justice, Attorney General's Task Force on Family Violence: *Final Report* (Washington, D.C.: GPO, 1984).

34. Richard Berk et al., "A Bayseian Analysis of the Colorado Springs Spouse Abuse Experiment," *Journal of Criminal Law and Criminology* 83 (1992): 170–200; Antony Pate and Edwin Hamilton, "Formal and Informal Deterrents to Domestic Violence: The Dade County Spouse Abuse Experiment," *American Sociological Review* 57 (1992): 691–97.

35. Franklyn Dunford. "System-Initiated Warrants for Suspects of Misdemeanor Domestic Assault: A Pilot Study," *Justice Quarterly* 7 (1990) 631–53; J. David Hirschel, Ira Hutchinson, and Charles Dean, "The Failure of Arrest to Deter Spouse Abuse," *Journal of Research in Crime and Delinquency* 29 (1992): 7–33.

36. K. Ferraro, "Policing Woman Battering," *Social Problems* 6, no. 1 (1989): 61–74.

37. Ibid.

38. Buckner, "The Police," 325; and Harris, *The Police Academy*.

39. Richard J. Lundman, ed., *Police Behavior: A Sociological Perspective* (New York: Oxford University Press, 1980), 19–20.

40. Ibid.

## CHAPTER 9: JUVENILES

1. A. Binder, G. Geis, and D. Bruce, *Juvenile Delinquency Historical, Cultural, Legal Perspectives* (New York: Macmillian Publishing Co., 1988), 273.

2. Susan E. Martin, *On the Move: The Status of Women in Policing* (Washington, D.C.: Police Foundation, 1990).

3. D. H. Bayley and E. Bittner, "Learning the Skills of Policing," in *Critical Issues in Policing Contemporary Readings*, ed. Roger G. Dunham and Geoffrey P. Alpert (Prospect Heights, Ill.: Waveland Press, 1989), 87–110.

4. Walker, *The Police in America*, 131.

5. Ibid.

6. President's Commission on Law Enforcement and Administration of Justice, *Task Force Report*, 18.

7. J. Van Maanen, "The Asshole," in *The Police and Society*, ed. Victor E. Kappeler (Prospect Heights, Ill.: Waveland Press, 1995), 307–28.

8. Nova, "By the Year 2000," *Policing the Police* (KCET, 7 May 1991).

9. L. T. Empey and M. C. Stafford, *American Delinquency: Its Meaning & Construction*, 3d ed. (Belmont, Calif.: Wadsworth Publishing Co., 1991).

10. M. Mead, *Coming of Age in Samoa* (New York: Morrow, 1928).

11. F. M. Thrasher, *The Gang* (Chicago: University of Chicago Press, 1927).

12. M. S. Rosen, "A LEN Interview with Professor Alfred Blumstein of Carnegie Mellon University," *Law Enforcement News* xxi, no. 422 (30 April 1995), 10–13.

13. R. K. Jackson and W. D. McBride, *Understanding Street Gangs* (Incline Village, Nev.: Copperhouse, 1986).

14. C. R. Shaw, H. D. McKay, and J. F. McDonald, *Brothers in Crime* (Chicago, Ill.: University of Chicago Press, 1983).

15. Buckner, "The Police," 215.

16. Muir, *Police: Streetcorner Politicians*, 127–28.

17. J. Q. Wilson, and G. L. Kelling, "Police and Neighborhood Safety: Broken Windows," *Atlantic Monthly* 249 (March 1982): 29–38.

18. R. Navarette Jr., "The Moral Dilemmas of a Tagger's Slayer," *Los Angeles Times*, 5 March 1995, M1.

19. During a major gang sweep in Los Angeles, for example, half of the arrested youngsters were not members of gangs (Nova, "By the Year 2000").

20. Black, *The Manners and Customs of the Police*, 24–25; I. Piliavin and S. Briar, "Police Encounters with Juveniles," *American Journal of Sociology* 71: 206–14; K. C. Davis, *Police Discretion* (St. Paul, Minn.: West Publishing Company, 1975); and R. Lundman, R. Sykes, and J. Clark, "Police Control of Juveniles:

A Replication," in *Police Behavior: A Sociological Perspective*, ed. R. Lundman (New York: Oxford University Press, 1980).

21. Buckner, "The Police," 329.
22. Ibid., 330.
23. Scott H. Decker, "Citizen Attitudes toward the Police: A Review of Past Findings and Suggestions for Future Policy," *Journal of Police Science and Administration* 9 (1981): 80–87.
24. C. Werthman and I. Piliavin, "Gang Members and the Police," in *The Police: Six Sociological Essays*, ed. D. J. Bordua (New York: John Wiley and Sons, 1967): 56–98.
25. Muir, *Police: Streetcorner Politicians*, 130.
26. J. Andenaes, "The Moral or Educative Influence of Criminal Law," *Journal of Social Issues* 27 (1971): 17–31.
27. H. L. Packer, *The Limits of the Criminal Sanction* (Stanford: Stanford University Press, 1968).
28. J. Braithwaite, "Challenging Just Deserts: Punishing White-Collar Criminals," *The Journal of Criminal Law and Criminology* 73 (1982): 723–63.
29. S. Spitzer, "Punishment and Social Organization: A Study of Durkheim's Theory of Penal Evolution," *Law and Society* 9 (1975): 613–37.
30. J. Andenaes, "The Moral or Educative Influence of Criminal Law," *Journal of Social Issues* 27 (1971): –31.
31. L. Coser, introduction to *The Division of Labor in Society*, by E. Durkheim, trans. W. D. Halls (London: Macmillan, 1984).
32. Durkheim, *The Division of Labor in Society*, 29.
33. Ibid.
34. Meyer and Jesilow, *Doing Justice in the People's Court*.
35. Andenaes, "The Moral or Educative Influence of Criminal Law."
36. Bayley and Mendelsohn, *Minorities and the Police*, 106; Albert Reiss Jr., "Police Brutality . . . Answers to Key Questions," *Trans-Action* 5 (1968): 10–19; Niederhoffer, *Behind the Shield*, 57–58.

## Chapter 10: Final Thoughts

1. Goldstein, *The New Policing*, 1.
2. Skolnick and Bayley, "Theme and Variation in Community Policing," 34.
3. Michael Norman, "One Cop, Eight Square Blocks," *New York Times Magazine* (December 1993): 62–69, 76, 86, 89–90, 96.
4. H. W. Eber, "Selecting Law Enforcement Officers for Community Policing: A Technology and Some Policy Implications," *Psychological Resources* (25 June 1993).
5. Goffrey P. Alpert and Roger G. Dunham, "Community Policing," *Journal of Police Science and Administration* 14, no. 3: 212–22.
6. Fox Butterfield, "As Crime Falls, Pressure Rises to Alter Data," *New York Times*, 3 August 1998, A1(N), A1(L); and D. Parsons, "Police Officers' Perceptions: A Comparative Study by Gender and Organization."
7. Jesilow and Parsons, "Community Policing as Peacemaking."

# Index

# About the Authors

DEBORAH PARSONS is an assistant professor in the Department of Criminal Justice at California State University, San Bernardino. She was a full-time police officer before entering academia and worked as a beat officer in Orange County, California. She also has served as a department's assistant chief. She has maintained her police officer status and occasionally fills in for vacationing officers. Her experiences were the impetus for this book. She continues to do research on policing and to consult with local agencies.

PAUL JESILOW is an associate professor in the Department of Criminology, Law, and Society at the University of California, Irvine. He has published extensively on criminal justice issues, including *Myths That Cause Crime* (with Harold Pepinsky)—a Seven Locks Press book and winner of the Academy of Criminal Justice Sciences—Outstanding Book of the Year Award; *Prescription for Profit: How Doctors Defraud Medicaid* (with Henry Pontell and Gilbert Geis, University of California Press); and *Doing Justice in the People's Court: Sentencing by Municipal Court Judges* (with Jon'a Meyer, State University of New York Press). He currently is preparing a book (with Frank Afflitto) based on the experiences of the survivors among the disappeared in Guatemala.